THE
SILENT TRAVELLER
IN SAN FRANCISCO

THE
SILENT TRAVELLER
IN SAN FRANCISCO

Written and Illustrated by

CHIANG YEE

W · W · NORTON & COMPANY · INC ·

NEW YORK

TO

Robert and Thelma Morris

Contents

Plates in Color

An Unnecessary Note

How MANY SEA GULLS have left their claw-marks on the San Francisco beaches? And since when? Have any of them ever looked at the claw-marks they left or bothered about whether they would soon be covered up with dust and sand by a strong wind from the Pacific Ocean? Wholly unnecessary!

Unlike the sea gulls I am a humble mammal born on the opposite side of the globe and have happened to walk round San Francisco not only once but ten times since 1953. Each time I traced my footprints here and there with rough sketches and illegible scribbles. "What for," I do not know, but I laughed at myself sometimes when I heard a sea gull squeaking over my head as I wandered. His words seemed to say: "How like men-mammals in the past! Is it really necessary? Fish is what I am after!"

On many an occasion I gave up writing and painting my impressions of San Francisco, for they were not necessary. However, the sea gulls did come to San Francisco and did leave their claw-marks on the beaches. These remained on the sand for a while till the coming of a strong wind from the ocean. I therefore kept on retouching my notes and sketches now and then. They are now published as a book. Dare I hope they will remain as long as the sea gulls' claw-marks on the San Francisco beaches?

Though unnecessary, I had better make clear that the book did not come out as soon as I expected and that the contents are not arranged chronologically, according to the times of my visits. It is not an historical book, nor a critical study. San Francisco changes all the time and so fast. Not only have the foreseeable changes taken place, such as houses filling up every open space, even the unforeseeable has happened—the deep-rooted prison on Alcatraz is no more in the Bay. I take change as change comes, but I feel it unnecessary to change my first impression of Alcatraz. So it remains. I am glad to find that Alcatraz as a grim prison has not been a sore to my pair of brown eyes only!

Again, there is always the inevitable in life: six friends of mine— Harry Cowell, John Little, Richard Short, Joseph Henry Jackson, John Howell, and Van Wyck Brooks, who all wanted to know what I thought about San Francisco—have since died. If there is such a possibility that they, all known to me as good men, could still live in Heaven, as I was told to believe in my young days, they might read my gratitude to them however inadequate.

July, 1963. New York.   C. Y.

THE
SILENT TRAVELLER
IN SAN FRANCISCO

I

Approaching Differently

SAN FRANCISCO is known in China as Chiu-Chin-Shan or Old-Gold-Hill. In the eighteen-sixties a large group of Southern Chinese were recruited and brought over as laborers to help build the Pacific Railroad in California. They were simple peasants and worked hard to save money to send home from time to time. Eventually the place where they were working became known among their kinsfolk and neighbours as one "where they have struck gold." Immediately after the discovery of gold at Sutter's Mill in the Sierra Foothills most of this group of Chinese went to work in the new gold-diggings and were able to send more money home. They sent for their sons and other relations to work with them. In their letters home they evidently referred to San Francisco as the Old-Gold-Hill to distinguish from the new gold field at Sutter's Mill. Since then many Chinese from Southern China have come to California to find ways of making a better living. At the first glance they may have looked like those early gold-rushers from the Yankee land and Europe, but in fact they just helped to rush out the gold for others.

Although San Francisco is mentioned in a Chinese official publication of the early nineteenth century, knowledge of the place at that time was confined to the Chinese living along the fringe of the South China coast, whose relations or friends had emigrated there. Even a century later, I myself, having been born in Central China, had never heard anyone talk of San Francisco till I left my native land. Certainly I never dreamt of reaching such a place.

One's birthplace is an accident, and life consists of a series of accidents which may turn out luckily or not. A single lucky accident can bring unexpected joy into one's life; that is what San Francisco has done for me. I came to see San Francisco through a chance meeting in

General Sutter at his mill

June 1946, when I was returning to London from my first visit to New York. Having lived in England for many years and having managed to survive the bomb which fell and smashed my London flat during the Second World War, I felt in need of a change directly after the war ended. It was very difficult to book a passage to the United States but I managed to get a berth on the Cunard Liner *Queen Mary,* which was carrying two thousand G.I. brides and seven hundred babies, in December 1945. I stayed in New York for six months and recorded my experiences there in my book *The Silent Traveller in New York,* a few months later. Eventually I travelled back to England on the S.S. *Erickson,* sharing a big sleeping quarter along with thirty passengers. I had just begun to dump my belongings on one of the lower bunks

when a cheerful voice sang out "Hallo!" It was Bob Morris, who occupied the bunk above me. We soon became good friends, sharing the
same table for meals and walking and talking together during the
whole trip. I learned that Bob was English by birth and had gone to
Canada when he was only fourteen. Years later he had married there.
Bob and his wife, Thelma, have been living in San Francisco for a
long time now and own a business there.

We met almost every day during his stay in England and he told me
many stories of the city of his adoption. Soon I began to think that it
would be interesting to pay San Francisco a visit and find out if all I
had heard was true. Bob returned home after two months in England,
but we corresponded regularly and in each letter he urged me to come
out. Eventually in November 1952 at the suggestion of my publisher,
I came to America for a year's visit, to spend six months in Boston and
the other six in San Francisco. I wrote to Bob Morris about my plan.
By then he and Thelma had established a new business in Sacramento,
the Capital of California, and had built a new home in Carmichael on
the outskirts of the city. They asked me to spend a few days with them
first, saying that they would then take me to a friend's house in San
Francisco for my stay. This arrangement sounded wonderful. I chose
to travel by train from Boston to the west coast. I broke the journey at
Chicago for a day to see the many fine specimens of early Chinese
bronzes in the Brundage Collection at the Chicago Art Institute and
also to see various jades in the Bahr Collection at the Chicago Museum of Natural History. I also spent two nights at Denver in Hotel
Oxford, which I chose simply because I had made my home in Oxford,
England, since 1940. I joined a Rocky Mountain Tour to see Buffalo
Bill's grave, the Red Rock Open-air Theatre and much beautiful
mountain scenery. I also had a good walk in Washington Park in
Denver before I took the train to continue my journey to Sacramento.

Bob and Thelma were at the station. This was my first meeting with
Thelma, whose smile expressed a ready welcome. Among the sights
of the city which they soon showed me, I specially remember the
Capitol Park round the State House where the celebration of a
camellia week was in full swing. Hundreds of camellias were in bloom,
an unforgettable sight. My thoughts suddenly turned to the north of

Buffalo Bill's grave

England where my good friend, Sir William Milner, used to show me with a proud and happpy grin two or three camellias in bloom in his greenhouse. I care specially for this flower, as it is a native of China, being introduced to Europe in the eighteen fifties and then brought to America by Ernest Wilson of the Arnold Arboretum of Harvard University.

The few days in Sacramento passed quickly and it was time to leave for San Francisco. After breakfast Bob got the car ready for the drive, and we were soon spinning alongside the Sacramento River. This is one of the two big rivers that join above Sacramento; the other is called American River. A big project had been planned to build ports and wharves in order to bring in large steamers and freighters. In the next few years Sacramento would grow enormously and become even more prosperous, I was told. Silently I asked myself: "Has not every American city been growing steadily since it was established during the past two hundred years?" As we passed Freeport, the first town after the capital, I caught a glimpse of the river, which was reddish yellow in color, and full of sand, reminding me of the Yangtse River on which my home-town Kiukiang lies, I could not help feeling some nostalgia. Suddenly a great flock of wild geese flew over towards the Sierra Nevadas, where the highest peaks, capped with snow, stood out against the blue sky.

A great flock of wild geese flew over towards the Sierra Nevadas

My eyes followed the flight of the geese until they became tiny specks, almost invisible. We had already reached Hood, the second town along the river, but Bob insisted on following the direction of the geese to give me particular pleasure, so we turned south to Franklin. He thought the geese would have landed on the rice-fields to pick up grain, for Sacramento Valley is extremely fertile and rice is sown by airplanes over a vast area. I chuckled to myself, wondering how I could explain to my fellow-countrymen in the paddy fields of China what I meant by rice-fields in Sacramento valley. By the time we reached them, however, the geese had already taken off for other pastures and there were none to be seen.

Along both river banks were many clusters of young willow branches turning bright yellow like gold threads in the sun. Again I was reminded of the Yangtse River near my home-town in China, where willows grow along its borders. Yet somehow there was a great difference. In the early spring, from March onwards, along the Yangtse banks there would be a mass of green grass and rushes as well as the delicate colors of apricot and peach blossom which added a mellowness in the sunlight, while the Sacramento riverside is sandy and displays weariness in the tropical heat. Presently row after row of pruned trees in a seemingly endless orchard fell behind us one after another, while we moved forward as if we were reviewing a military maneuver. Thelma told me that these were Bartlett pear trees producing the best pears in the world. Soon afterwards the first swing bridge in the United States was shown to me. I was even more interested in seeing the bright blue slopes of Mount Diablo in the distance. What a contrast with the huge stretch of level plain in the Sacramento valley through which we had come!

The next two river-towns, Walnut Grove and Ryde, were quickly passed and we came to Isleton, famous for its asparagus, which is shipped all over the United States if not beyond. As our car was moving along at a good speed, I did not see much of this valuable crop, but the glimpse I caught was of fields full of long thin grass like finely woven carpets. This reminded me of the late Reginald Farrer, a well-known English botanist, who went to China to collect new plants for the Royal Horticultural Society, and who was surprised to see in the residence of the Governor of Lan-chou-Fu, Kansu Province, a few asparagus plants growing as a rarity in a beautiful Chinese porcelain pot. Asparagus, known in Chinese as Lung-hsi-tsao or Dragon-beard-grass, does not grow freely in China, and I imagine it was brought over to China in the mid-nineteenth century when Europeans, in particular the English, came to live in Shanghai and other big cities. Asparagus then became known to the Chinese as an edible plant with a delicious flavor, but for some reason the Chinese never took it very much as food. Instead, it appears, Chinese scholars were attracted by its delicate stems and fragile, beautifully patterned leaves, and began to grow them in porcelain pots as an additional ornament for their study. I even remember seeing a painting of asparagus on silk by a Ching court-painter of the nineteenth century. This shows how true is the Chinese proverb "Hsing hsiang chin, hsi hsiang yuan"—"Human nature brings men close to one another, but human habits keep them apart." In other words, there is no difference in human nature between the peoples of the earth, but they have different habits and customs according to their environment. I wonder, for instance, how an Eskimo would react if he suddenly found a beautiful fresh flower growing out of the icy wastes, while many of us pay no heed to flowers when they are blooming in profusion.

However, the great advancement of modern science has lessened the grievances and regrets in many human hearts. It has helped to grow things in places where their natural conditions are lacking; it also provides means to bring special foods to cities where these foods could not grow. It is not impossible that nowadays in some of the main centers in Alaska, the Eskimos may look without surprise on fresh flowers, and even eat asparagus, while their not-too-remote ancestors did not know what either was. While I was meditating in this way, I was roused by being told to look at the many Del Monte fruit plants on the other side of the river. It seemed an enormous business concern and I could not imagine how a fruit cannery could cover such an area, until I remembered all the supermarkets in the many American towns and cities I have visited. I know Del Monte fruits very well, for a British friend of mine loves their small-size cans and I try to send some over to the other side of the Atlantic from time to time. I know that I shall have no difficulty in buying Del Monte fruits in any small village in the United States where there might be only a tiny grocery store. This is the great advantage of modern transport. One can eat the same things anywhere under the American fifty-star flag. My idea in visiting a new place is to see its special characteristics and whatever may show its unique quality. Food may still claim to do this in France and China, but I fear that this will not be so in the years to come owing to the fast means of transportation available nowadays as well as the continual movement of inhabitants from one place to another. Any small town in Europe or China shows its unique history in the construction of its buildings dating from various periods. Most American towns on the other hand seem to have been built to the same pattern; each has at least one same-type Post Office, bank, drug store, and supermarket. They all look alike to me, but when I said to Bob that the few river-towns which we had just passed through were all similar to one another and in fact not very different from towns I had seen in New England and other states, he laughed and cautioned me, "Don't speak too soon; wait till we get to San Francisco!"

We had now come to Antioch Bridge over the San Joaquin River. The Sacramento joins the San Joaquin here to flow to the Pacific. Bob told me how in 1926 and 1927 he used to travel between Sacramento and San Francisco by river-boat. There were two of them, called *Delta Queen*, the same sort of river-boat as those which Mark Twain describes operating on the Mississippi. It appeared that in those days when the *Delta King* and *Delta Queen* were running, there used to be a good many Chinese junks and sampans moving up and down the river, all manned by Chinese. All the riverside towns we had passed had been full of Chinese shops and Chinese people. Each was a Chinatown then, like the one in present-day San Francisco. At last I understood why one of the first Chinese students at the University of California some fifty years ago described the Sacramento River as a completely Chinese river like the Yangtse or the Pearl River with activities on the water exactly the same as in China. How appropriate it was for me to approach San Francisco along a Chinese river! I remembered that only a few days before when Bob and Thelma had taken me to see the Mother Lode Country from Donner Lake we had come to a place named *Chinese Camp,* which used to have a population of over four thousand Chinese, among whom an elderly lady acted as Grandma to every gold-miner, Chinese or American, in those early gold-rush days. The Chinese who were employed to dig for gold must have encamped here. They built their houses, streets and even small gardens like those they had left in China. As they had all come from South China, and were chiefly Cantonese, they called their streets *T'ang-jen-chieh* or *Street of Men of T'ang,* for the Cantonese Chinese have been proud to address each other as Men of T'ang since the Southern part of China came under the rule of the T'ang Emperors in the seventh century. T'ang Jen Chieh must have been the first Chinatown. But *Chinese Camp* was almost a ghost town when we were there. We saw a young man trying to mend a broken bicycle in front of a dilapidated house, standing apart from two or three other houses. That was all; not a Chinese shop, nor a Chinese, not even a Chinese word could be traced. There have been many cases in the long history of China of cities once prosperous and famed throughout the whole empire becoming deserted and forgotten.

"Time is the extension of motion" says some early Greek philosopher. We cannot stop "motion" extending and therefore we have to accept "change." I tried not to regret the vanished Chinatowns of the Sacramento River.

Meanwhile we had been driving through the industrial town of Pittsburg, having nearly the same name as the well-known city in Pennsylvania. But Bob said this is the home of one of the largest steel manufacturing companies in the U.S., which ships its products to all parts of the country and all over the world. In the open country when the car moved fast I involuntarily felt not only that other cars on the same highway were much smaller than ours but that even the towns were no more than villages, with inhabitants the size of pygmies. The *highway* system is one of the greatest achievements of modern America, but I think it has made those who move along it more self-centered and even more self-important than they might otherwise have been. Inside this non-stop speedily moving car I felt the road so endless, the distance between places nil, America itself a vast, unobstructed and featureless land full of parallel lines with big circles and curves at intervals, on which masses of colored beetles ran on in endless chain. There were no inhabitants, no shape or form to the hills, mountains and rocks, and all the trees looked like big or small blobs of dark blue or green ink spilt at random. Not a single bird could be seen in flight, for they had become like tiny insects too small to recognize. What has become of man then? I asked myself. My mind felt strained and my eye-balls seemed to be swelling in order to grasp quickly enough the ceaselessly moving scene. No wonder modern art accentuates so noticeably the point to which it wishes to draw attention.

Bob got the car over a bridge among many other cars and followed on and on in one of the parallel lanes. We were now in Vallejo, and the faint shape of Mount Diablo had vanished. Instead, many small bun-like hills, of a fresh green color, kept rolling back on both sides of us so fast that I felt I was sitting in front of a movie screen. Suddenly vast stretches of water came in sight and we had reached San Pablo Bay. Far, far away in the distance and behind some hills rose a lofty mountain, which, I learnt, was Mount Tamalpais. Our car moved on still with many others in front and behind. Not one hesitated a moment, nor stopped. I would never have connected so much activity with the sup-posedly quiet countryside. In China there is a striking difference between the country and the city; the former is tranquil and full of fresh air, the latter noisy and dirty with dust. Many well-known pas-sages of Chinese prose and poetry describing the serene beauty of the countryside could never have been applied to this countryside that we were travelling through now in California. There must have been quiet patches sometimes, no doubt, but the tropical sun, glaring so brightly, beat down on my eyelids so that I had a struggle to keep them open, and drove away any tranquillity from the scene for me. The sky had been deep blue all the way, as blue as the immensely long sheets of indigo cloth that we Chinese use to make huge canopies over our courtyards to shield them from the summer sun. But the canopy that I was passing underneath was infinite, without supporting poles, and the sun blazed on. The brilliant rays seemed to have beaten up the dust from the road and scattered it round the edges of the hills, far and wide, so that it looked like a sort of yellow smoke. It even made the hills and trees in their young greenery look tired and withered from being baked all the time.

The parallel lines of the highway now turned into a complicated mixture of lines, very confusing to my eyes. The activity on them seemed to be more intense than ever. There were now many houses and motels lining both sides of the highway. The neon signs, red and green, shone in the relentless sunlight like veins on a microscope slide. The scene all round became increasingly dramatic. The little faint image of the top of Mount Tamalpais was now like a huge sheet of gray-blue paint with a slanting unevenly cut line, standing upright on the flat ground to my right, while on the left were twinkling silver lines, probably of water, in the distance. Close by the foot of Mount Tamalpais, round hills with a luxuriant growth of trees, dotted with white-mushroom-like houses, emerged quickly one after another. On the opposite side sprang up hills like steaming hot buns in the brilliant sun with no trees at all, but with a large number of small houses like colorful fungi scattered over them. We were now in Marin County.

My friends had planned to show me whatever they could of interest on the way, and our car now turned off the highway to follow the sign for Sausalito. Soon numerous masts appeared on a water-front lined with warehouses. There were all types of luxury yachts and sailing boats belonging to the wealthy inhabitants of the Bay area. Sausalito is planning to be one of the best yachting centers in the world. I looked over the masts to the vast expanse of water; far beyond and over on the other side where white dots and sparks gathered together San Francisco was pointed out to me. Unconsciously I wiped my face with my paw like a cat and then it was gone, for we had come to a turn in the road and left the water-front. A unique first glimpse of a city, I thought, but what is it actually like?

My head was next completely bewildered by the sudden disappearance of the sunshine. Only a moment ago in all the sky not a wisp of cloud had been visible. Now we were confronted with masses of infinitesimal particles moving and whirling as if directed by some supernatural being to display some curious magic for us. They were not high above us as clouds usually are, but were bearing down to earth fast and were about to swallow up all the hills in front of our car. Of these, some were quickly covered without a trace, some thinly veiled, and others still stood out clearly. The scene was like a Chinese landscape in mist painted by some master of the Sung dynasty. At the same time I seemed to see the voluminous clouds and mists rotating continuously, thickening here and thinning there, so that it seemed as if all the hills were racing one another; one would appear and disappear again as another came to take its place. The whole scene was dramatically alive. It filled me with excitement. I imagined that I was back in north-eastern China at Tunghai, where I taught in a school some thirty years ago and where, one Sunday morning, a colleague and I rode on horseback up a famous rocky mountain there, Yun-tai Shan, by the Yellow Sea. This mountain became famous because one of the earliest known Chinese painters, Ku K'ai-chih of the fourth century (an example of whose work, *Admonition of the Imperial Instructress*, is in the British Museum in London), wrote a treatise on how he painted it. It is a huge mountain full of grotesque and fantastic rock-formations; very few trees grow on it and hardly any bushes or grass. The whole district of Tunghai is almost barren—a poor country with few inhabitants. Being interested in both art and adventure I could not help wanting to pay this famous mountain a visit. "Not many people go up there," we were told, but a man who kept horses for people to ride over the mountain was introduced to us. We hired two and my friend rode off before me. It was a sunny morning and for a time we had a lovely, clear view. All of a sudden the scene in front was wiped out by massive clouds storming along. They seemed to be rushing towards us on our narrow footpath. I had fallen some distance behind my friend and watched him moving on slowly, myself filled with awe and inspiration. I felt that the following two lines from a well-known Chinese poem by Li Po described the view most appropriately:

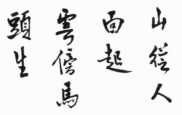

The mountain rises up from the human face;
The clouds grow by the side of the horse's-head.

Gradually my friend and his horse became a faint image and then were lost. I and my horse were completely engulfed in the clouds and mists. All of a sudden a great gust of wind drove the scudding clouds over us. My friend was unprepared and was blown off his horse. He was a trained wrestler, so only his body hit the rock, and not his head. He was not really hurt and laughed as he scrambled on to his horse again. We were both young and enjoyed the thrill and beauty of the moment. We did not know where we were, nor did we care when we would reach the city again; we had been up the mountain for four hours already. We had no fear of being lost, for we had complete faith in our horses. Presently a big shaft of sunshine broke through the thick cloud-mass to reveal the formations of some of the rocks shaped with ethereal and incomparable delicacy. My friend's horse made a turn towards the sunshine and we eventually came out of the clouds and rode back along a sunny footpath, home for dinner. More than thirty years had slipped by and not once had I given this trip a thought.

What a joy it was to me now to be reminded of it, as we motored fast along this well-paved highway of America. Most of the cars ahead of us were losing their shape, and soon were visible no more. We were all engulfed in the dense clouds, or mist. There were no more hills except one sweeping flowing line slanting down on my right. At this moment, to my great surprise and delight, up there appeared in the air a distinctively Chinese vermilion-painted Gate of Heaven, though blurred by the continually rolling clouds. A glorious, heart-stirring sight indeed! I was no longer riding up the Yun-tai Shan but instead was climbing up to the Nan-tien-men, the Southern Heavenly Gate of Mount Tai in Shangtung Province, where Confucius was born more than two thousand five hundred years ago. Mount Tai is one of the most sacred mountains of China; its spirit was worshiped by the early kings and emperors even before Confucius' day. On the very top of its highest peak, a Chinese temple was built, and to approach it one must pass through the Southern Heavenly Gate, built on the gap between two enormous rocky gorges. While walking up we would see from far below the Southern Heavenly Gate as if suspended in air, either through the mist or the sunny haze. I felt that the faint gate that had appeared in the air before me now must be Chinese, for China has always preferred vermilion for her palace gates, Pailous or gateways, pillars of temples and monasteries. How could I not be moved by this unusual yet familiar sight from my own past of some thirty years ago? Indeed, it quite carried me away!

Being, however, an earthly creature I came back to earth and realized that I was being motored over a bridge—the famous Golden Gate Bridge—as Bob and Thelma told me at the same time. "But why painted in Chinese red?" My friends had no time to answer nor I to listen, for my eyes were greeted by yet another red archway, redder than the first, and also floating in air. A moment later another section of it appeared from below and the whole looked like a red ladder suspended in the air so that I could climb to Heaven. It was the second tower of the Golden Gate Bridge that we were passing. The clouds and mist became denser than ever and I could hardly see a few yards beyond our car. The noise of other cars sounded clearly but there was no visible sign of them. Tiny yellow lights on both sides made a great struggle to penetrate the mist. It was impossible to tell whether we were again in the open countryside; our whole surroundings were invisible and mysterious.

Presently the fog grew thinner and revealed a straight street lined with houses and shops that seemed to continue endlessly. At long last we came to a halt, for me to be shown the Coit Tower and a rapid view of its surroundings. We stopped again at the top of one of the Twin Peaks, but the wind was far too strong and we could hardly stand against it. Then, we had a meal in Chinatown. Finally I was installed in the house of a friend of Bob and Thelma's at Lake Street, and they departed to their hotel, for the night. What a day I had had and how my head swam with so many sights to be taken in all at once! I could hardly say a word to my friends on parting; I needed time to sort it all out.

Lying on my bed, I gathered together my first impressions of the city: surrounded by water, clean and fresh, yet mysterious and unapproachable, sprawling like numerous rattlesnakes as well as stretching out with more arms than an octopus, pioneeringly strange yet traditionally familiar, subconsciously poetic, externally indifferent yet internally human, distinctively American and unmistakably San Francisco. I let my imagination wander and looked forward to testing my dreams by reality.

II

Walking Reflectively

Market street, I was told, used to be commonly termed the "Path of Gold." That was some eighty or ninety years ago. When I walked along it for the first time in February 1953, it did not seem to inspire such a name. Yet each time I walked there I could not help reflecting on this poetic name. After all, the city of San Francisco became world-famous not as an historical battlefield, nor as the seat of government of a nation, but through the chance discovery of gold in its neighborhood. The whole city can be said to have been built on gold. But had gold not been discovered and rushed for nearby, would San Francisco still have become world-famous? I have no doubt that it would. Its natural setting, its moderate climate, and its friendly air all make it attractive. But the finding of the gold and the rush it caused have had no match anywhere in the world at any time in human history. The tales told about it still ring fresh in the ear. No one can ignore them. Each time I had a walk along Market Street, from the beginning near the Ferry Building to the Civic Center or vice versa I was reminded of the famous Chinese proverb "Fire melts gold and gold melts man." Indeed many men were melted by gold in San Francisco, not too long ago, yet the City has steadily become saner and healthier. I find this a wonderful comfort in my thinking about the future of man despite the storm-clouds which have been gathering continuously these past few years. I mean political upheavals!

Strolling easily—in the literal sense of the word, for the pavement on either side of Market Street is quite wide and one can walk completely at ease in this most frequented thoroughfare of the West coast —I thought of Montgomery Street, where the masses of gold were first assembled so that it soon became the financial center of the West. Montgomery Street ranks as the first street of importance in the history of the city, for it was directly connected with the seashore where ships were anchored and near where the first settlers lived round Telegraph Hill. Out of this the city grew. When Market Street was designed by Jasper O'Farrell, a Dubliner and civil engineer who first worked for the Mexican Government, surveying land grants in the Bay region, and later for the American authority, the inhabitants did not like the abnormal width of the suggested street which was going to encroach on the rights of land-owners; they decided to lynch him. O'Farrell had to run away and hide out of the public reach for some time. The people had the law in their own hands then. A hundred years or so have slipped away, and though the pavement of Market Street is still wide enough, the street bed seems even too narrow to take the full volume of traffic nowadays. And how different the scene is now, though some may still wish to have the law in their own hands!

Market Street

From time to time my thoughts would return to the past as I walked along Market Street. It is said that directly after gold was discovered at Sutter's Mill along the American River, all the inhabitants, whether butcher, shop-keeper, iron-monger, fish-monger, bartender, barber, or street-sweeper, if there was one then, laid down their tools and locked their doors, putting up the notice, "Gone to the diggings." Some had wives who were left to await their man's return with a sackful of gold. The city must have looked deserted and empty without men: it could have been called a "City of Women." Though perhaps it is misleading to suggest calling it a "City of Women," for there were very few women about at first. In the early pioneer days only a handful of women dared to cross the country with their husband or lover in the covered wagons. However, the city would not have been without men for long. Soon the news of "Gold" spread through the world and load after load of fresh faces appeared on ship after ship which anchored in the Bay. Each load bolted at once to the diggings. There must have been a great commotion all the time in the neighborhood of Montgomery Street. Very few cared to stay behind to run even daily provision shops. The price of every kind of commodity soared high; eggs cost a dollar apiece, for example, and whisky was sold for $10,000 a keg. No one was available to do the washing. Tons and tons of dirty clothes, collected from the gold-miners, were shipped to the Sandwich Islands, now the State of Hawaii, to be laundered. Being a China-born Chinese I chuckled to myself on discovering how so many Chinese got into the laundry business. It is a fact that a good many Chinese from Kwangtung Province were already emigrating and some had settled down to make a living in the South Sea Islands, including Hawaii, soon after Captain Cook discovered them. The Cantonese, the name by which the Chinese born in Kwangtung Province are generally known outside China, are a seafaring lot, for they live near the sea and are used to seacoast life as well as island life. Those who had settled in Hawaii now seized this golden chance to make a better living by agreeing to wash the dirty clothes of the gold-miners. When they had made enough money, they moved to San Francisco. Many of their relations were brought over for manual work; they became servants or went into the laundry or restaurant business. The Cantonese are known in the rest of China as "good businessmen, honest and keen in work." They soon proved their ability by spreading their business to almost every State of America. They also earned a special reputation for all of us, whether Cantonese or otherwise: "A Chinese laundryman does the best laundry and does it by hand." I myself have been politely asked countless times where my laundry shop was! In San Francisco I often joked about having a chain-store business under the name of "Yee." "Yee" is a very common family name in the Cantonese pronunciation, but my family name is actualy transliterated "Chiang."

My friends, Thelma and Bob Morris, once told me a very interesting story about the gold-rush days. Though many men failed in their digging, many more succeeded, and their pockets were full of gold dust and nuggets day after day. They would come to town to empty their pockets at night and return to fill them up again at the next digging. Gold shone and sparkled from their pockets; it made their eyes pop out and their mouths gape with longing. A certain clever businessman thought of building a luxurious hotel near the digging place, so that the miners could all spend their gold there. The railroad was finished and soon the hotel was completed too. He engaged a number of women from the New England States to be servants in the hotel. When the train bringing them reached a small station ahead of the one near which the hotel was situated, thousands of the gold-miners climbed into the train, displayed their pockets full of gold to the women, and asked for them in marriage. Not a single woman, young or old, was left to get out of the train when it reached the next station. It was impossible to run the hotel and it never opened for business at all. Women were so scarce. Hundreds of men looked miserably at their gold and spent it all on kegs of whisky. A city without men is empty; a city without women means chaos.

However, the scarcity of women in San Francisco could not last for ever. Many were drawn to the new city of gold from all corners of the earth. The Barbary Coast soon became cosmopolitan and world famous. Girls of other lands featured in all kinds of stories, but Chinese girls seem to have got more than their share in the book entitled *The Barbary Coast*. China has long had stories like those in the *Arabian Nights* and the *Decameron*. *Chin Ping Mei* or "Golden Lotus," a famous sixteenth-century Chinese novel a complete translation of which has recently appeared in Western book stores, shows that the nature of the Chinese race differs little from that of any other. The unusual events on the Barbary Coast less than a hundred years ago were not so fantastic after all. The Barbary Coast has now lost its notoriety, but has human nature undergone a change? I do not know if the ancient Egyptians and Greeks had an answer to the problem of man's baser nature, but the ancient Chinese had none. People in the West have now heard of Confucius, but many do not know that there are two schools of thought in Confucianism. One advocates "the nature of man is good and should be cultivated," while the other believes that "the nature of man is evil—his goodness is only acquired by training."Maybe the second school of Confucian thought supplies the explanation why the doings on the Barbary Coast have disappeared from the San Franciscan scene nowadays.

Why did Market Street become known as the Path of Gold? I read somewhere that a certain Doctor Jones—who must have been well-educated to call himsef Doctor—had suffered from a genuine gold-fever for a time. He used to scatter gold dust on a white sheet, which he had spread over the floor, and then walk through the gold-dust in his bare feet. He even took off his clothes and rolled his naked body in the gold-dust. Finally he scooped all the dust up in his hands and poured it over his head before he dropped on the floor and fell into a deep sleep. Another story tells of a man who in frenzied dreams thought he had piles of gold and must begin to build a palace where thousands of slaves would work for him and thousands of fair maidens vie to win his love. However, Market Street did not earn its special name from either of these eccentrics, but from William C. Ralston of San Francisco, who built the Palace Hotel, not with gold, strangely enough, but with silver from Nevada, where he had the largest share in the Comstock Lode mines. Unfortunately, though he had planned and begun to build the hotel, he did not live to see it ceremoniously opened for business. Hundreds of fantastic stories about Ralston's life in San Francisco have been told and retold even to the day when I first visited the City. I found no trace of the old Palace Hotel on Market Street, but I discovered a lonely, not at all flattering monument with a bas-relief portrait of Ralston on a cement pedestal when I walked along the shore of Marin Road. The monument looked small and insignificant in the middle of a broad green lawn. Very few people notice it. I was told that Ralston had drowned himself near here when the Palace Hotel was nearing completion on account of a rumour about a deficit of millions of dollars in his bank of California. He could not stop the rumour. He had done so once before with the help of a Hungarian friend who was the Mint's assayer at the time. This time he had no Hungarian friend to help him; he could think of no way out but drowning. What a tragic end to a dramatic life! I wonder how long this insignificant monument to Ralston will remain in fast-changing San Francisco?

Though the monument will disappear sooner or later, the fame of Ralston will continue in San Francisco for many a generation to come. I can well believe that Ralston had a strong love for the City and that he wanted to do something to make it known in the world. With his fantastic brain he planned and achieved Ralston's Palace Hotel, known as *Bonanza Inn*—America's First Luxury Hotel. The building was completed in 1875 and the whole place was destroyed by the earthquake and fire of 1906. It had thirty years of life, but what a full thirty-year life it enjoyed! It helped to create the bonanza period of San Francisco, colorful, extravagant and almost unbelievable. It was opened with a magnificent reception given in honor of General Phil Sheridan, who delivered a speech. Cheers rose to the roof from the thousands who filled the public rooms and hallways and the six balconies crowded to capacity when General Ulysses S. Grant entered it on September 20, 1879. Later King David Kalakaua of Hawaii, Queen Kapiolani and Princess Liliuokalani stayed there, and the King died there too. Emperor Dom Pedro of Brazil, the Queen of Holland, the Grand Duchess of Russia, the kings of Württemberg and Prussia—not the Empress-dowager, Tzu Hsi, of China, though—all dined here. Can any modern hotel, though grander and more lavish, boast a more distinguished list of patrons? The world has fewer kings and queens now, and even fewer emperors. Perhaps the visitors' Book of London's Dorchester Hotel or that of modern New York's Waldorf-Astoria could show as big a score, but San Francisco has never been a great political center. How could one single hotel, far away from the center of world affairs, gain such fame? Ralston, it is said, spent $6,500,000 on building it; many modern luxury hotels must have cost double or treble that sum yet have no spacious marble-paved public rooms, nor such an immense and splendid courtyard to let carriages of the great pass through. It seems to me that this type of enterprise has earned for America as a whole the reputation of enjoying a bonanza type of life to this day. There are still people outside America who believe that all modern Americans live like those who struck gold in the bonanza period of San Francisco. The pavements of Market Street leading to the Palace Hotel were strewn with gold-dust in those days, hence the name "Path of Gold."

Another enterprise which came to my mind while walking along Market Street was Bancroft's History Factory. It was not a factory in the usual sense but a five-story brick building built by Hubert Howe Bancroft to house his thriving book and stationery business. Bancroft

The Mint

himself lived on the top floor and there wrote his monumental history
—five volumes on the North American Indian Races of the Pacific
States, three volumes on Central America, eleven on California, six on
Mexico, and many others on the eleven Western States and Alaska.
How could one man achieve so much? Bancroft admitted that he did
not do all the work himself, but that he employed twenty people all
well-educated and competent, and some knowing six or seven different languages, to help him sort and compile material from his accumulated sixty thousand maps, books and manuscripts, and hundreds and
thousands of newspapers in different languages. Bancroft as the chief
editor supervised them all like the manager of a big factory. This must
have been an entirely new venture in the writing and publishing
world of that time, a sort of encyclopedic work and the first of its kind

in America. Works of a similar nature have been produced in China centuries ago; for instance, the *Shih-chi* or Historical Records, written single-handed by Ssu-ma Ch'ien, who was born about 145 B.C. It is a history of China from the earliest ages down to about a hundred years before the Christian era in a hundred and thirty chapters of up to 526,500 words. The Twenty-four Dynastic Histories of China were produced in 1747 in a uniform series bound in two hundred and nineteen large volumes. In the past two decades or so a large number of encyclopedic works have begun to appear in America too. Boswell's *Journals* may perhaps be regarded as the first noted person's work to be treated in this compresensive way. My friend, Wilmarth Lewis, who gave his whole collection of Horace Walpole's papers to Yale University, once took Van Wyck Brooks and me round his "factory," as he jokingly called it, and told us that he hoped to have all of Walpole's papers published in twenty or thirty volumes, and that he was editing them with a staff of eighteen scholars. Two other friends of mine, Lyman Butterfield and Wendell Garrett, have been working on the Adams family papers and have just published the first two volumes, which are to be followed by many more. A third friend of mine, Julian Boyd, who is Chairman of Bear Lake Congress, of which I am a member, is to bring out numerous volumes on Thomas Jefferson's papers at Princeton University. There is work of this type going on in almost every large university and publishing house in America. Having seen the labor involved, I cannot help admiring Bancroft more than ever. He worked at his huge task without any financial support or encouragement, and with comparatively few helpers. His pioneering spirit was indomitable. It is this pioneering spirit in the air of San Francisco, as well as the beautiful natural setting of the city, which has often compelled me to linger there longer than I should. Bancroft's red-brick building vanished in the 1906 earthquake and fire, and unfortunately his name seems to have disappeared with the building. I have asked many people for more information about his life and character, but few had even heard of him. San Francisco should feel proud to have harboured so many fine men, pioneers in many fields. Bancroft was one of them.

There was a third building on Market Street, near Powell Street, which may have contributed more than the Book Factory to the name "Path of Gold." It was Lucky Baldwin's $2,000,000 House of Gold. Unfortunately, though Baldwin was lucky, his fabulous yet less dramatic life was always overshadowed by Ralston's, as was his Hotel by the Palace.

It was difficult for me to imagine how Market Street looked before the 1906 earthquake and fire. The Ferry Building at one end and at the other the Twin Peaks must have remained the same, though the former's name has lost its significance. On the three-mile-long street one landmark, maybe the only one, could be regarded as representative of the older days of the City. It is Lotta's Fountain, an uninteresting, unsubtle, and insignificant monument, but one which has a past with many sentiments attached to it. It could easily be overlooked in the swarming traffic of the street, with tall buildings and high poles on both sides, yet its rather disagreeable dirty-yellow color caught my eyes each time I came up the street from Kearny or Geary. It was erected in memory of an actress bred, though not born, in San Francisco; Lotta Crabtree, famed in the eighteen-sixties and seventies. Many memories of the old days cling to this fountain and many an old-timer spoke of it. But how many old-timers are left now in San Francisco? The few I came across thought there would be a violent controversy if the Lotta Fountain were to be removed from Market Street.

This made me ponder over the purpose of monuments. I used to think that the many monuments I saw in European cities were simply personal tributes. This is true, of course, but now I realize that the continued existence of a monument provided neither earthquake nor war nor any other disaster causes its destruction depends on two other factors besides admiration of the person it portrays. It can continue to exist if it is linked with an important event in politics, religion or culture, or if it ranks as a work of art. Many early Greek sculptures, though obscure in their historical significance, are still admired as art. However, there are fashions in art too, and tastes sometimes clash. I recall the controversy caused in London some twenty-five years ago by the erection of the monument to Field-Marshal Haig of First World War fame, and how violently the design was criticized.

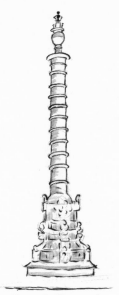

Lotta's Fountain

Such monuments have given rise to many committee meetings to raise funds, to select a site, to choose an artist and to decide the date for the unveiling ceremony. The committee members have all had to scratch their heads at times and some have even felt so annoyed that they would be prepared to fight a duel! After the monument has been in position for a while, quiet reigns on every front, and it is soon neglected. This is the way life goes on. I am glad I noticed the Lotta Fountain and I enjoyed wondering how the design and site of this monument had been chosen. I was fortunate to have seen it still standing on its original site.

Between 1953 and 1960 I noticed three new additions to San Francisco: the building of a Buddhist church (a name I could not quite understand), at the end of Grant Avenue, the more than life-size carved figure of Columbus on Telegraph Hill, and the many-sided glass building of the Wells Fargo Bank right on Market Street. This last item is a striking feature of the Street, for there is no other building like it yet. The craze for glass and steel buildings will spread to San Francisco, I am sure; and though there may not be another building exactly like the Bank, it will be lost in the mass. However, for the moment, it catches everyone's eye both from pavements and from inside the street-cars. The charming ladies in fashionable clothes and handsome men behind the glass are like figures in a movie. Unfortunately Ralston did not live to see the beginnings of this modern time of ours or he would surely have been the first to build a hotel of glass and steel.

Curiously enough, the present many-sided glass building of the Wells Fargo Bank reminds me in some ways of a little building from the past—the famous Octagon House in Gough Street which my friend, Don McPherson, told me about. Mere curiosity seldom moves me, but it had its way this time. Just as I found the spot, I met four workmen who were putting the old house on wheels to transplant it to the other side of the street. They all seemed to know why I had come and jokingly asked me if I wanted to see "Inkwell House." I could not understand their question and enquired "Is this the Octagon House?" They explained that it had been nicknamed "Inkwell House," as its shape resembles an ink bottle. The original Octagon House belonged to the McElroy family, but it became rubble in the 1906 earthquake. The moving of the present one was organized by the California State Society and the National Society of Colonial Dames of America, who own it. It interested me to learn that of the fifty octagonal houses built throughout North America some hundred years ago, when it was a fashion, five were in San Francisco, four on Russian Hill and the fifth on Rincon Hill. The only other one now remaining is in Green Street. They had been designed in this curious way in order to present eight sides to the sun. The present many-sided glass building of the Wells Fargo Bank should catch even more sun! Can it do so? I cannot help chuckling to myself when I read that the architect invented this new form for a bank building.

The Civic Center of San Francisco always received me at the end of my walks along Market Street. Not that I have a special interest in the Center; I just ended there to have a good rest on one of the many public benches. It was there I met my friend, Don McPherson, for the first time in 1953. Since then we have been together on many excursions. Don was then tending the garden of the Civic Center. He

"The Inkwell House" and Wells Fargo Bank

not only told me about Octagon House but also about the two
crooked streets, one the famous Lombard Street and the other along
the way to Pacific City. He even took me on a drive to point out the
second one. What I most enjoyed at the Civic Center was walking at
leisure round the walls of the City Hall, particularly on its south side.
The lower part of the granite foundation has been so cut as to leave a
good portion exposed and to give the impression that the whole structure—from the pointed top of the dome to the base of all the windows
—has been erected on a solid base, a squarish pedestal. I am sure the
architect who designed this Center did not dream that this granite
shelf would become an ideal bench for many office employees during
the lunch hour. I often managed to get there about noon. Usually a
number of people were already sitting there or standing around.
Gradually more and more would come until most of the space along
the whole wall was occupied. I always found this an interesting
occasion; every type of sitting or reclining pose was sketchable, and I
also overheard animated discussions from one group or another from
time to time. Though I could hardly follow any of their topics, it interested me, for it reminded me both of the Sunday free lectures and
discussions in Hyde Park, London, and of similar gatherings on Boston Common week-end afternoons. Don Mcpherson told me that this
wall had been dubbed the "War Street." But he also remarked that

this "War Street" has long been condemned as disfiguring the city and would soon be overshadowed by some new structures. Freedom of speech is one of the symbols of democracy. If the free discussion with "soap-box-orators" disappeared from Hyde Park, Boston Common and San Francisco's Civic Center, where else should I find such a genuine symbol of democracy?

It is true that Market Street of San Francisco is not what it used to be in the early days of its history, but it still has some picturesque customs. I shall always remember one of the sights I saw there on a New Year's Day. I had spent a strenuous New Year's Eve in Chinatown on Grant Avenue. Market Street looked much quieter than usual.

Not many people and cars were about yet. But the air of the whole street was very full, full of masses of white strips of paper fluttering down from every window of the tall buildings. At first they looked like big snowflakes. Then I noticed that many of them caught the bright sunshine as they fell and were transformed into broken pieces of *silver* or gold leaves. I learnt that it was a City custom to tear up the

"War Street"

pages of calendars of the year just past and throw them down from the windows. The whole street was soon littered to an inch deep in places. I have not met this custom in any other city I have visited so far, and it was a memorable event for me. So I wrote the following little poem to conclude:

火灼金兮金灼人
三藩市裡頹垣因
皇宮逆旅無餘迹
待渡高樓依舊新
漫說雙峰時隱現
且看浮世嚼沙塵
唄行一事堪汲記
元旦家家散碎銀

"Fire melts gold which melts man";
San Francisco reveals its old foundation:
The Palace Hotel has left no trace any more;
But the Ferry Building is as fresh as ever.
Idly talking about the Twin Peaks now clear and now obscure,
As usual the floating world is still chewing the sand and dust.
In my silent travels one thing remains really memorable:
On New Year's Day house after house scatters broken silver!

III

Listening Receptively

SCIENCE CAN ONLY DESCRIBE the myriad objects in the Universe: it cannot analyse the minds which apprehend them. Take "sound" for instance. Science divides "sound" into two main categories; "cacophonous" and "musical." Cacophonous sound is mere noise, while musical sound is a composed melody where "sound" and "sounds" are associated together in succession. "Sound," whether cacophonous or musical, can encounter "like" and "dislike" in different "minds." Also, the same "cacophonous" or "musical" sound can affect different minds similarly. Being a China-born mammal, I was familiar with Chinese music and unfamiliar with western music in my first few years outside China. Now I can say that I am familiar with western music but am still unable to say why I like certain compositions and not others.

I have tried to listen receptively to many unfamiliar sounds in the western world. Unfortunately some of the sounds, whether "cacophonous" or musical, such as the roaring auto-horns in a congested street, the droning madness of an aeroplane overhead, the loud broadcasts from next door, the guttural clucking of a subway train passing by, or the mob muttering below a tall apartment-building have all forced themselves to become familiar to me against my will.

Happily for me, there are three unfamiliar sounds in San Francisco that have never forced themselves on my ear: it is I who have listened to them receptively and with pleasure. These three sounds, though the scientist might describe them as "cacophonous," have contributed to giving San Francisco its unique character. One of them is the fog-horn at Golden Gate.

London has a reputation all over the world for being a "City of Fog," and though the fog there is reputed to be as thick as pea-soup (I must state from my own experience that I only met such a fog once in many years), no special sound-warning is placed anywhere along the river to protect shipping. On the other hand, London fog seems to provide the Englishman with scope for his sense of humour. The next morning after that pea-soup fog in 1935 I read that seven Londoners had walked straight into the Thames River. I exercised my sense of humour too by composing the following little poem:

不知人世有江河
怪汝掉頭狂笑去
對此茫茫喚奈何
全城都上夜中過

The whole city passes into night;
"What on earth shall I do?" I say to myself.
"I marvel at you, as you look back, laughing
    uproariously, and keep moving on:
"As if not knowing that there are rivers in this
    human world."

The last line implies that many Londoners treat the fog as a joke, and do not bother themselves about the possible dangers. Of course London is some distance from the sea and big ships can only come a certain way up the river. In many parts of the City the sound of the fog-horn would never be heard.

Halifax, on the coast of Nova Scotia, is very frequently shrouded

by fog. Though I did not stay long there, I heard many stories of fishermen being engulfed in thick fog. Once a fisherman kept sailing his
boat forward, as he thought, yet in fact was never more than a few
yards from the same spot. A shout came to him from another boat: "If
you don't know your way about in the fog, you can't be a Nova Scotia
fisherman!" Yet no fog-horn sounds a warning from the Halifax coast.

I first heard the fog-horn in Sausalito in my friends', the Morrises',
car as we approached the Golden Gate Bridge in February, 1953. It
made me start but only for a moment, as I was then engulfed body and
soul in the fog as we moved over the wide bed of the bridge at the
same speed as the other cars in their parallel lanes. The next morning
when I woke up at Lawson House in Lake Street the fog-horn entered
my ears clearly at regular intervals. Then it stopped for a while, only
to be taken up again and again. My first reaction was one of surprise
and alarm. It had immediately sent my mind back to the wartime days
I spent in England. Three out of four full years of World War II, I
was forced to listen to the air-raid warning siren almost daily. I should
have grown accustomed to it, but each time it tore me to pieces. It
seemed to hammer on my head and force me to quicken my pace. I
never thought a sound could be so unbearable as that siren. Modern
life has much to drive one off one's balance; I think no authority
should sound the siren for the sake of a prepared exercise.

The sound of the fog-horn, once I had grown used to it, became
quite agreeable to me eventually. It is a warning and sounds mournful, like moaning, but it does not attack one's constitution. "Mourn-
fulness" can imply concern for others—parents, relatives or friends.
For instance, a cow utters a mournful moo when calling her strayed
calf, or to express content at being well-fed. San Francisco's fog-horn
must have been installed quite a good distance outside the Golden
Gate in order to guide ships as they come in and out of harbour. Those
who live around the Golden Gate hear it frequently, and it came to my
ears almost every morning when I lived at Lake Street. It can also be
heard occasionally far away from the Golden Gate, but it comes at its
own will on the wind, its sad tone softened to a soothing one. I once
listened to it receptively in a strong gust of wind on my way up Mount
Tamalpais and felt as if back on a Swiss Alp hearing the echo of a

shepherd's yodelling. I realized that San Francisco, in spite of being a great metropolis, still retains her rural serenity at heart. I have also listened to the fog-horn unexpectedly on Russian Hill, Telegraph Hill, and somewhere near Twin Peaks. One night I realized that the following morning would be the Easter Festival and that there would be a great choir singing round the Cross on the top of Mount David-son. I slipped out of the house very early in the morning and eventual-ly managed to get a taxi to take me to the spot. The ceremony of the Festival had already started and a great mass of people was singing to-gether. I am not a Christian, but I listened to this choir with the sub-dued, respectful feeling I have for all religion. Suddenly a soft, gentle, slightly-moaning sound, borne on the wind, entered my ears: I listened attentively and found that the fog-horn fitted into the tempo of the choir melody. I went on listening until fog-horn and singing had both died away.

Whenever I was in San Francisco I would be sure to hear somebody remarking that they could not bear the sound of the fog-horn. But to me the fog-horn sound is associated with my affection for San Fran-cisco. Once or twice, when after a few days' stay in the city I had heard no fog-horn, I went purposely towards the Golden Gate to listen for it. Whenever my thoughts turn to San Francisco the fog-horn begins to sound in my ears. I am sure that many natives of San Francisco who never gave a thought to it before they left the city must have found themselves saying now and again when they were far away, "I wish I could hear the fog-horn sound again!"

The sound of the cable-cars affects me in the same way. When it came to my ears for the first time, it did not sound entirely unfamiliar, as the fog-horn had done. It took me right back to the Shanghai streets where I rode on tram-cars as a young student some forty years ago. These vehicles have long disappeared from Shanghai streets, and I do not think any opposition was raised by her mixed population of Europeans, Americans and Chinese when they went. Not because the tram-car had no connection with the history of the city but because few people, particularly the Chinese, had any feeling for the history of Shanghai. Though Shanghai, from its origins as a stretch of flat, marshy land, had risen to be one of the wealthiest and most populous

Only in San Francisco

commercial cities in the world, the days of her glory never belonged
to the Chinese. At the height of her development Shanghai was divided
into many foreign concessions and the larger part was called the "International Settlement." The tram-car business was run by a group of
non-Chinese who had the sole voice in keeping or abolishing the enterprise. The Extra-territorial rights accorded to the Concessions and
Settlement were only waived in 1942 when China became a publicly-
recognized ally in World War II. It is sad to think that only a war
could bring that about, but on the other hand war did some good in
wiping out a black spot in human history. I lived in Shanghai for two
years but never got to like it. But the sound of the tram-car bells was
firmly stamped in my memory.

I relate the above in order to illustrate why the sound of the cable-
car has a special meaning for me. On first hearing it I thought it was
similar to that of a tram-car. After listening to it again and again, I
realized that it was announcing the arrival and departure of the cable-
car rather than sounding a warning like a tram-bell. The cable-car
driver has a definite way of ringing the bell—one hit on the front part,
one on the side towards the striker and then a quick repetition of the

process three times. The sound is not just a noise which science might call cacophonous; it is a series of sounds associated together in a fixed rhythm—loud but not unpleasant. By and by I began to like it quite well—especially when it made me forget the swift-rolling autos. It has

the strange effect on me that even when I hear it quite faintly from a good distance away it seems to overpower the loud honk of a nearby Cadillac or Jaguar. I like to listen to the sound of the cable-cars from the top of Nob Hill. If the car is coming up, the sound vibrates pleasantly, giving a feeling of relief and causing a smile. If the car is going down the sound fades from loud to soft and softer till it almost vanishes, lingering on affectionately as if a young child were turning round constantly to call good-bye to some well-loved person, until the voice can no longer be heard.

The sound of the cable-cars can only be heard in a limited area of San Francisco, centering on the busy streets linked with Market. In my first few visits I heard more of them, for there were three cable-

car lines then. Now they have been cut down to one line only—the California-Powell line. During my latest visits I heard more and more talk about abolishing them altogether. They do not pay their way. I never bothered about the abolition of the tram-cars in Shanghai, but this talk of doing away with cable-cars in San Francisco stirred me to say repeatedly: "It would be a great pity!" From what I have read, the cable-car played a significant part in the past history of San Francisco. I have read of Andrew S. Hallidie's joy on completing his design for it and putting it into execution, and of the great enthusiasm it aroused when it was first ceremoniously set in motion. It was one of the early human achievements in the city and it remains an attraction. Many cities try to find ways of attracting tourists and sightseers; why cannot San Francisco spend enough to keep this attraction going? To me it is a typical feature of San Francisco, and I am glad to be able to record my appreciation of it.

The third sound that I specially associate with San Francisco is the barking of sea lions. I am not thinking of that lonely sea lion in a small water tank outside a curio shop on Fisherman's Wharf, but those that frequent the Seal Rock out in the Ocean. They can occasionally be heard, if the wind is favorable, on the terrace of Cliff House, along the beach and on Sutro Height. In spite of its name, Seal Rock cannot be the playground of ordinary seals, whose barking would hardly carry to the shore. In this connection, I must quote a passage by a certain J. G. Wood who wrote in 1875:

> They [Californian sea-lions] are marvelously blatant animals, keeping up a continual chorus of vociferations as long as they are on land. The old males are the most noisy of the party, snorting discordantly, and roaring like magnified lions. The females answer by loud bleatings, and the young of both sexes add their voices in a less degree. The united cries of a large herd of Sea Lions are so deafening, that human senses are almost stunned by the clangorous uproar.

So the mammals who have their kingdom on Seal Rock are not common seals but Californian Sea Lions. I do not care for the word "blatant" to describe the talk of this fellow mammal of mine. "Blatant" means "vulgarly clamorous" according to the Oxford Dictionary. No matter how vulgar their clamour might be from near at hand, it would be reduced to much softer tones when carried through fog and mist, or for a long distance over the water, to the navigators and their crews and passengers, both in olden times and today. It would undoubtedly give them indescribable joy, for they would realize that they were close to land. In all my sea-travels this joyous sensation at the thought of approaching land, after watching a wide expanse of water for days on end, has never diminished. Unfortunately I have not yet had the opportunity of approaching San Francisco by sea, but I can imagine how much satisfaction the clamour of the Californian sea lions on Seal Rock would give me before the first, faint outline of San Francisco came in sight. While the fog-horn provides a kindly warning of danger ahead on the way to the Golden Gate, the clamour of the sea lions on Seal Rock can be likened to a large band playing welcoming tunes to approaching visitors. How fortunate San Francisco is to have this unique natural band!

I wonder why the sea lions have established their kingdom on the group of three rocks opposite Cliff House and not on any other rock along the Pacific coast, many of which I have seen, from Pillar Point on Moss Beach to Sir Francis Drake Bay. I once watched their antics through a telescope and listened to their clamour from the terraces of Cliff House as well as from the beach. The clamour that entered my ears from time to time was a gentle barking filling the air with a sense of contentment. I found it an agreeable contrast to the monotonous washing of the great waves against the shore and to the sounds from that Coney-island-like playground on the other side of the highway beach. It is common knowledge that the seal's and sea lion's cries are similar to the barking of a dog. I personally prefer to hear a dog's barking from a distance, although I know very well that this form of greeting does not always mean that the dog is hostile to my approach; in fact it is most likely greeting me enthusiastically.

Sea lions on Seal Rocks

When the fog-horn was first devised and installed for use, I do not know. It is an artificial sound created by man. But no doubt it will stay as long as fog gathers round the Golden Gate. The sound of the cable-cars, though also man-made, will disappear sooner or later, I must regretfully admit. Whether the sound of the sea lions on Seal Rock will remain or will disappear in the remote future, it is difficult to say, for the cunning and dexterity of the smartest mammals, men, in their new invention—oceanography—is so unpredictable. However, I can congratulate myself on having been able to listen receptively to these three sounds, so characteristic of San Francisco, at the same time.

IV

Climbing Perilously

An UNEXPECTED TREAT resulted from a casual remark of mine. I happened to ask if one could go up the tower of the Golden Gate Bridge. "Why not"? was the answer of my good friend, Milton Liang. Milton is a noted engineer in San Francisco and has worked in association with Mr. John Goulding Little, structural engineer to the office of the Golden Gate Bridge. He began to make arrangements for my visit and one morning (1953) I was asked to go to the office with him to meet Mr. Little. We were treated to a hearty breakfast at a restaurant on the Bay side of the Bridge. Mr. Little, seventy-six years of age, had a most engaging personality, and plenty of anecdotes about old San Francisco. Smiling all the time, he related one story after another about the great fire and earthquake of 1906. The office in which he had been working vanished in the quake. In fact, the present Montgomery Building was the only big building left standing then.

But what really absorbed him was bridge engineering. His talk always came round to the building of more bridges across San Francisco Bay. The traffic in and out of San Francisco by 1935 had become so heavy and congested that a way of easing it had to be worked out. It was estimated that when the Golden Gate Bridge was first opened in 1937, the traffic was handled at the rate of 2,280,000 vehicles annually, on six traffic lanes. Since then the volume has doubled and trebled.

Milton asked for me if we would be going up the tower. The reply was "No, we shall not. What do you want to go up there for? Nothing to see." Mr. Little kept his pioneering manner in leading us about, while Milton demonstrated his Confucian upbringing by obeying his superior without argument. I felt like a dog, following step by step, tail between legs. Presently we were inside the concrete structure by the foot of the rock close to the water surface on the San Francisco side. At once Mr. Little's eyes opened wide with enjoyment, for it was here that the ends of the steel cables, suspenders and accessories were tied up together. Nothing could go wrong here. The diameter of cables over wrapping was thirty-six inches, length of one cable 7,650 ft., number of wires in each cable 27,572; number of strands in each cable 61; size of wire (no. 6) diameter 0.196 in.; total length of wire used 80,000 miles; and weight of cables, suspenders and accessories 24,500 tons. I soon realized that I was with two great lovers of figures.

Later Milton and I found ourselves standing by a concrete wall while Mr. Little climbed up an absolutely vertical steel ladder through an open hole. He did not wait to ask whether I would follow him. Presently Milton climbed after him. For a moment my mind wandered; it was far away on the English Yorkshire moors where I used to roam with my friend's Labrador dog when I stayed at Parcivall Hall. Before reaching the moors we usually crossed a number of fields. Round the Yorkshire fields are low stone walls; low to me, but rather high for the Labrador dog to jump over. He never cared for scrambling over the walls even if there were some stepping stones. Each time I got over a stone wall, he would stare at me sadly and indicate that he needed help. In the concrete hole by the side of the vertical steel ladder I could not communicate in any way with Mr. Little and Milton who were already up. Eventually I emerged beside them from the hole and felt quite triumphant, but neither of them even turned his head to look at me. We were now standing underneath the bridge span on the Marin pier. The huge steel structure, bar by bar in parallel arrangement with diagonal traversing lines all the way, was explained to me. Each single steel bar looked colossal from directly underneath. It could easily have crushed me into pieces, yet it was suspended there above my head so majestically as if without support from anywhere, for both ends were too far away to be seen. My companions seemed exceedingly small in the presence of the steel bars. Thousands of cars were passing incessantly in either direction above, but standing where I was, I heard little of the great commotion. It was a marvellous human achievement. Far above and far away on one of the suspenders I detected a darkish spot—a man was repainting the steel cable of the suspender. A few more men were repainting the steel bar on the side of the bridge span. I was told that this repainting is an all-the-year-round job; sixty-two painters are at work every day. When the men reach one end they turn back and repaint the steel on the other side all the way along to the other end again. The whole process is repeated continuously. A single steel suspender might take one or two days to repaint. Any type of night fog moistens the steel surface and so it has to be painted over and over again to prevent the damp from causing deterioration of the material.

Golden Gate Bridge has the longest suspension span in the world between two towers. Despite the heavy load constantly moving over it, it shows no sign of vibration to our human eyes, yet it is vibrating all the time. We had come to a vertical pole with an indicator moving up and down the main span. Normally it sways within one or two feet. But on December 1, 1951, it swayed up to eight or nine feet. The terrible west wind, worst of all kinds in this region, blew at over sixty-nine miles an hour and an unheard-of storm raged for the whole day. The traffic on Golden Gate Bridge had never been stopped since its construction, but it was brought to a stand-still for almost two hours that day. The directors and the general manager must have had their first real anxieties about their bridge; fortunately it stood up to the test. Mr. Little tried to explain to me why the engineers who built it had over-estimated somewhat the strength of the crossing steel bars in not using a much longer diagonal bar to intercept the main span, so that it would not sway violently in even the heaviest storm. Mr. Little used a good many technical engineering terms which were beyond my comprehension. I realized that he was in the habit of explaining the structure of Golden Gate Bridge when showing engineer-visitors round from time to time, and was really forgetting that I was no engineer, although he did ask repeatedly: "Do you understand . . . ?" For a time I managed to satisfy him with a smile. Then he seemed to demand an answer in words. Hesitatingly I ventured: "Well . . . yes." "Oh, no, you don't." was his quick retort. He then patted my shoulder, gave a hearty laugh, and shoved me into his car beside Milton. Unmistakably he had enjoyed talking about the engineering, regardless of my inability to understand.

Standing on Lime Point overlooking the Bay I tried to visualize

Berkeley on a clear day. It was hidden in a dense midday sunny haze. Perhaps Berkeley can never be seen clearly from Lime Point, for there is always morning and evening mist round Golden Gate Bridge. Mr. Little picked up a bit of rock where we were standing and squeezed it into powder, telling me that the rocks on the surface on the Marin side were either sedimentary or igneous. Then pointing to a crack in the earth where we were standing he said that the rocks here might change form one day. He showed me what the chief engineer, Joseph B. Strauss, had said in his report: "It is reasonable to assume that once or twice in a century San Francisco will be shaken by a violent earthquake. The trace of San Andreas fault, upon which a sudden slip occurred in 1906 with disastrous results to San Francisco, lies six miles to the west of the bridge site. But there is no evidence that the Golden Gate itself is in danger of a dislocation such that differential movement between the bridge-ends might be caused. Even when we contemplate the possible destruction of the Golden Gate Bridge by an earthquake of exceptional violence, it should be borne in mind that any earthquake so violent that it would destroy the bridge would also completely destroy San Francisco." So the "supreme, indifferent-to-fate" San Francisco goes on building more bridges across the Bay. Mr. Little had his plan for a new bridge in mind all the time.

Neither side of Fort Baker in Marin County is open to visitors, for both areas are military reservations. But the warning placard did not deter Mr. Little's car, and I was glad to be taken all along the rocky shore down to Lime Point Lighthouse. A beautiful-looking rock stood not far from the shore. But the Lighthouse itself seemed quite puny, when I lifted my head to catch sight of the massive main span of the bridge stretching out far, far away. The Lighthouse is a whitewashed building, like a tiny white dot amid the colossal red-painted steel structure of the Golden Gate Bridge and the countless green waves in the open Bay. On the San Francisco side there is at old Fort Point a massive stone building still standing, almost unnoticeable when the bridge as a whole is being viewed. In the olden days before the bridge was built, Fort Point and Lime Point Lighthouse must have been the sole authorities in command of the largest land-locked harbour in the world. For the past twenty-odd years since 1937 their authority has been almost completely wiped away. The old Fort is now an empty, dilapidated structure, though the Lighthouse still functions in a modest way. "Change" appears everywhere and always will. It is simply futile to lament change, or to glamorize it. Another change will come to take the place of the Golden Gate Bridge sooner or later; the chief engineer who designed it did not have in his mind a "once-for-all" notion.

Coming to the other side, opposite the lighthouse, on our way to Fort Barry Mr. Little had something to say about land development. What an active and progressive mind he revealed. He was thinking of big open spaces free of military installations on these hill slopes. We must have come near to the Rodeo Lagoon, for I was intrigued by two or three whitewashed rocks standing out of the sea against the bright sun. They were quite a distance away. I said I would like to get out of the car for a better view of these rocks. Mr. Little booed: "Oh those! Those are bird rocks. Lots of seagulls helped to paint them white!" His mind was really engaged on how to develop the land which he had heard was for sale. The road was not meant for cars but we kept driving on. Presently we encountered three riders on horseback, a bearded man, a younger man, and a girl. All were in blue jeans and looked as if they had stepped out of some "western" movie film. A short distance away stood a wooden corral with some cattle and horses enclosed in it. There must have been a big ranch somewhere nearby. I was amazed that we had come so soon into the typical deep West. Only a short time ago we had passed over Golden Gate Bridge, yet these were the romantic-looking figures of the Western ranches. They talked as in the movies. Mr. Little was quite at home with them, for he had come to San Francisco originally from the deep West. He was now trying to persuade Milton to buy some of the land. "Only $500 per acre." He was sure that in a few years' time the price would soar and the land be developed into a housing project or township. It seems that the West is still a land of opportunity for a pioneer spirit.

When I was a young child at home, my grandmother, who at eighty still ruled the big household of forty members, used to instruct us youngsters by way of well-known Chinese proverbs or sayings. One of her favorites was "A peach-stone will grow into a peach tree, but no one can foretell how the peach tree will grow." She taught us not to be too cocksure about anything. I thought of this proverb and wondered how long both sides of the Marin end of the Golden Gate Bridge would remain a military reservation.

That evening I happened to go into a shop near where I was staying. The proprietor of "Hobby Center" chatted with me as there were no other customers about. No sooner did I mention my visit to examine the construction of Golden Gate Bridge than he told me how he had climbed up the main suspension cable before the two main-span travelers met at mid-span and the stiffening trusses were joined together in November 1936. He had just been fascinated by the structure and had done it for a dare. He slipped out of his home one dark night. Two uniformed guards were on duty at the bridge, but they must have taken him for a motorist who had stopped there to have a look at the structure or at the scenery by night. He began to climb up the cable higher and higher until he felt a light being shone on him. The wind carried no sound to his ears, nor were the rays of the torch strong enough to reach him as he climbed on. He had the illusion, though, that someone was following him, and he clambered up faster than ever. He reached the top of the tower and fought his way down along the tower wall. As there was still a gap between the end of the span and the land, he climbed down to the fender close to the water-surface where the temporary pier structure was still attached. He arrived home for a good, sound sleep. He told me that he did not see anything when he reached the top of the tower: it was dark and he did not dare linger there. He seemed to agree with Mr. Little's "Nothing to see up at the top." Next morning the newspapers reported that someone had possibly attempted to climb up the cable of Golden Gate Bridge the previous evening, but that the guard had found nothing. The daring young man kept quiet at the time; a year later he began to tell people about his adventure. Many did not believe him and regarded it as a joke.

Three months went by quickly and I had to return to Boston for some research work before arranging my trip back to England. Before I went Milton and Biwei, his wife, insisted on entertaining me for dinner at their home which, like that of all my other good friends in the Bay area, was on Grizzly Peak. I could reach their house by bus, but I chose my own treasured method of progress—walking. Setting out in plenty of time, I enjoyed myself strolling and looking around all the way along Euclid Avenue. I met no one, yet I felt many were watching me curiously from their windows. The people on the West coast seem to have more time to spare than those in the East, much more than New Yorkers. But as for walking, it seems that only crazy people do that in the West as, on an average, each home has two or three cars. I spent some time in a rose garden a few steps down from Euclid Avenue. No sooner had I emerged on the road again than Shih-hsiang Chen, Professor of Chinese Literature at Berkeley, greeted me with a roar of laughter saying that at Milton's they had all been talking about my mad craze for walking and he had come to fetch me. He then shoved me into his car, saying "Get in, screwy brother!" and we drove away. He was very fond of saying "We two screwy brothers." During the evening we spoke of my visit to Golden Gate Bridge three months before. Milton remembered that I still hankered after climbing the tower, and the result was a phone call from him a few days later, telling me to be at the Administrative office of the Golden Gate Bridge at ten o'clock next morning.

Mr. Little was waiting at the entrance to introduce me to the General Manager, James E. Rickets. He said that James had made arrangements for someone to take me up the tower and that he was not going with me. "Nothing to see up there," Mr. Little shook his head in puzzlement, "I still don't understand what you want to go up the tower for." Before I could express my gratitude, he got into his car and drove away. Mr. Rickets called for Harry Walford and handed me over to him. "It is a nice morning for you," remarked Mr. Rickets. "I shall be here when you come down."

Harry told me that he got his job as a fire mechanic through his father-in-law, Ralph Patsel, who worked at the Golden Gate Bridge for seven years. "You must have courted the right girl," said I. This earned a wide grin from my guide as well as a pleasant hour afterwards. Nothing can go wrong if one praises a man's ability to find a good wife! We soon came round the Toll Plaza from underneath and stood before a small steel door at the Bay-side tower on the San Francisco end. The door led into the elevator which could only carry three people at a time. On the way up I learned that Harry had been truck driver, auto-mechanic and fire mechanic as well as travelling much before he married. Now married, he could not travel but enjoyed his job and family. Photographs of Roy and Rachelle, his little son and daughter, were shown to me.

Words left me for an instant and my mind was dazed when I was plunged out of the little door into *space*, really SPACE, except that my feet were attached to something solid. A moment ago I had my back pressed to a stiff, steel wall. A moment ago I had felt my breath circling round and crossing Harry's. A moment ago my eyelids had seemed rather heavy under the one small electric light. Only a moment ago the flesh of my body was about to quarrel with the bones for taking up too much room. What a difference now! My back stuck to nothing. My breath became buoyant and floated away. My eyelids moved without restraint and my bones and flesh stopped quarrelling. I felt free, detached, high above everything, yet infinitesimally small in the wide expanse. Can it be described as a sensation? A sensation of what—of pleasure or pain? It was neither. It was a sensation that I could not describe either in English or Chinese. But to me it meant that I was on the top of the tower of Golden Gate Bridge at last.

While I was drawing a deep breath and trying to compose myself, Harry called me to follow him up a steel ladder to the airway beacon above—Harry sees to this light every day. Up that absolutely vertical ladder in the open? I soon ceased to feel triumphant and became an ordinary man, not trained like Mr. Little as a structural engineer, nor like Harry, a fire mechanic. Climbing up the vertical steel ladder down below had proved almost too much for me; to do a similar climb on a taller steel ladder in the open air was unthinkable. It was no use pretending I could, but neither did I like to refuse. Fortunately Harry, unlike Mr. Little, was younger than me and I did not feel obliged by my Confucian upbringing to obey him. So I simply told him to go ahead while I looked round where I was. I moved to the center of the bar between two towers and watched Harry climbing up unconcernedly one step after another, until his body looked minute on the ladder under the round beacon-light rotating on its steel structure. On the other hand he seemed more than half as big as the Island of Alcatraz lying on the left far away and far below in the blue sea. It was a very clear morning; not only had the early sea fog long disappeared, but there was no morning haze shrouding the Berkeley hills. The few skyscrapers of San Francisco, placed a little apart from one another, looked like white candles ready to be lit up for some special festival. Every house was dressed in white satin. The faint towers of the Bay Bridge seemed to be flag-posts standing at equal intervals; an impressive procession might have been passing between them. The sky was an enormous canopy made of azure silk. The fresh green of the Berkeley hills opposite the pure white of San Francisco City, enclosing the deep blue of the Bay, made a perfect color scheme pleasing to my eyes.

On top of the tower of Golden Gate Bridge

Harry had reached the end of the ladder and moved to the other side, perhaps to inspect the beacon light. While watching the light rotating at regular intervals, my mind went back to early mornings and evenings when I had been driven over the bridge in a friend's car

which I try to make the most. In Heaven there may be wonders unobtainable on earth, yet I, unlike Chu Yuan, prefer to gaze at heaven and to linger on earth as long as I can. Just at that moment in my daydream Harry called to ask "How do you like being here? "Fine," I replied, and thanked him for having brought me to earth again.

Indeed how agreeable earth was to me, as I stood on the tower of Golden Gate Bridge, gazing at Heaven and all around. There was not a tiny dot of cloud anywhere. No artist could have painted so vast an area so evenly with his blue pigment. The bright sun shone directly on me but I did not feel hot. There was wind blowing on both sides, yet I did not feel cold. I breathed without hindrance. My sight reached as far as the horizon. My body felt lighter as if I was floating high above the water. My thoughts darted here and there, far and wide, completely carefree. Unlike being on the summit of Mount Tamalpais, I was actually detached from the earth, lifted by a steel bar six hundred and ninety feet above the water. And unlike being in an airplane I was not confined to looking through a tiny porthole at a small portion of an embossed map, while propellers revolved fast and noisily. From the top of Golden Gate Bridge I could detect someone walking round the Lime Point Lighthouse as well as a fisherman by the old Fort. They looked no bigger than ants. The sight of a huge ocean liner with its grayish-white body against the dark blue sea, gliding along in stately manner, was unforgettable. It did not seem to belong to the present machine age but to be rowed by enormous white oars created by the forking waves, sweeping both sides. Far away, row after row of houses along Lombard and around San Francisco Peninsula no longer looked like houses but rather like sheets and sheets of shining white silk unrolled and spread on the hill slopes to air, a sight familiar in the Chinese silk country outside Han-chou or Nanking.

Presently Harry appeared and asked if I was ready to go down. I followed him into the service elevator. He had a great deal to say about his work as a fire-mechanic. There are two lights on each tower, one of which is on reserve. The weather, through the Golden Gate into the Bay, can be very bad, but no matter how bad it is the light must go on. The terrible storm of December 1, 1951, whose velocity, Mr. Little had told me, reached sixty-nine miles per hour, was again described.

Market Street and the Bay from Twin Peaks.

Harry had had to go up to see to the lights but could not open the
door of the elevator when he reached the top. Had it not been jammed
he might have been blown off the ladder. I thought we would leave
the elevator when we reached the main-span, but Harry had something more to show me. Having stepped out, I found myself standing
on the fender wall that encloses the foundation of the tower. From
here, only forty feet above the water, I could see it rushing by and
could well believe that it was flowing at eight to nine miles an hour.
The fender is one thousand one hundred feet from the tip of San
Francisco peninsula, and I felt that Harry and I had become two lonely Islanders. Two big holes, eighteen inches by twenty-four inches, are
left open down below the fender to keep the water flowing more
steadily. Masses of fish swim inside the fender, for they like the quietness of the water there. Harry told me with a grin that he had a com-
pensation sometimes after bad weather; he fishes round the fender,

with the General Manager's permission. "This is my private pool," he joked. He caught ling-cod, blue cod, perch, smelt, sea trout, bass, salmon, capozone, and eel. He also got a leopard shark once, the hind part of which was good eating. I asked if he had ever tasted Chinese shark's fins' soup, but I could not tell what kind of shark it was whose fins made the delicious soup I am fond of. In contrast to the stillness on the top of the tower the commotion around the fender was intense. Not only did the water rush swiftly by, and the wind blow keenly, but the commotion was heightened by the darting hither and thither of flocks of hell-divers, like well-disciplined troopers in battle. The hell-divers are black birds which fly faster than wind and water. They flew so close to the water surface that I could not have noticed them from higher up. While watching their flight, I also noticed a number of starfish in the water. Occasionally cuttlefish came along close to the fender wall. In a Chinese book entitled *Tan Kai* compiled by Feng Meng-lung of the Ming dynasty (1368-1644) there is a passage about these fish:

> The cuttlefish has five pairs of arms which it can draw into its mouth, and also can hide its mouth under its belly. Being equipped with an additional precaution against danger, it ejects black fluid to screen itself whenever it meets a fishing boat. Whereupon the fisherman casts his net on the black spot and takes it out of the water.

So do people get themselves into trouble sometimes by being over-cautious.

Back in the administrative office, I was greeted by Mr. James E. Rickets with a numbered copy of a red-covered book, *The Golden Gate Bridge*, signed by the general manager. I was delighted. Mr. Rickets added to his kindness by giving me a lift back to town. On our way I learned that he was very fond of fishing and did not mind the cold and rough weather, for he came from Newfoundland. Unlike the managers of many big offices, he is free-mannered, unreserved in conversation and friendly. I thanked him for all he had done for me.

A few days later I had to return to New York and Boston. Before I left I tried to see Mr. Little in order to thank him personally, but he was occupied elsewhere. Now the gatekeeper above has admitted him to Heaven. I write this to render him my homage. I want him to know that as he expected I did not see very much on the top of the tower of Golden Gate Bridge, but I *felt* a great deal while up there; and ever since, when I look back on the experience, I realize my good luck in having come to know Mr. Little in time.

V

Cruising Hypnotically

THE FOG-HORN sounded less and less, and the sky became clearer and clearer, as I set out to meet Alan White at his hotel. He has been my friend-and-publisher in London ever since 1935 when he helped to bring out my first book in English, *The Chinese Eye: An interpretation of Chinese Painting,* in connection with an International Exhibition of Chinese Art at Burlington House, London (1935-1936). When I met him for the first time I had not been long in England and he was then one of seven directors of Methuen & Co. Gradually he rose to be the managing director and now chairman of the one-hundred-year-old publishing company; he has himself carefully supervised the production of sixteen of the twenty-one books I have published so far. On the day (December, 1952) I left England for Boston, he and his wife Margery and his two sons, Richard and Julian, came to see me off at Waterloo Station. It was then that we arranged to meet again in San Francisco when he would later be making a business trip round the world. Now I had learned that he would be arriving in San Francisco from Melbourne.

Alan had no business to deal with in San Francisco. He was making a necessary break in the flight to New York and had decided to stop off for a few days' rest, and also to see something of this famous city of America's West while I was there. He agreed with my plan to take a trip round the Bay by boat the following day. We reached Fisherman's Wharf in the afternoon in time for the second run of the Bay Cruise. It was a pleasant sunny day but not too warm. No sooner was the anchor rope loosened than a loudspeaker began to announce the various buildings and landmarks within sight, with the usual tedious explanations. Alan and I were standing in the bow gazing ahead towards the Golden Gate Bridge and were not sorry that the wind carried those words away. The Bay water was not at all smooth and I have been told that it has never been known to be quite calm since the first Spanish Captain, Don Manuel de Ayala, entered it in 1775. This accounted for the merry dancing of the human structures on the shore as seen from our small cruising boat.

Alan wore at that time a type of Robert Louis Stevenson hair style. His hair was blown over his face and flapped behind his head in competition with the little flag of Stars and Stripes near where he stood. The much-tossed hair did not seem to bother him, for he kept looking straight ahead, at the oncoming scenery, as we all did except three children who were running from side to side of the boat. The skyline of the City had a hypnotic effect on the adults' minds. After the boat had passed the long fishing piers near the Aquatic Museum, thousands of dark-plumaged birds came flying very low, almost touching the water, and following one another as swiftly as the squadron after squadron of bombers that I used to see in the London sky during the Second World War. But to watch the bomber squadrons from far below caused a severe strain on the eyes, while to observe the quick motion of the water birds a short distance over the water kept the eyes alert and mobile. They were on our right, they were on our left, they were ahead of our boat and they were following behind us. They never stopped, but just flew on and on. Each flock passed us almost in a flash, yet the birds seemed to be always there, for one large flock would fly in constantly to take the place of another. How many there were it was simply impossible to tell; and how much activity there was over the water surface! The three young children kept running to the left, the right, the bow and the stern as if they were directed to do so by an invisible hypnotizer. One of them would suddenly scream at the sight of a new flying birdsquadron and jump about with upstretched arms; the other two immediately followed suit; they did it again and again. If their young minds were not under the influence of a sort of hypnotism, why did they keep on doing the same thing? Someone told me that there were many Pacific loons on the Bay water. Perhaps these birds were loons. A Pacific loon has a reputation for craziness, because of its wild, fiendish cries. I did not hear them crying but their swift troop-like movement hither and thither to no purpose seemed very crazy indeed.

Alan still had his eyes fixed straight ahead and his long hair still blew in the wind. He looked a little tired after the strenuous air-journey from England to Australia and New Zealand and on to San Francisco, but he gave the impression too of being lost in thought. We were now approaching the Golden Gate Bridge, though still a good distance away. Every one of us, including the youngsters, seemed to be in a trance—all watching as we moved nearer and nearer to the

Alan White on the Bay cruise

huge gap between two rocky mounds which appeared to be connected by a long, thin wire-like rope tightly stretched between two bamboo poles thrust into the water. It was a faint elusive picture. Gradually our boat drew nearer to the two rocky mounds with their constant bobbing motion, and the two bamboo-poles with the long rope between them became thicker and took on the shape of a bridge of a reddish color. I can well understand the choice of vermilion for Golden Gate Bridge. If it were painted silver like the Bay Bridge, it would be indistinguishable most of the time, for the glossy surface of the water under the sun or the morning fog and evening mist would obscure it. On the other hand, if the Bay Bridge had been painted red, it would be too conspicuous and even an eyesore amid the surrounding light-colored buildings.

Suddenly I saw a rather thick but fluffy white-cotton blanket un-rolling and swaying up and down like everything else ahead of us, then coming nearer as if trying to get underneath the bed of the Golden Gate Bridge to come and wrap us all up against the cold wind that had been blowing ever since we started. Indeed, it managed to squeeze underneath, then swelled out immediately covering up the bridge-bed and the lower part of the two towers, which I had at first thought were bamboo-poles. The upper structure of the two towers now hung in the air like two red Chinese lanterns. Our pilot turned the boat more to the north and then east to avoid the oncoming steamer. As we turned I saw Angel Island in front of Mount Tamalpais dressing for dinner in a thin bluish-gray silk gown. Secret veils came from nowhere and soon formed a black velvet wrap for her when our boat turned farther east in the direction of the Bay Bridge. There was a soft, im-passive beauty and dreamlike mystery around Angel Island and San Rafael.

A shout of "Alcatraz!" from the announcer created the strangest hypnotic effect over all of us. A sight of outstanding loveliness on the north side of the Bay gave place to the horror of the barren aspect and grim significance of Alcatraz. Alan and I moved with the rest to the other side of the boat where we all craned over to see if we could catch a glimpse of anyone moving on that twelve-acre rock. Is it not human nature to enjoy the sight of a wrong-doer more than of a well-behaved person? Since 1933 Alcatraz has been notorious as the jail of eternal silence. It is said to have rigid discipline; its elaborate system to pre-vent escape is based on the "electric eye" which detects any metal on an inmate's body; the swift currents that flow around the rock make escape by water virtually impossible. The whole island of twelve acres was covered with high walled buildings.

I once tried to pay a visit to the rock, but the friend who had promised to make arrangements with the Warden died; I went to see San Quentin instead. After all, the inmates of these prisons are all human beings. Why should they be so rigidly guarded on a rock which is situated in the center of all kinds of human activities connected with pleasure-seeking, beautiful sights and comfortable living? It is quite understandable that the rock should have been fortified by the

Spanish in their day and that it should have been used as a military prison in the middle of the nineteenth century. Why it was chosen as a Federal penitentiary in 1933 is hard to understand. Could it not rather be turned into a most attractive pleasure-ground for all to enjoy? Is it there to serve as a reminder that there are incorrigible wrong-doers in the human world? I had learned about this rock from "The Birdman of Alcatraz," a well-known book made into a movie, and this made me move as hypnotically as the rest to have a keen look at it as we passed by.

The next focal point for our eyes was a huge metal buoy with a bell on it which sounded with the movement of the Bay water. The bell ringing by itself over the water was one attraction; another was some fat cormorants sitting there and overbalancing from time to time as the buoy bobbed up and down. Cormorants appear in many Chinese water-color paintings since the tenth century. They are seaside birds, good swimmers with voracious habits. Chinese fishermen train them to go out with them in a boat and sit quietly on the edge until they receive the order. They then dive into the water, seize a fish in their beak and bring it back. If the fish is very large two or three cormorants carry it together in a businesslike manner. Once in London when I was discussing a landscape of the Sung Master Ma Yuan showing cormorants on a boat moving down a stream, a lady in the group refused to look at the painting, declaring that it was most cruel to treat the birds in that way. I was surprised at the remark and asked her what she thought of the great English animal painter Landseer's work showing dead stags, rabbits and pheasants piled up together with the blood still flowing! How illogical people can be. I was glad to see the cormorants on the buoy in the Bay still looking as carefree and paintable as in the Chinese scene.

Again and again during the cruise our conversation came round to human behaviour and the contrast between the inhabitants of the West coast and those living in other parts of the U.S.A. I seldom indulge in generalizations. I think a New Yorker may seem rather bad-tempered and even quite rude when he is caught up in the forced frenzy of his business life, but if we meet him at home when he is relaxing, he could be as amiable and friendly as anyone. However, I could not help recalling what Mr. John Goulding Little, the consultant engineer, had once told me about the people of San Francisco when he showed me round the construction of the Golden Gate Bridge. He had come to make his career in San Francisco at the beginning of the century and had experienced the havoc of the great earthquake and fire of 1906. "That great event in human history," said Mr. Little, "has left this city of San Francisco an everlasting soul guiding all of us to judge our lives properly, though none today realize it." His point was that in that one night, all San Franciscans became equal: wealth meant nothing any more. In the sudden catastrophe, no one knew what would happen in the next hour and every one became reasonable and thoughtful for others. There was no apparent panic and little looting, for every one was in the same boat. Every one in the camp, the former rich and the still poor, shared food and clothes and cared for the very young, the old and the sick. The whole population of the city became a big friendly family. The instinctive friendliness created in that horrible night was still in the Bay air, affirmed Mr. Little. Indeed although that was the first time we had met, he himself treated me like one of his kin. Alan kept nodding his head and agreed that there was apparently something, as Mr. Little said, in the San Francisco air.

At this moment something appeared to be hindering our boat from going through the Bay Bridge. A commotion occurred in front of us and five or six rowing boats rushed underneath the enormous structure with the tide. Alan is a Cambridge man and I have lived in Oxford for sixteen years or so; rowing boats full of Blues were familiar sights to us. But we were both surprised to see these boats being rowed in the good old Oxford-Cambridge fashion on San Francisco Bay.

We paid no attention to Treasure Island, man-made for the 1939 Golden Gate International Exposition and now a forbidden naval territory. To pass directly underneath the Bay Bridge was a unique experience, though it reminded me of passing under George Washington Bridge over the Hudson River. But the Bay water does not flow smoothly like the river; I wondered how rowing races could be managed on such water. There is a constant wind blowing over the Bay

Boat race on the Bay

and this together with the ebbing and rising of the tide keeps the waves in a lively, dancing movement.

Oakland Harbor and Alameda were next pointed out to us, then the boat made another turn to the right and the skyline of the entire city of San Francisco came into view. Something seemed to be bewitching my eyes, though they were focused straight ahead. For the heights of the tall buildings were not static; some were shooting upwards while others were shrinking down. All the windows looked the same size at a first glance, but a moment later some grew bigger and some smaller and many even became fine dots hardly discernible. A few blazed with sparkling rays, and masses winked incessantly as our boat rocked on the water. Before the coming of dusk I seemed to hear the movements of a number of invisible painters who were busy covering the pure white walls with flesh tints, then pinkish, then purple colors. All the buildings were shaking their heads and jumping up and down —music and merriment floated in the air. I felt intoxicated. The City of San Francisco was exhibiting her beautiful obscurity in contrast to her dazzling splendour under the sun a moment ago. I said to Alan that the sun must be setting very slowly over on the other side of the Twin Peaks. He nodded and gave me a gentle smile hypnotically. He did not bother about what I was saying. How could he know about the Twin Peaks after one day's stay?

Again we were moving underneath the Bay Bridge, this time on the San Francisco side of the tiny island of Yerba Buena, the only reminder that this was once the name for the whole Bay Region. One morning my Chinese friend, Tong Min-fong, a cabaret performer working in one of the famous night-clubs in San Francisco, drove me round Yerba Buena but was soon turned back when we approached the man-made Treasure Island. The American army and navy occupy the best scenic spots in San Francisco Bay.

We sailed on, into the magnificent assembly of mists whose array was encompassing the rock cliffs by the Golden Gate, the Bridge, the hills of Mill Valley, Mount Tamalpais, and Angel Island. Alcatraz was almost blotted out; it became an imaginary, ether-bound palace fit for fairies or kings. It was faintly visible but unapproachable. The mists rolled on and on. I hailed them voicelessly. The moment of transition from splendour to obscurity is even more beautiful than that from obscurity to splendour. White-capped waves appeared now in increasing number. We were all released from our hypnotic condition by the cold wash of the flying foam spraying upwards from the bows.

The after-effects of hypnotism are hard to shake off. Neither Alan nor I showed any inclination to talk about the many beauties of water, earth, and sky we had just been seeing. Our legs were not inclined to bestir themselves either. Alan rejected the idea of eating cross-legged in a Japanese restaurant at Fisherman's Wharf, and I was not keen to get a pair of chopsticks busy again in his hand in a Chinese eating place on Grant Avenue, though Alan had long become expert in using chopsticks. We agreed to try a German restaurant under the Coit Tower on Telegraph Hill, where I had found the food excellent and the atmosphere very agreeable a few nights before. We were politely received by the head-waiter and shown to a table by the window, from which we could see the lights on the Bay shore. On each table a candle was half burned down, the tiny wick on its grotesquely fat body dripping with candle grease. We both laughed at the ingenuity of the human mind which will go to any extremes if there is a "gain" to be had. "Give it a romantic air" is the cry when all the incentive for romance is lost. Since the lovely lighting of chandelier days was replaced by blazing neon lights, a tiny candle flame has come to meet the need of the never-satisfied human mind. Most of the tables were occupied by young couples. Alan knew something of German food and the dishes he suggested were very appetizing. Of course we became quite gluttonous after the long time we had spent on the windy Bay water. We talked while we ate, touching on all kinds of subjects and often reminding each other of days spent together on Black Heath near London, where Alan used to live, at Hampton Court, in Oxford and many other places in England. "With a Bay like this in San Francisco," Alan remarked, "no one would want to dash about." "There is a Bay in New York too, you know," I reminded him. Though environment may influence people, the real nature of a man counts most. Many human beings are inclined to take things easily if they can, but there are some who simply cannot. By way of entertaining my friend I then related a famous Chinese joke about two men, the one very excitable and the other very deliberate. They were sitting together having a drink round an old-fashioned Chinese stove with live charcoal burning in a brass bowl on a wooden stand. The long gown of the excitable man touched the stove and was beginning to burn, just as he turned his head to look at a painting on the wall. The deliberate man, seeing this, tapped his shoulder and said in a very polite, slow manner:

"There is something I should like to let you know, which I have noticed, but which owing to your uncontrollable temper I hesitate to mention, though the result will be the same for me whether I mention it or not."

"What is it? What is it? Say quickly!"

"Well, well, a corner of your long gown has dipped itself into the charcoal bowl and is now on fire."

"Why ever didn't you say so before?" The excitable man pulled out the gown to extinguish it and jumped at his friend in a rage.

"People do assert that you have a very excitable temper, and now I see that they are not far wrong," came the reply!

VI

Rising Elegantly

ALMOST THREE MONTHS had slipped by since my arrival in San Francisco Bay. Almost every day the same whimsical thought arose in my mind. And almost every time I walked round the Bay, the outline of Mount Tamalpais in mist, in haze or in blazing sunshine, appeared, urging me to put my thought into action. I had the wish to camp up on Mount Tamalpais for a night and watch the day break.

I was told that a certain Jacob Lesse was the first person to climb the peak a hundred years or so ago in order to disprove the Lacatuit Indian legend that evil spirits haunt the mountain. Lester Jaspovice told me that when he was a youngster in San Rafael school, his teacher used to take the class for outings round the wide bay. In those days, it was a wild region edged with sand dunes. On one occasion, while the children were playing, a huge Red Indian in feathered cap and with painted face jumped out from behind one of the sand-hills. Lester and his classmates ran for their lives. But the Indian was no other than their teacher in disguise! Lester remembered, too, how his teacher used to take the class up Mount Tamalpais by the wooden-trestled railroad of the Mount Tamalpais Scenic Railway, drawn by oil-burning logging engines. They had all the fun of going up then and did not mind whether they found Indians or not. I met Lester Jaspovice in the Hobby Center Camera shop along Geary, and he told me that that railway was known as the "Crookedest Railroad in the World." But of course it had long been abolished when I came to San Francisco.

I myself have been taken up Mount Tamalpais by friends several times. I know the view of the distant Bay and have also walked among many strangely-shaped rocks to the Fire-Watch Tower on the tip of the West Peak. Mount Tamalpais presents a thousand aspects, and each time it seems to respond to my mood. I was told that many different groups of Indians used to live scattered among all these hills some two hundred years ago, but nowadays the hills are left in peace. How I wished that I could be the only remaining Indian walking along the trails silently for hours and days, living on acorns and gazing at the changing scenery!

My wish to spend a night on Mount Tamalpais kept burning inside me. I tried to find a way of staying behind there after one of my trips but it was useless—even a bus conductor insisted on my joining his touring party back to Mill Valley. My return to England was becoming imminent, so at last I ventured to explain my project to Jimmy Lawson and ask him if he would take me up Tamalpais one night and leave me there. He readily agreed, and even offered to keep me company. Some days later Juanita said that she had decided to join her husband and me in the adventure, but they would have to return to the city early the following morning for their Sunday services. She is a musician and plays the organ for the church and Jimmy is a Christian Science reader. I was ready to agree to anything, for I was more than happy at the prospect of a night on Tamalpais at last.

Juanita made everything ready, including food and sleeping bags. About nine o'clock at night Jimmy motored us through the Golden Gate Bridge where the lines of brilliant lamps on both sides seemed like rows of glossy yellow pearls of unusual size. In the company of my two good friends, I had a satisfied and grateful heart. Up the Mill Valley the road was clear for driving. It was pitch dark all round, except for an occasional light or two from some distant houses appearing through the thickets of trees, then disappearing and reappearing as if winking at me.

Presently our car turned on to the Observation Point, for the Lawsons wanted me to have a look at the night scene of San Francisco Bay far down below. We were the only people there and none of us uttered a word. The solid blackness everywhere overpowered the lighted area in the distance, making it look so very small, yet dazzlingly bright. Was it a floating magic carpet well-equipped with modern neon apparatus? Or was it Vaissavana, one of the four Indian Maharaja-deva kings, crossing the ocean with his retinue in full armour and insignia with torches and lanterns in a slow-moving procession? The scene was entrancing

—a fairy land yet real, or a near-at-hand reality yet remote and untouchable. Neither shapes of buildings nor human forms were visible. All the viable lights were floating, floating on as if attached to nothing, some winking and some moving a little faster than others. They gave me a nostalgic feeling for an experience I had with my father high up a hill near my native city on a festival night.

It was long a custom in China, though it may be discontinued now, to keep the festival of All Souls on the fifteenth day of the seventh moon. Scriptures were read by Buddhist and Taoist priests and elaborate offerings made to the Buddhist Trinity for the purpose of releasing from purgatory the souls of those who had died on land or sea, so that they could go back to where they belonged in their lifetime. The custom is said to originate with Sakyamuni, whose disciple Maudgalyayana is represented as having been to purgatory to relieve his mother's sufferings. Sakyamuni told him that only the united efforts of the whole priesthood could alleviate the pains of the suffering in hell. After dusk on that date many families took out lotus lanterns, made of red grease-proof paper in the shape of lotus flowers, in which were some cabbage oil and a tiny wick and went down to the riverside to light them and set them adrift on the water. These lotus-shaped water-lamps were to guide and carry all the wandering souls, newly released, to where they wanted to go. My father, being an artist with a liberal mind, loved this custom dearly. He busied himself setting off a number of the lotus lamps down the river and then went up to higher ground to watch them floating. He used to tell me that he could not say whether the lamps really helped wandering souls; his enjoyment lay in the entrancing sight of so many bright-red floating dots. My first experience of them was when I was about twelve years of age. I helped my father to set off the lamps on the Yangtse river and then we went up a nearby hill called Yen-chih Shan to watch. That was more than forty years ago, and I have been wandering outside China for the past twenty-six years. Whether there will be a red lotus lamp to carry my soul back to my birthplace is doubtful.

When we had gazed our fill at the San Francisco lights far away below, Jimmy drove us to the Camping office to make the necessary arrangements. A few tents were already set up and occupied, so we warned ourselves not to make much noise while finding a pitch. All our provisions were laid on a picnic table. The Lawsons established themselves not far from me. I had a comfortable sleeping bag and felt glad that I had no tent over me. This was the first time I had spent a night in the open air on a mountain since I had left China. I had a little wooden hut on my native Mount Lu. A small mountain stream half circled the hut and then joined a waterfall down below. I had a huge rock hollowed to take my bedding and I would fall asleep there listening to the delicious sound of the flowing water. But the hut was situated over two thousand eight hundred feet above sea level and it could be very cold in the earliest hours of the morning. I never managed to spend the whole night outside the hut. Now I was ready to enjoy a full night in the open, for Mount Tamalpais is in the semi-tropical zone, dry and warm. I shut my eyes for a moment to recall all that I had just seen and was filled with pleasurable anticipation of the new experience before me.

When I next lifted my eyelids, to my surprise I saw that the moon was looking directly down on me. Why had I not noticed her a moment ago? Nothing could have been better than this pleasant surprise. The moon revealed to me that I was lying in a beautiful pine grove with lofty trunks rising all round me. The clear light had a tranquillizing effect: all my thoughts were stilled as I idly watched the intricate patterns formed by the twigs among the top branches of the pine trees. The very pine needles seemed to stand out separately against the clear dark-blue of the night. The moon was full but I could not see her full face behind the intricate patterns. She seemed now to be evading my direct gaze. Some white clouds had appeared and must have caused the impression that the pine branches were vibrating, for there was no wind. While watching them I could not tell whether it was the moon moving, or the clouds or the tops of the trees.

The stillness of my mind at that moment was a little disturbed by the upward movement of something on a pine tree nearby. It moved and then stopped, and a moment later it started again. The faint rustlings were repeated until a small black spot revealed itself against the upper part of the thick trunk, and soon disappeared to the other side of the tree. Again it appeared. It moved swiftly along a branch right to the tip, where it lifted up its two forepaws in front of its chest in the Chinese fashion of a person ready to worship and pray. It was a squirrel. The black outlines of the branches and twigs and of the body of the little creature against the round face of the bright moon formed a perfect composition for a Chinese monochrome painting. The deeper the night sank, the vaguer my mind became. The outlines of the branches and the squirrel began to fade and mingle in my thoughts—then vanished completely.

A little after three o'clock I woke up. The moon had departed. It was still dark. I managed to slip out of the sleeping bag without making any noise and went to have a quick wash. When I returned, the Lawsons had also got up, and Juanita hastened to tell me that the raccoons must have eaten my breakfast, for there were no slices of ham left in the paper bags. Fortunately a few pieces of bread were intact, and I nibbled two of them with a glass of milk. My friends soon busied themselves packing up. Jimmy suggested that I should go alone to the spot where I could watch the sun rising: They would expect to see me at home in the evening.

To hear was to obey. Through the darkness I walked on steadily and slowly following the footpath round the edge of a steep hill to the spot where I had been several times before. All the way I saw only a great blackness; neither sea nor hills were visible, just my own form and a short stretch of vaguely whitish footpath in front of and behind my feet. I did not go down the steps to the observation point but remained by the footpath above, and settled on a rock. Never before had I peered into the massive darkness so eagerly and intently. All of a sudden—literally in the wink of an eye—appeared the silhouettes of land and sea on a still blackish background. Who could have cut them out so swiftly in such a vast scale? Bit by bit the heavy darkness grew less solid: The blackish background of a moment ago was now the color of fish-milt. It was the sky, distinguishable now from the earth. The day had broken! Gradually the light strengthened, and the fish-milt sky changed to gleaming red close to the horizon through the burning golden beams somewhere behind the land mass. The bluish part of the sky soon joined the splendid shiny reddish tint to draw upward bit by bit the source of all the light and color. At first only a curved rim appeared, then a quarter-circle, a semi-circle, three-quarters, till at last it floated above the horizon—the brilliant, red-hot, golden ball of colossal size. At least, it looked red-hot, but its heat did not yet penetrate. On the other hand, it seemed to spread a universal mirth over land and sea, far and near around me. An indescribable warmth rose within me and caused my eyes to sparkle.

This was not my only experience of watching the sunrise, but it was a very memorable one. As a young boy of a little more than twelve, I was once taken up by my father to the highest peak of my native Mount Lu. It was about four thousand feet above the sea level. Up there, even in summer, though dry it was not too hot—about seventy degrees in daytime up to the last thousand feet. On that early morning, the higher we moved up, the colder I felt. My father knew what to expect and had brought thick clothes for us both. After the dawn broke I realized that we were completely encircled by white woolly clouds which seemed to reach to infinity on all sides. Except for the big rocky cliff where we were standing, there was not a scrap of land in sight. I watched the huge golden-red ball of the sun gradually pushing its way up with great effort through the thick woolly clouds. Perhaps I was still too young to appreciate the sight as my father did: I was feeling too cold and was soon taken down to where we were staying. Another time I watched the sun rising up slowly but strenuously from the bottom of the Atlantic Ocean while great waves seemed to beat against its face all the time. This was when I was sitting on the bridge deck not far from the big funnel of the Cunard Liner, *Queen Mary*, soon after the end of the Second World War. The Liner was not yet reconditioned from its troop-carrying service. On this first trip after the war it carried two thousand three hundred G. I. brides and seven hundred babies. We men, eighty altogether, were cornered and could not move about much on the decks. I spent my time mostly on the bridge deck, and that early morning was cold on the open ocean; the glowing rays of the rising sun brought me a little warmth. On Mount Tamalpais I found the sun neither rising out of thick clouds nor from the bottom of the ocean. It sailed up gently and elegantly in the grand manner but with a faint rosy blush over its face like a well-bred Chinese lady during the traditional wedding ceremony. According to Chinese custom she would not utter a word for almost the whole day, but would appear to blush and glow with an inward warmth.

I suddenly noticed the emergence of a mass of yellowish matter in odd shapes, dotted above the white clouds close to the water edge. The white clouds appeared tinged with violet by the influence of the yellowish matter, which in turn became brighter and shinier. Apparently it was the City of San Francisco, a tiny spot in the remote distance. It sparkled under the sun yet remained vague.

The slope on which I was standing on Mount Tamalpais stretched down to San Francisco Bay. It displayed now an unusual color effect, in which the green leaves of the manzanita trees and the brown surface of the soil with patches of the typical dark green-and-red succulent San Franciscan grasses blended into a subtle and soft purplish hue under the burning beams of the rising sun. Some heavy mists had gathered just over the Bay surface and seemed to have swallowed up the foundations of the distant City, leaving a number of faint, thin, tall buildings, apparently of silver or crystal. While the sun still rose upwards, the crystal city grew magically bigger as the Bay mist thinned.

A little distance to my left there appeared a faint image of the peak of Mount Diablo. Curiously enough Mount Diablo could easily be mistaken for the Japanese national pride, Mount Fujiyama, which is seen in so many Japanese paintings and woodcuts, except that Diablo lacks the cap of snow. The whole view—the rising sun between the image of Mount Diablo slightly above on my left and the distant City down below on the right—together with the soft curve of Richardson Bay from the corner of Sausalito right round to Belvedere near the base of Mount Tamalpais presented me with a beautiful composition for a painting.

The sun—the universal-mirth producer—was now heaving his broad shoulder over the edge of the world as the poet, John Keats, once expressed it. Its radiant beams made me avert my eyes. All the mists had evaporated—not a single wisp remained over the Bay. The coastal line that had seemed like the image of a rattlesnake a moment ago was now clear. The haphazard hiking trails, zigzagging along the hill ridge or around the hill waist, revealed themselves as a vague pattern of curved red lines on an uneven-surfaced canvas of thick green paints—an abstract painting in the modern style.

I now looked back along the footpath which I had followed in the darkness. A mass of billowy white cloud was creeping along far beyond where the Golden Gate Bridge lay. Nothing of that great engineering feat was visible. The motion of the vast shroud of endless white clouds was hardly perceptible, yet it continually advanced and spread still wider. According to ancient Chinese belief, it might have been a majestic dragon stretching its royal body and legs towards where I stood. A place where the dragon dwells, so the belief holds, possesses "lung-mo" meaning "dragon's vein" or "ling-ch'i" meaning "living element." Unlike the monster of western tradition, the Chinese dragon has long been the most honored animal in our legends, a lively spiritual being, full of wisdom and benevolence, exercising influence for the benefit of all. In its unseen presence everything grows and flourishes. Perhaps this explains why San Francisco holds an indefinable attraction for all who come to know it: it must possess the "dragon's vein." At any rate, that is my explanation!

The sun was now far above the horizon, and high over the city. It was no longer a big red-golden disc but a much smaller, bright mirror —too bright to look at. Its burning beams made me feel quite warm so that I had to take off my jacket. I suddenly remembered an intriguing problem about the sun that had once puzzled Confucius. It was said that Confucius was driving with his disciple, Tzu Lu, when they met two young boys in heated argument on the road. Confucius told Tzu Lu to get down and find out what it was all about. They were arguing about the distance between the sun and the place where they were standing. One boy said that the sun was nearer him in the morning than at noon time, because it was bigger in the morning than at noon, and the bigger the nearer. But the other boy argued that sun became hotter at noon time than in the morning, and the hotter the nearer. Both boys asked if Confucius could say who was right. Confucius could not say. The boys went away, shouting laughingly: "Who says that Confucius is the wisest man on earth?" Being no Confucius myself, I do not mind admitting that I could not say who was right either. I then moved on down the hillside to find the friend who was coming to meet me at the Mountain House.

After walking a short distance along the footpath I felt hotter and hotter. I caught sight of two or three hummingbirds suspended in the air while their wings seemed to be revolving incessantly rather than flapping like those of other birds. They could even fly backwards. This backward-flying by the humming-bird that hums and flies like a bee has shattered my conventional knowledge about birds! No humming-birds have ever appeared in China.

As I neared the Radar Station on the mountain-side I remembered the open-air Mountain Theatre not far from there, and which I had been taken to see the previous month. It must have been an imitation of the Greek open-air theaters, though this one on Mount Tamalpais does not much resemble the ones I saw at Delphi or at Athens. The theater on Mount Tamalpais is said to be the only mountain amphitheater of its kind in the world. The stage is approximately two thousand feet above sea level. The audience that comes to see a play can also enjoy the beautiful setting of the surroundings from the top of Tamalpais. With a few exceptions, notably those of the Second World War years, each third Sunday in May is the "Mountain Play Day." The first play, produced in 1913, was *Abraham and Isaac*, a miracle play—together with some scenes from *Twelfth Night*. A play entitled *Tamalpa* by Dan Totheroh was first presented in 1921 and is repeated about every five years. The play tells the following story:

> On the mountain lies a maiden asleep on a bed of eternal purple, and it is she who gives the play its name and its theme. When Tamalpa walked upon the mountain-top the tribe in the valley whispered her name in fear and called her a siren.
>
> Her mother was Ah-Shawn-nee, an evil witch, who ruled an evil tribe and sent plagues of death to the tribes of man.
>
> At last the Great White Spirit offered the shining gift of Healing to the world, and Piayutuma, of the tribe in the valley, was chosen to climb the mountain's slope, attain the gift from the Great White Spirit and return as the world's first medicine man.
>
> Tamalpa, young and beautiful, was sent by Ah-Shawn-nee to turn him from his mission and succeeded, but in doing so fell truly in love for the first time in her life.

After a long and bitter struggle she tried to make him give her up and go upon his way but, blind with love, he would not heed and hastened the morn of marriage.

Seeing no other course, Tamalpa made the supreme sacrifice and was borne in solemn triumph to the mountain-top, where she sleeps forever in the eyes of the world.

I should like to have seen this play performed, though the story is so different from the legend of Tamalpa I had read elsewhere. This legend relates that centuries ago the God of the Sun assumed human form and descended to earth on a mission. After he landed on the mountain, he fell deeply in love with the beautiful daughter of an Indian Chief. When the time came for his return to Heaven, he seized his love in his arms and mounted into the sky. Unfortunately one of his feet struck Mount Diablo, and he plunged headlong into the great lake whose water is now that of the Bay, formerly divided by the mountain range. The mighty arm of the God of the Sun broke a gap through the mountain barrier, which is known to us now as the Golden Gate. But the lovely Indian maiden was crushed to death when hurled from his arms. He gently picked her up and laid her to rest on the drier part of the mountain. The soft outlines of Mount Tamalpais are the outlines of the graceful form of the lovely Indian maiden in her eternal sleep.

By now I had begun to feel very hungry, and I noticed a hiking trail near the Observation Stage, which would lead me to the Mountain House, the only eating place up the Mountain. Sir Edward Appleton of the British Association for the Advancement of Science once remarked: "Man is at his best when facing the challenge of the unknown." I did not want to be at my best but had to find the way. After a good deal of trial and error I managed to hit the right trail. The hill was dry and the slope on this trail very steep; with each step of mine the sand and pebbles rattled down the hillside. I tried to keep erect with a slight tilt backwards; but as soon as I leaned back, my foot would slip and upset my balance. Many times I nearly fell flat. Noticing a chipmunk munching its nut on a stone with evident enjoyment, I remembered with chagrin the raccoon's breakfast which should have been mine. When I stepped forward to have a closer look at my fellow creature, it disappeared. It must have been afraid that I wanted to share its nut. I then became interested in the shape of the little stone on which the chipmunk had perched. When I picked it up, I found it was very light; in fact it was not a stone at all but part of a knobbly root of a manzanita tree. It had a wonderful shape and could have been used for some indoor decorative arrangement. I kept it, intend-

Chipmunk

ing to bring it back to San Francisco. Gradually many similar dry knobs of the manzanita roots presented themselves to my eyes and I could not resist collecting them. I selected the five best and with them my hands and arms were full. No sooner had I realized that I had come to a steeper slope than my feet lost their firm hold and began to carry me away. To my great alarm a rather big rock underneath my left foot gave way and I must have caused a little earthquake to be recorded in a nearby seismological laboratory. My body did not roll but slid down until I opened my hands to grasp the strong root of a living manzanita. Lo and behold! the five, beautiful, dry knobs of the manzanita roots went tumbling down the slope without saying good-bye to me! Nothing seemed to them so enjoyable as to be absolutely free. I shook my head and looked up at the brilliant sun which shone directly on my face with spite. The God of the Sun was telling me not to take anything away from his beloved!

Wearily I got up and managed to reach the Mountain House eventually. While having a cup of coffee, in dashed Mrs. Olive Cowell, excitedly announcing that she had everything fixed and that it was about the right time for us to set off for Russian River. We climbed in the car and speedily moved off. She did not ask what I had been doing up Tamalpais since the previous night, nor did she spare a moment for me to tell her the Indian Maiden legend, which she said she knew all about already. She had so much to say to me all the way. But I insisted on telling her that the God of the Sun had shown a "miracle" to me. She only laughed and went on with her own remarks. It seems to me that our modern life has become much too realistic; very little is left for imagination. It has also become too civilized. For myself I prefer to paddle in muddy water rather than in a well-paved swimming pool, and I enjoyed my night in the sleeping bag up Mount Tamalpais more than in a comfortable bed. Thanks to the Lawsons, my wish came true.

VII

Blowing Mysteriously

Mr. FRANK WILLIAMS, the great self-trained architect of Sacramento who has built more than two thousand houses there so far, wanted to take me to see some beautiful dwelling houses in Grass Valley, an old mining town, and Hirshman's Diggins, where he used to play with wagon-men as a kid, and Nevada City where he was born some seventy years ago. Bob Morris drove us. On our way Frank had a great deal to tell me about how he went to work in Oregon when he was thirteen years old and then to the gold field in Nevada at seventeen. Later he worked for Charles Dean of Dean & Dean, a marvellous craftsman, and studied hard to train himself as an architect to build houses for people to live in. He then used to have ten or fifteen houses being built at the same time. After having seen a number of beautiful little houses of charming New England style in Nevada City, I marvelled at their uniqueness and wondered how they could have been built in such an out-of-the-way town and also why there are so few New-England-styled houses in San Francisco, as most of the gold-rushers came from the East. Frank explained that in the days of the gold rush, few people actually stayed in San Francisco for long, and that when they got money the cheap labor and good climate encouraged them to bring material from New England and to build their houses like the old homes they knew. San Francisco's cold weather was no good for most of them. Besides, San Francisco's steep hills and narrow lots of land did not lend themselves to the building of big houses. "Architecturally speaking," continued Frank, "San Francisco has never been famous for good houses. But it has always been a fascinating city in which to study ways of building houses." He always came to roam in it whenever he could. In the eighteen-fifties all Victorian-styled houses, chiefly on Nob Hill, were built by fabulously rich families who had the money to spend but no idea of how the houses should be built, so they were all strictly English, since this was the prevailing style at the time. Then after the great fire and earthquake of 1906 the Mediterranean type of residential house and landscaped house was built. Later came the jigsaw era when there were no more fabulously rich people but many who became upper middle class and could afford to build houses in the way they liked. This has opened new developments and enriched architectural activities in San Francisco ever since. Gradually California Modern, a style typically Californian, has been created and many houses with Japanese influence combine the simplified form in craftsmanship and decoration. Labor, change of material, transportation, and the function of electricity have all contributed to the change of styles in architecture. Good line, good proportion, color scheme, light and air have all come into the process of architectural design. Arrangement of windows to provide good views is of much more value in San Francisco than in most places. "Building a house," Frank then remarked with a broad smile, "is one of the greatest adventures in life. I never forget a single house I have built."

Though no student of architecture, I was interested in all Frank had to say about San Francisco houses. To me they seem to include a bewildering variety of styles, Moorish, Spanish, English, Italian and French château, Romanesque, Moslem, Japanese, ultra-modern and pseudo-Chinese. Perhaps no other cosmopolitan city has accumulated so many different types of house. The Sentinel Building, now called Columbus Tower, between Columbus and Pacific Avenues, stands out from the rest as the symbol of a bygone era. How long will it continue to stand there? Space seems to me to have been the paramount building problem in San Francisco and the modern housing method of building hundreds of similar dwellings has crept in everywhere around this big city. However, I was often surprised to find some ingenious houses built on the smallest possible piece of land awkwardly situated on the corner of a hill slope. On many an occasion when I was travelling by car and we seemed to have come to the end of the road, by making another turn we unexpectedly arrived at a tiny cosy place, like a hermitage. Once I was driven into a garage by the roadside, within which a door opened wide to reveal our hostess greeting and

Columbus Towers

beckoning us to follow her down the steps. At the bottom of the first flight we made a turn, followed down some more steps, and emerged into the living room, which is actually far below the garage. The lower slope of the hill offers a better view, so the living rooms are built below and the car has to stay above! I feel that San Francisco postmen ought to have a better wage than those of other cities for they need such skill in delivering letters. All San Francisco houses seem to have been unconsciously arranged like those paddy-fields on Chinese hillsides where no inch of land is left uncultivated. I was interested to realize that the architects in San Francisco have a similar outlook to the Chinese peasants who do not like to see any ground wasted.

It is natural that houses built on the hillsides should enjoy the great advantage of commanding good views. The most important thing for a San Francisco host or hostess to show me after I have entered the house is the beautiful view through the windows. Most of the houses built on the hill slopes are arranged like the steps of a giant staircase ready for the giant Gulliver to climb one by one in the Lilliputian San Francisco. And at Christmas that busy person, Santa Claus, must be able to carry out his task much more easily here, for he can start dropping his Christmas presents into the chimney of the first house on the very top of Russian Hill and then gradually walk down step by step, dropping the presents into the chimneys at the same time!

Santa Claus delivering gifts

It is fortunate for the city to have so many hills which protect her from the strong winds blowing from the Pacific Ocean. So far as I can judge, the cold fog seems to come to a stand-still around the Presidio and Twin Peaks. There is more sunshine down Market Street, and I was told that beyond Mission Street towards the Bay it is always warmer throughout the whole year, even in summer. Apart from Twin Peaks, though, none are hills in the rural sense, for all are covered with roads and buildings, from the bottom of the slope to the tip. Perhaps I could best describe the San Francisco roads as "tall land-waves" comparable with those on the high seas. Inside a friend's car I always felt like travelling on a boat, rocking in and out of the tall waves of the sea, until the car had to stop at the traffic lights.

From the distance, Twin Peaks are deceptive. Geographically they stand out as the highest point and command the view all round. But can we see the view all round from up there? Not in my experience anyway. On the first day of my arrival in February 1953, Bob and Thelma Morris drove Shih-hsiang Chen and me there to get a bird's-eye view of San Francisco. Parts of the city were visible but a thick sea-fog was swirling below. The car door had to be forced open against the wind with a hard push when I begged to be let out for a look. Shih-hsiang followed me up one of the peaks while Bob and Thelma remained in the car. I just managed to stand on the tip for a moment before we both were blown off our feet. There must be days when one could stand up there; but none of my friends gave me much encouragement.

The Twin Peaks are the remaining top of a huge hill which has been systematically cut away from its base upwards to make a spiral-like road with houses in terraces all round. There is nothing much of interest at the top except a big open space which has been made into a City Park, though hardly any people were to be seen there when I was taken by. I remember my pleasant trip up the Hill of Howth outside Dublin, Ireland, for a good blow, which I recorded in my book *The Silent Traveller in Dublin*. The Hill of Howth is a peninsula, bare, high, and projecting right out into the Irish sea; it catches the full force of every sea wind. There is a common saying in Dublin: "If you've got a cold, go and have a blow on the Hill of Howth." I thought, even without a cold I needed no inducement to return to it. Wind—except when of destructive tornado force—is exhilarating. It makes one laugh gleefully, and not merely because its invisible hands make one's clothes caper comically. For some time I was hankering for a blow up the Twin Peaks. One day when I was staying with Rudolph Schaeffer at his School of Design on the rock at the top end of Mariposa Street, I woke to find there was no sign of the Twin Peaks from the window—they had been blotted out by mist. After breakfast

I asked Rudolph if he would drive me up to the top, but he hesitated a little over my request, for he knew nothing could be seen there. Later, in his usual friendly way, he agreed and we set off upwards. Upon reaching the Twin Peaks Boulevard Rudolph drove his car very slowly indeed, almost inch by inch, quite close to a low wall, only a small part of which could be seen at a time. Though our car body was almost grazing it, the wall appeared to be farther away, on account of the masses of tiny particles combined together into a veil that softened its rugged lines and created a distance between us. Beyond the wall I could see nothing. A dense white fog lay upon the whole hill, clothing the Twin Peaks from summit to base and then down to where we were and again down, down to the deep waters of the Bay in a vast edgeless shroud. Our car seemed to be drifting or floating in space far above the earth. No other car was about, for no other owner had a friend as crazy as I. Sitting in his driver's seat, Rudolph cautiously fixed his gaze straight ahead through the dark rims of his glasses, saying nothing and seemingly enjoying himself in perfect calm. Occasionally we exchanged a smile; the only sound we heard was the ticking of the engine. At times, a faint, almost inaudible sigh breathed behind the vast shroud of white fog in one direction or another. I only detected it when the breath came our way to puff at the side window of the car. It was the hill-wind or the Bay wind that was blowing and blowing all round us. Now and then the side windows rattled a little faster for a moment or two. A faint cry from a lonely, bewildered seagull far down below came haltingly through the sodden atmosphere to my ear too. Was it calling to remind us that we had company? All was engulfed in an absurd enchanting mystery.

Rudolph gladly consented to my suggestion of getting out of the car for a while. It was blowy, but the masses of white particles were jostling each other in a sort of merry-go-round fashion instead of dashing along in a rapid sweeping flow. They all seemed to keep to their own places, though circling, moving and rolling all the time. Here and there, a slight drift of one group of the mass disclosed shadowy clusters of objects, while another group became denser. Then the veils would billow and interweave, and the old impermeable obscurity prevail again. The great commotion never seemed to be diminishing.

Down in the valley when the sky was clear, I often gazed with great wonderment at the various formations of the clouds, sometimes taking the shape of a bear, a lion and even a Chinese dragon, an enormous monster of prehistoric days. In recent years I have travelled long distances by air and the aeroplane was always high above the clouds, whose formations are even more amazing and alluring from that aspect. I remember with particular vividness the clouds on my flight from New York to Antigua and then on to Barbados in the Caribbean. They took the shapes of towered citadels in the grandest manner, such as St. Peter's Basilica in Rome and all the magnificent châteaux of France and castles of Spain; some looked like the spire of the English Salisbury Cathedral; one suggested the Blue Mosque of Istanbul, yet another resembled the structure of the famous Indian Temple at Somnath; even a few tall columns of the New York skyscrapers were represented, but none of them suggested to me the Kyoto Shinto Shrine or Peking Palace. The scientist may explain this by saying that clouds tend to rise upwards instead of spreading sideways in sections or layers like the curving roofs of Chinese and Japanese architecture. Quite apart from this, it seems to me that the ideas in my mind have changed during my many years outside China, which in turn have influenced my eye-view somehow or somewhat.

Now I was actually inside the clouds on the Twin Peaks and realized that there was continual movement among the masses of white particles that built up those magnificent, serene-looking structures seen from down below or high above. I felt completely bewildered by the way the forms of Nature changed with my own position. "I" or "my eyes" play the vital part in my personal reaction towards "reality" or "non-reality." Can I definitely call anything "real" or "unreal"?

Indeed, some things looked "real yet unreal" to me while I was still engulfed in the mist and clouds over the Twin Peaks. There was some brightness behind the mass of vapour which made the particles buoyant and light and yet more mysterious. The sun was there. Gradually part of the mass moved and drifted away and left a brighter gap, till eventually there was only a very thin veil there. A huge shaft of sunlight streaming down from above lit up a cluster of white houses as if it was a miniature model of some housing project, made of silver,

A cable car coming up California Street.

artistically displayed in Macy's window not far from Union Square. They looked so unreal, yet real! The next moment they seemed to be floating in the air while the masses of moving particles surrounding them kept blurring my sight. Was the cluster of houses afloat on the mist? For a while I stood there hypnotically watching the unusual scene, then I called to Rudolph to get out of the car: "There's a *mirage*!" I said. But when he joined me the cluster of houses was no longer visible. The mirage had appeared only for a moment and we were engulfed in the old impermeable mass again.

Presently we drove on as slowly as before. While gliding through the shrouding fog, many of the white particles passed by the car window and knocked gently on the glass as if to soothe me. I had never seen a mirage before, though many ancient Chinese books recorded it. In *Han Shu* or History of Han Dynasty (206 B.C. - 220 A.D.) it is claimed that a certain sea-serpent breathed out a vapour which formed buildings and pavilions in the air. Those towered citadels I saw above the clouds might well have been the breath of an ancient Chinese serpent! Another book, *P'o-wu-chih*, says that sometime between spring and summer in Teng-chou-fu of Shantung Province, three sides of which is surrounded by the East China Sea, a sea-market would appear above the sea with city walls and a market place full of people moving to and fro—a mirage. A great Sung poet, Su Tung-po (1036-1101), is said to have regretted that on leaving his position as local governor of Shantung, having been recalled to the Capital, he had not seen that mirage during his time of office. It is recorded that he then made an offering in the Temple of the Sea-serpent Spirit and at last saw the sea-market the next morning. The Oxford Dictionary gives the meaning of *mirage* as an illusory image produced by atmospheric conditions, for instance, of a lake in the desert or city or trees in the sky. So it actually exists in the Western world as well as in the Eastern one, and has been seen in Europe and America before. It looks "real," yet it is an illusion. What I had seen a moment ago was a mirage, an unreal thing, yet it was real to me. How bewildering and mysterious!

All of a sudden a bright spot appeared in the massive fog, and shone directly against the window pane where Rudolph was sitting, so that

Brown pelicans in flight towards Golden Gate Bridge.

he had to pull down the little shade. Immediately we saw another huge shaft of sunlight that lit up a large group of trees apparently in the air. "That is Sutro Forest" said Rudolph. A moment later another shaft revealed some more miniature-model-like houses, like the first group I had seen. Perhaps one great ray of sunshine was shifting hither and thither to show us one scenic mirage after another. Each was a reality yet each was revealed to my eyes as a mirage. I felt greatly enchanted at having seen the mirage-like reality of San Francisco City high up the Twin Peaks.

I was deep in thought when our car started moving again. Rudolph was as cautious as before and silent too. In my mind I had been battling with a challenge—a real challenge that had not occurred to me before. I was thinking of how to record with my brush this mirage-like reality of San Francisco City. Making a few rough pencil marks on a small pad from my pocket I decided to try.

We had been up the Twin Peaks for a good while; yet neither of the Peaks had managed to reveal its face to us before our car turned to go downwards. Rudolph wanted to show me the house where he had spent his first twelve years in San Francisco, more than a quarter of a century ago. The City had undergone many changes, but this house he had once lived in was still there. The wind was blowing harder than ever on our way down. The masses of white particles rolled in greater confusion. Then the mist in front of me began to thin out; houses, trees and lines of rattlesnake-like moving road all appeared, though blurred, and those in the distance were still vague and veiled. It was no mirage this time: we had come to the lower part of the hill.

After a swing and a turn of the road Rudolph pointed out to me a three-story house on the side of a hill facing Sutro Forest. He used to call it "Swish Castle" years ago, and that is still its name to him. We drove up closer to have a look, though we could not go in to disturb the present occupants. Outwardly there was no change as far as Rudolph could see. He told me that he had taken possession of this house in 1917 or a little earlier. It was then supposed to be haunted by a lady who had sailed on a ship which was wrecked and sank off the coast of California near Eureka. The lady was said to have come back to inhabit her old home, so the house was without tenants for some years. Rudolph moved in without knowing this. He was quite alone in the house, but tough and young in spirit. One night an unusual sound made itself heard, as if garments were swishing up and down the stairs and along the walls. Though not easily scared, he began to feel uneasy at the persistence of the noise. He lay awake and could not think what to do. After a while he plucked up courage to get up and investigate. The night had sunk deep. There were few other houses nearby, and no light was to be seen. The rain poured down hard. The wind rattled one of the broken windows intermittently. Water dripped constantly through the eucalyptus trees all round the house. The swishing noise must have come from the rain and wind among the leaves—a mysterious sound yet a reality! He went up to bed again but still could not sleep. No explanation why. Next morning he found a trunk full of photographs belonging to the former owner of the house, a lady who had conducted a matrimonial bureau there. One of the photos, the picture of a certain "Susie," was supposed to be the like- ness of the poor drowned lady, so he christened her "Susie Swish" and the house "Swish Castle." He knew nothing more about her, nor about the shipwreck in which she perished. But the long hanging eucalyptus branches never ceased to produce a hissing sound around the house at night, nor was it rare to hear the rain dripping through the eucalyptus leaves with a disturbing "swish, swish." To this day, Rudolph could not be sure if Susie Swish had ever really existed and whether it was she who came to haunt the house at night. It is still a mystery.

"You must have been the first person to live in the first haunted house in San Francisco," I remarked. Rudolph had accumulated quite a few "firsts," as I learnt from time to time. He was regarded as one of the pioneers in the City after the great fire. He was the first to start a School of Design there, the first to arouse interest in Oriental Art by gradually building up an East-West Art Gallery, the first to inaugurate a special course on the study of colors in all American schools, the first to dye table-linen and to paint doors in bright colors years ago. He was also the first, about 1930, to teach flower-arrangement. All these things are now commonplace. With a smile and a wave of the hand, he dropped me now at the house where I was staying.

After the pleasant, mysterious blow high up the Twin Peaks in the morning and then the visit to "Swish Castle" my mind had been actually haunted by "reality" and "unreality" chasing each other. We all know that ghosts as well as mirages are unreal, yet we talk about them as if they were real. Now I had, so to speak, met them in reality, yet I felt them to be unreal. Life needs the intermingling of these two elements: purely realistic living brings irritations from time to time. When irritations come to me I would hope to go up Twin Peaks for a blow if I can.

Thinking of the early ghosts in San Francisco, I recall how I found that the ghosts and witches in early Boston, as described in my book *The Silent Traveller in Boston*, were not native Indians but came over the Atlantic with the Pilgrims. I was just as interested now to find that the early ghosts or spirits that haunted San Francisco were not native Californian-Indians either. Curiously enough, one of these was a Hawaiian. How he turned up, no one has ever questioned. He appeared in a house, or rather a white, many-gabled Swiss chalet, now non-existent, on the western side of Russian Hill. At the time, the occupant of the chalet was a Colonel J. P. Manrow, an Englishman and a celebrity who served in the San Francisco Vigilance Committee of 1856. During his service on the Committee, a certain James King of William was assassinated in the City, and some months later Colonel Manrow reported that some strange happenings had begun to occur in his house. Tables were tipped and noises heard from no-body and nowhere. Two disbelieving friends of his, William H. Rhodes, a science-fiction writer, and a mining engineer, Almarin B. Paul, accepted the Colonel's invitation to witness the scene in his house on September 19, 1856. Six of them—Rhodes, Paul, the Colonel and his wife, his wife's sister and niece—all sat in a circle with joined hands. All of a sudden, knocks sounded everywhere and the door-bell rang vigorously and continuously. A table tilted and swung about in mid-air, while books leaped from shelves and sofa cushions flew all round. Almost at the same time each of the six received a blow on the head and a kick from some invisible agency. Then a book jumped

Graveyard of the Mission Dolores where lies James P. Casey who killed
James King of William

across the room and hit one of the three ladies. Paul picked it up and
put it on the table. It flew open, and opened again after being closed.
Later the Colonel managed somehow to exchange words with the
ghost who insisted that it was the ghost of James King of William. On
cross-examination it later admitted that it was the spirit of Capitana,
a Kanaka crone of Hawaii. They then asked it to show up in a more
recognizable form. Immediately a bush outside the window vibrated
terribly and a visible form appeared for a second and then vanished.
A moment later, another form with a horrid look and repulsive mien
frightened them all to death except Paul, who saw it entering the
house and disappearing into the wall. At a request to it to be kinder,
each felt soft hands patting his cheek and caressing him (or her). This
was repeated for three nights in the presence of Rhodes and Paul, who
vowed that it was a genuine fact and no fake. The Manrows were
plagued by this Capitana for many more months; at times it threw
things about and at other times it played gleefully. Never once did it
do any bodily harm to any one in the household. From the evidence
of the science-novelist and the mining engineer, the existence of Capi-

tana was a reality in years gone by. Had Capitana left for Hawaii after the disappearance of the many-gabled Swiss chalet, or where is her spirit now?

Evidently ghosts need not pay for their travels: neither long distance nor mountain nor sea seem to cause them any hindrance. For instance, it is told how David Belasco, the great San Francisco-born actor and producer, lay down in bed after two exhausting nights of producing *Zara* at New York's Garrick Theater in January, 1899, and saw his mother, who came to his bedside calling him by his familiar nickname at home, and telling him not to grieve, for she was happy. The next morning he had a telegram informing him that his mother in their old home South of the Slot (actually South of Market Street) in San Francisco, had died at the exact moment when she had appeared beside him. Evidently she, being a ghost, travelled fast, far faster than a jet plane. Belasco said that as a young man, he visited the scene of every murder that he heard of—and they were many. . . . He also knew every infamous and dangerous place in San Francisco in the eighteen eighties. Only his mother understood him for she, though worried, knew that he was curious about life and wanted to see everything for himself. To this he probably owed his professional success. But without that understanding mother of his, he might have encountered some difficulties in his youthful adventures and wanderings. A mother's care for her children is one of the most genuine manifestations of the goodness of human nature. Even before Mrs. Belasco departed into the spirit world, she had to bring her son a last message of love.

Ghost-talk and haunted houses seem to belong to the old World chiefly, or to New England as far as the United States are concerned. No one would think of such happenings in the golden city, or so I believed before I visited it for the first time; now I know better. Only recently I was dining at a friend's house in Berkeley, where Dr. C. M. Li, professor of Economics at the University of California, insisted on telling us of an event which happened in his friend's house at the end of Virginia Avenue. After his friends had been in the house for a while, they found out that it was haunted. Both husband and wife are scientists, and took no notice of the rumours, yet they admitted having heard strange noises late at night from time to time. Not only that, the wife occasionally noticed that her young daughter of three, playing happily under a tree in the garden, was laughing and talking. She did not pay much attention at first, for she thought it was nice for the child to play so well by herself. Gradually she began to feel differently, for she felt that she was watching her daughter playing with somebody else. This happened repeatedly, and they started to question the little girl. Sometimes she gave a sensible answer and sometimes not, but they were sure that she was playing with someone whom they could not see. Eventually they decided to move.

The unreality of ghosts and mirages, all the mysteries in the world of "creation" or of continuity of life often obsessed my thoughts, but that day on the Twin Peaks they affected me more than usual. My experience in the mysterious blow high up those hills helped me to compose the following verses:

Since my young days I heard of the sea-market,
Longed to see it but no chance came.
Now reaching the summit of the Twin Peaks
Suddenly I perceive a way opening to Heaven's capitol.
The car's humming never leaves the human world,
Yet the dense fog pursues us as if we were riding the wind.
Now dark, now bright, the misty veils are playful;
Rising and sinking they drift east and west by turns.
Unexpectedly the sun's ray comes to dazzle my sight;
The strong and the soft yielding to each other
    break up the wholeness;
Many-storied houses emerge, silvery in color.
I seem to hear the commotion of a market high up above.
Is there no division between immortals and men?
How can the earthly world appear in the sky?
Though the common saying about the sea-serpent's
    breath be an empty tale,
Let's enjoy the Creator's ingenuity
    at this very moment!
How strange, my cherished wish is now fulfilled.
Reality and mirage, mirage and reality, are
    one throughout the Universe.

奇哉竟償半生願　真幻幻真寰宇同
漫説俗傳蜃吐氣　且樂此時造化工
豈是仙與人無別　何來塵世落上空
顯出層樓銀樣色　似聞市集鬧哄哄
忽爾陽光爭我視　咧柔互讓開鴻濛
時暗時明多戲謔　亦昇亦降任西東
車聲証未離人境　濃霧追隨如御風
而今來到雙峰頂　頓覺天都路可通
自幼即聞海上市　欲觀海市總無從

VIII

Marvelling Literally

IN THE PREFACE TO *Liao-Chai-Chih-Yi,* a collection of Extraordinary Tales, written by Pú Liu-hsien in the seventeenth century, T'ang Meng-lai wrote:

> People generally tend to attribute an existence only to such things as they can see day by day with their own eyes, but they are apt to marvel at whatever appears to them in one moment and in the next moment disappears. They do not marvel at the sprouting and falling of leaves and flowers, nor do they pay attention to the coming and going of the insects; they only marvel at the manifestation of something supernatural or something they have not seen before or something they cannot trace afterwards. It is true that the soaring of the wind and the flowing of the stream, as well as the flying of the snowflakes or the shining of the moon at night, may well all be regarded as extraordinary phenomena in nature, but we are accustomed to them and therefore do not marvel at them. People marvel at ghosts and spirits but not at men.

I, however, am ready to marvel at man, the men of San Francisco, particularly the men in the early history of the city. I have never given special thought to or marvelled at those who made Peking, Athens, Rome, Paris, London, or even Washington into Capitals; I have taken these cities for granted. Before they became Capitals and cities of importance, they must have long been inhabited; their growth was a gradual one over centuries.

With San Francisco, on the other hand, the building up of the city is so recent that I still can see and meet those who had a hand in it. Those who may have inhabited the area before this modern city arose have left no traces for me to study. Anything they may have left behind has been completely wiped out by the men of San Francisco—

the founders. They thoroughly demolished any Indian relics in their determination to build the new. I marvel at the men of San Francisco for this. Those who were well-versed in history, geology, and modern science raised objection after objection against the construction of the Bay Bridge and the Golden Gate Bridge. Yet they built them. They leveled hills; they constructed cable cars to draw people up the hills which they did not want to flatten, and now they have persuaded everyone to drive their cars upwards without fear and also to park their cars in the middle of a steep hill without danger. This is the second respect in which I marvel at the early men of San Francisco.

There is a third respect in which I must marvel at them. That is that they created possibility out of impossibility and made us all forget the existence of such impossibility and instead regard the result as an absolutely natural occurrence. In other words, they created Nature. What Nature did they create in San Francisco? Golden Gate Park! The man whom I marvel at most is one who came from Scotland, John McLaren!

I must admit that I had no idea of the size of Golden Gate Park nor of its history when I first came to wander in it unexpectedly. I was then staying with my friends, Mr. and Mrs. Lawson, at Lake Street above Presidio. My preference for exploring any place on foot, without a map or a guide book, keeps me alert to anything I may encounter and in a constant state of surprise. It was on the third morning of my stay that I strolled westward from Lake Street and then from Seacliff along the coast to Cliff House as I had done the day before. By chance I entered a gate and walked along a beautifully shaded lane lined with trees, which I thought might lead up to some fine mansion or castle such as I used to find in my travels in Britain and France. And I of course was ready to be turned back by an unfriendly gate-keeper or a fierce barking dog as I had also experienced there. Surprisingly neither expectation came true. The lane opened out into a huge open space with nicely-cut meadows and lawns where a number of water sprays in action made the grass look fresh and unusually green. I was surprised, too, to see so many fine, healthy-looking pine trees of enormous size and height, together with many other tall trees well-grouped in natural settings. I thought I had not seen a big estate so well-designed and kept anywhere in Europe. The Palace of Versailles has extensive grounds, it is true, but the gardens are laid out in a stiff, symmetrical arrangement. While I was strolling slowly and at random I could not help wondering if I had unwittingly strayed outside the City boundary. None of the great cities of Europe that I have visited has so big an open space within its borders. Later I saw many trees of interesting shape—not very tall, with many finely twisted branches interwoven in rugged antique patterns, on which a number of young boys and girls were sitting or playing a game of climbing through the looped branches. Close by those twisted trees was a good-sized lake where many more young children were sailing their toy boats with great merriment. Then I moved round the lake shore and came to a point where a Greek-styled marble archway made a *Portal of the Past*; it had come from one of the well-known homes destroyed in the fire of 1906.

Presently I found myself in a grove of thousands of rhododendron bushes, many in full bloom with large white, pink and purple flowers. The next moment I was walking by a big enclosure, in which many animals such as deer, goats, and American buffaloes (bison) were idly grazing. Because the paddock is so spacious and wide, all the animals grazing there looked as small as artificial garden-ornaments. Three of the deer were white, and a stag lying on the rich green grass was just a tiny white dot in the shape of a stag. Even the huge bison, about ten of them, could have been mistaken for rather large chow dogs. The eyes on a bison's head are very small; I could not even see the eyes of the bison standing not far from where I was. When I first saw an American buffalo in the Bronx Zoo at New York, it looked cramped and unhappy in its narrow enclosure. In San Francisco now I saw ten of them together in much happier surroundings. Perhaps they did not realize they were inside an enclosure, or did not care whether they were or not. With a pair of such small eyes set in a rugged and well-battered face fringed by a massive never-combed beard they look as worldly-wise and experienced as if they did not care even if heaven and earth turned upside down. Recently I read that someone had compared the best type of beatnik face with that of a bison! How appropriate, I thought, for San Francisco has long declared that the first beatnik appeared in the area of Pacific and Columbus Avenues.

Bison in Golden Gate Park

I do not know, however, if I can agree that the beatnik is a San Francisco creation. When in Paris at the end of the Second World War, I used to go and sit in the Café des deux Magots in Saint Germain des Prés for hours, in order to see some of the Existentialists. I remember that the people I saw there were not very different from those I have met in Columbus Avenue, except that the former spoke French and the latter English or American. This reminds me of some Chinese people in the first or second century who formed a sect with a belief in certain deities who would grant good health and long life. The followers of this sect held a ceremony called "The Fast of Mud and Soot" at certain times. In the description I have read of one of these ceremonies thirty-eight participants of both sexes approached an outdoor altar in single file, holding each other by the hand. Their hair hung loose and their faces were blackened with soot and smeared, too, with a handful of mud. Then the leader gave the signal for them to begin jumping (not exactly dancing) to music, and they continued shouting or lamenting for hours. This was repeated several times in a day and at the end of the fast they were all "psychologically straightened out." Thereafter, I believe, they were all supposed to have enjoyed good health and long life. When I tried to visualize in my mind's eye what these people looked like during their *fast* days, I saw them as not very different from bison-like beatniks, perhaps even more bison-like than the beatniks, as we Chinese have rather small eyes as a rule. I wonder if there was any type of person in ancient Greece who could have been called a bison-like beatnik? I think the holy men of ancient India might well have looked like that, if we only take their appearance and manner of dressing into account. Curiously enough I recently took part in a Beatnik Party in England. My good English friend, Major A. E. Allnatt, invited me to join his four-day Beatnik Party specially organized on his own Island of Osea at the mouth of the Black River in Essex. I went there straight after a cruising trip round a number of Greek islands. There were fourteen of us, men and women; much good food, plenty of games, and the warm air of the south of England. A set program was announced to us all and every one of us was kept amused and not left one minute idle. Our friend took the lead in all the games. The last and most important moment came. Everyone had to dress up in his or her own fashion as a beatnik. To my great regret I had brought nothing to dress up in nor could I dance. But I set myself to sketch the rest. The winners of the beatnik dress and dance contest were Polly and Donald Hall, an English writer-and-poet. They looked like many a pair I had seen dancing at one of the waterfront cafés of Marseilles. Afterwards I asked Donald why he had dressed up like a Marseilles longshoreman in a French beret and horizontally-striped T-shirt, saying that I had heard the "beatnik" was a San Francisco creation. Donald just roared with laughter at this idea. However, San Francisco certainly created "Beat Zen." Whether "Beat Zen" is spreading all over the United States is not my concern. What interests me is that I was able to compare the faces of the beatnik and the bison in San Francisco.

I went to the Park again another day. I missed the direction of the American Buffalo Paddock and found a place where there were row-

ing boats for hire. I am fond of rowing and have rowed alone on the
Isis, a branch of the River Thames at Oxford, but the boats here
looked smaller. I strolled on, watching two young boys on the water.
They were paddling on, instead of rowing, for the stream was growing
narrower. From one bank rose a rather high hill, while the other was
lined with trees and bushes in luxuriant growth. All this vegetation
seemed to have been there for centuries, only trimmed back by man
along the water's edge and footpaths. The two boys had now entered
a very narrow channel; I thought they would be in trouble if they met
another boat. They managed to squeeze under a small stone bridge
and emerged on to a big open stretch of water—a lake. I soon realized
that it was not deep enough for the Oxford type of rowing-boat; a
squarish paddling dinghy did very well there. Three colored dinghies
were already bobbing on the lake, one bright red and the other two
green. They did not show up on the water very well, for there was not
much water-surface left clear of birds—all kinds of water-birds, ducks,
swans, seagulls and, the most prominent of all, coots. Such a mass
accumulation of birds on a limited water-surface was a new sight
for me, nor had I ever encountered so many coots living together as a

happy community. I understand that coots are known in the British
Isles to be very quarrelsome water-birds, but they did not seem to be
so here. Each has a white horny plate on the forehead and walks with
a rather eccentric gait caused by a wide flattened membrane on the
edges of each toe. They suggested to me a group of dark page- or mes-
senger-boys, their light-colored caps tipped over their foreheads, rushing out of a big hotel somewhere on Nob Hill.

Quite a number of young children came with their elders in cars to
feed the birds. Behind the squeaking of the seagulls, the quacking of
the ducks and the chattering of the boys and girls I heard the roaring
sound of masses of falling water somewhere in the direction of some
tall pines and palm trees. I moved round the water's edge and sat down
on a bench facing the waterfall, which hung down like a sheet of
white silk, well-shaded from the sun. The lake is not a big one, yet it
became quite impressive with the view of the waterfall far away inside the trees. I have seen many waterfalls in different places, but a
few palm trees together with tall pines standing nearby made a new
setting. I began to sketch the whole scene but found it difficult to get
the shape of the Fall very well. Someone sitting on the same bench told
me there was a footpath in front of the Fall and that I could walk there
to have a closer look at it. I learned from him that the lake was called
Stow Lake and the hill Strawberry Hill. The entire hill was surrounded by water but a small bridge had been built on each side so
that people could walk around it. He told me he had come from Den-
mark. He worked downtown and lived near the park. Whenever he
was free from work he would come and sit looking at the birds on Stow
Lake. I made a round of the hill and resolved to come again in the
morning to make more and better sketches.

To my surprise I next came upon an original Japanese Temple
gate carved in wood. Inside I saw many Japanese dwarf trees growing
and a most conspicuous three-quarter-circle arched bridge with two
young boys climbing up on one side and looking as if they would fall
backwards at any moment. Finally I refreshed myself with a cup of
green tea brought by a young Japanese lady in her national costume.
The whole set-up, being somewhat exotic, deserves attention. But I
felt that the healthy growth of trees and plants had outwitted the

original plan for a miniature Japanese garden; the crowded, overlapping foliage seemed on the point of pushing the onlooker down into the narrow stream or tiny pool. If the foliage were thinned, many other Japanese structures would be revealed. I wondered if there is something like a miniature western garden with girls serving wine in the costume of Colonial days in any of the public parks in Japan!

Japanese Garden in Golden Gate Park

It was natural for me to step inside the de Young Memorial Museum as I was so near it. I enjoyed looking at many objects of Mayan, Incan, Aztec and pre-Columbian American Indian art, such as could hardly be seen in any big European museum. Nevertheless, I felt a little disappointed and could not understand why San Francisco had no art connoisseurs or collectors interested in making up a worthy presentation of Oriental art for this museum. Many have wondered about this before me, because San Francisco is so close to the Orient and had earlier connections with China and Japan than any other cities in the United States, except perhaps Salem and Boston of Massachusetts, where the Yankee skippers had a flourishing China trade. Yet Seattle has a wonderful collection of Chinese and Japanese art in the Seattle Museum of Art. So have Toledo, Cleveland, Detroit, Kansas City, Boston, etc. Of course no city can have everything. Interest in art is a matter of individual taste. Early San Franciscans were perhaps kept too busy with their practical problems, and also the population came from many different parts of the world and must have had different tastes. But I understand that some good pieces from the Brundage Collection will soon be coming to the de Young Museum, and one of the finest of all Chinese objets d'art, a Shang bronze in the form of a rhinoceros, which I am particularly fond of, will be housed there in the near future. This alone would bring me to Golden Gate Park as often as possible. I must say that no museum is more fortunate than the de Young Museum in having so beautiful a natural setting within a huge, well-laid out park. Any visitor would be as happy as I was to go out for

Shang Bronze

fresh air and for a casual look round at the many different tropical plants after a pleasant tour inside the Museum.

As planned, I brought my tools and media to do some more and better sketches around Stow Lake the next morning. I found the spot easily enough and the bench, but to my great surprise, the striking, big waterfall had disappeared. I could not believe my eyes and walked all round Strawberry Hill; not a drop of water was falling through the rocky gorge and a number of big rocks stood out in the former bed of the Fall. It bewildered me and I seemed to have lost my own reality. Giving up sketching, I walked on slowly. By chance a uniformed Park keeper appeared in the distance and I made my way to him as quickly as I could. The water in the Lake was as high as ever; how could the waterfall have dried up so suddenly? "It was turned on for a special occasion," the keeper answered. This confused me even further. The keeper left me to continue his beat and I took myself back to Stow Lake for meditation. Afterwards I crossed the small stone bridge and met three young teenagers busy climbing up Strawberry Hill, and chasing one another. Eventually they reached the top of the hill and disappeared. I became curious about their behavior and followed their path up the hill. On the way, I saw two water tanks of enormous size, half buried in the soil. A young boy shouted that those tanks kept the water for the waterfall and only the keeper had the key to turn them on. At last I was enlightened! In my book *The Silent Traveller in Dublin* I recorded that the great Irish artist, Jack B. Yeats, brother of the poet, once told me that when the English King George IV came to visit Powerscourt Fall in Ireland, the owner had a vast hall, one hundred and eighty feet long by forty feet wide, specially built for the reception of the royal visitor; and to ensure a good flow of water over the fall a reservoir was dug at the top of the hill. Unfortunately, after dinner, the King no longer felt inclined to have a look at the fall. Had the waterfall of Strawberry Hill been turned on the day before specially for me? I felt lucky to have seen it at work, but now I was sad because I wanted to see it again and it was not turned on, which meant I was no king after all!

Still visualizing its beauty and resolving to see it again sometime, I wandered on aimlessly. To my great surprise I came across lake after

Waterfall and Stow Lake

lake; Glen Lake, Mallard Lake, Matson Lake, and then Chain of Lakes, and marvelled that a metropolis with its ever-growing population could afford the space for such a huge park with hill, woods and so many lakes in it. Among many other water birds, the coot was still the most conspicuous one in and out of every lake.

Before I left the park for Ocean beach I saw thousands of shortish trees, like cypress and fir with strong trunks, growing densely together with no space left for a thin man to squeeze in between any of them. Their branches were closely-knit and interwoven together above as if they were a very thick blanket spread over myriads of small poles deeply set into the earth. All these short trunks, which can neither grow thick nor tall from being so closely packed together, slant inwards towards the park. They have foliage like the cypress, not dark blue-green but black, filthy with much dirt and sand. They make a striking contrast to the fine, tall trees and beautiful green meadows everywhere inside the park. Obviously the ocean wind has caused all the suffering to these stunted trees; on the other hand, their suffering and indomitable spirit in withstanding the tempest and wrath of the so-called Pacific Ocean had brought me much enjoyment in the past few days. Like men throughout the ages, I turned away from the sad and unhappy look of these thousands of short trees. However, I salved my conscience by giving them a wave of admiration when I realized how much good they had done by keeping the park from being blasted away by the ocean wind.

Many cars streamed through the ocean gate to the park but nobody stopped to take a look at the enormous windmills on either side of the entrance. The two huge windmills, Dutch and Murphy, were not in a happy state; in fact they were dilapidated and will soon disappear from their sites. One of them had its wings or fan-sheet broken and neither had been in use for a long time. They had been built to draw water for the plants and trees and had played their useful part in fostering the growth of all the living things inside the park from the early days. The wind, whether squall or tempest, from the Pacific ocean had its good side, although it ill-treated and tossed the short trees around the windmills so fiercely, I chuckled to myself. There are two sides to everything. Now San Francisco has a better water system that runs through the whole city, thanks to the advances of modern science, and the windmills have lost their usefulness and are to be demolished. Creation comes from necessity; improvement takes over the earlier creation: that is the natural law of change. Outwardly man has not changed much since the old days, but inwardly modern man's mind is far more complicated than that of his ancestors. I have seen

Ocean Beach entrance to Golden Gate Park

many who just motored through Golden Gate Park as fast as they could; they went there simply to avoid traffic jams.

Although I have not yet seen a better laid-out public park than this one, I think the San Francisco air contributes more to its success than mere money. London has her mild and not-too-hot sunny days to keep its park grass green and the flowers in full bloom, but it can be chilly and rainy too. In summer all the Paris trees become dark green and oppressed by the heat. Rome and Athens are too hot in summer. Peking has her unbelievable sand-wind days in winter with heavy snow, and it is much too hot in summer too. San Francisco has the London-like calm, soft days, a little overcast in the morning but always clearing up in the afternoon, which produced a hazy, mild, and undisturbed atmosphere, spreading over the many, many fine pines and redwoods and other trees a sweet, gray tint, and making them look especially lovely from a distance. And the various clumps of distant trees are also wonderfully softened by the haze or thin mist; many forms and differ-

Band shell in Golden Gate Park

ent hues seem to melt together in harmony. Nothing is more beautiful than trees like the fine-shaped pines and the lofty redwoods a little removed from the eye, standing out against those nearer at hand. San Francisco summer fog can be quite dense, but it generally thins out when it passes over Golden Gate Park Stadium and becomes thinner and thinner on its way to Stow Lake and eastwards. When the weather was like this, I gazed simply to enjoy the general mass of softened harmony and sober coloring. The mists were sometimes white, which enhanced the composition of the whole scene. Sometimes when the mists passed behind and formed a soft bluish background to the trees which intercepted them, their foliage and ramifications appeared to greater advantage. I did not manage to watch the dawn in Golden Gate Park, but I often tried to imagine the first sun rays catching the summits of every tree, then gradually penetrating downwards and outwards. I was once fortunate enough to wander there in the setting sun, which tinted the general softness of the atmosphere with purple all over the trees, so that radiance and obscurity seemed blended together: an unforgettable sight and experience.

I sketched and sketched in Golden Gate Park. In the first three days I spent there during my first visit to San Francisco my rough scribbles

Listening to the Band

filled two thick blocks. Then through sheer absentmindedness while gazing at the varied scene, I lost those sketch books. I went back to the park in search of them but where could one start looking in such a huge expanse? I comforted myself that I had time to do better sketches still. After a week, the lost sketches came back through the post; there had been an opened letter of mine inside one of the books. I naturally had a friendly feeling for the park after this very kind action on some-one's part.

On one occasion, I entered the Conservatory to see the famous col-lection of rare orchids and begonias. I had never seen such a colorful display of orchids before and expressed my admiration to the only other person there, the gardener, adding praise for the large flower-bed in front of the Conservatory, on which a number of words were spelled out in flowers. I remarked that that flower-bed with a message reminded me of the huge floral clock in Princes Street gardens in Edinburgh, Scotland. Breaking into a wide smile, the gardener re-plied: "That's just it. Mr. McLaren never stopped talking about the floral clock at Edinburgh; he was determined to make something like it. This is the result."

Who was John McLaren? I then enquired of my San Francisco friends. Some had not heard of him like me and others knew a lot about him. Apparently he was a Scotsman, born in Bannock in the eighteen-thirties, had worked as a dairy hand and a shepherd, and later became an assistant gardener in the Royal Botanical Gardens in Edinburgh, where he gained much knowledge of horticulture and developed enthusiasm for growing trees. He developed a new strain of grass known as "sea bent" to help hold the sandy soil along the Firth of Forth. He arrived in San Francisco in 1870 and vowed to grow redwoods, thousands of them, as fine as those he first set eyes on. At that time much of the ocean shore-land had remained in more or less the same state as when Bret Harte and Mark Twain used to drive their old hackney coaches through long stretches of sand dunes and muddy patches from the lonely Cliff House at the turning point from the north. No one thought of growing trees there, being sure the strong wind would uproot them in no time. From Presidio to the ocean the building of houses on the dunes was considered another impossibility at that time. However, it was no impossibility in the mind of John McLaren. His great success in growing trees on desert land and barren hills had become known along the west coast. So his advice was sought concerning building on the dunes and he took up the task under agreed conditions. In 1894 the Midwinter Fair was held in Golden Gate Park; not many of the thousands of visitors realized that the site of the Fair had been formerly covered by sand dunes. John McLaren was still superintendent of the park in 1939 when he was over ninety years of age. Looking at all the trees and plants, and hills and glens, the playing grounds for old and young, the de Young Museum of Art and the California Academy of Sciences, the Steinhart Aquarium and the Simpson Africa Hall, the masses of living creatures, squirrels, chipmunks, quail and many other birds, particularly the thousands of coots, and the beatnik-like bison, etc., it is just impossible to believe that the entire park was a thousand acres of sand dunes not so long ago.

John McLaren must have encountered many difficulties and much opposition. He managed to get his own way except in one respect—the statues. He was known to dislike statues in parks; he only loved to plant trees. But statues were part of the old European tradition to commemorate the local gods and great men; John McLaren's personal dislike had no weight with the City authorities. However, each time a new statue was erected in the park, it is said that he would busy himself growing trees to hide it. I am sure that he made an exception for the Robert Burns Statue not far from the de Young Museum. I have never known a Scot who did not raise his eyes with joy whenever I mentioned the name of Robert Burns, the one Scottish poet living in the heart of every Scotsman for generations. Through Professor Carrington Goodrich's introduction I once went to see Mr. Robert Bruce, a Scotsman and an authority on the irrigation of sugar plantations, on Maui Island in the State of Hawaii. At our first meeting I happened to say that I had written a book about Edinburgh and translated two short poems of Burns into Chinese, whereupon Mr. Bruce began to dance in the Highlander's fashion and to recite several long poems of Burns without a moment's hesitation. Burns helped me to several enjoyable days on Maui. In San Francisco, Donald McPherson, who was born in California but had never seen Scotland, wanted to take me to the Burns Society for the Festival. I declined, for I just could not risk having to eat the *haggis*, a special Scottish dish, after the experience I had had on the Festival day of the Burns Society in Scotland years ago. My warm feeling for Scotland has been expressed in my books, but I cannot bring myself to try *haggis* again.

John McLaren well displayed his indomitable Scottish spirit and faith in the creation of Golden Gate Park. Not only did he imitate the Floral Clock from Edinburgh, he also planted masses of rhododendrons, which have since become an outstanding feature of the park. It is well-known that two or three Scottish botanists were sent from the Edinburgh Botanic Gardens to collect plants in China in the middle of the nineteenth century and that they brought back many species of rhododendrons, which are hardy plants and flourish in the

Drake's Cross in Golden Gate Park

British Isles; I have seen rhododendrons blooming everywhere in Scotland. The rhododendron is even considered a cousin of the Scottish heather and so it is no wonder that John McLaren planted so many rhododendrons. When they were in full bloom, I found that part of the park a huge shroud of white, pink and red fluffy balls packed together supported by dark green leaves. It was a magnificent sight. The most prominent Scottish tree and one which I found everywhere in Scotland—the Scots pine—is lacking in Golden Gate Park. Why did John McLaren not try to plant them here? I have had a great liking for the Scots pine ever since I first met it, because of its smooth orange-brown trunk and branches, twisted to indicate strength and hardiness, with fresh green needles on the tips and dark-green ones next to them. Wherever they grow on the Scottish hills or glens they stand out from the other trees. However, they have very slender trunks and this might be one of the reasons why John McLaren did not plant any in the Park, for they would have been lost in comparison with the tall and massive stone-pines from Australia, and the local redwoods, which are even taller and so striking with their dark red trunks and branches.

When John McLaren first decided to turn sand dunes into a Park, many laughed at his idea, and others doubted, as they did not know how he would find fresh water to keep the plants alive. But he was undaunted. The two enormous windmills at the ocean entrance were designed by him to draw sea water, which would then be filtered. It was his idea, too, to plant those masses of cypresses so thickly that the ocean wind could not blow them down and they could serve as a screen for the other trees and plants, and the buildings inside the Park. In addition, he arranged to have the branches and twigs which were pruned from the Park trees thrown in bundles all along the beach. When the sea washed sand over them and covered them up, he repeated the process, again and again, for about forty years. The ocean helped him to build up the now smooth esplanade and highways along the beach from Cliff House towards the south. San Francisco was not built by one man. It seems to me that literally one ingenious mind built Golden Gate Park out of a thousand acres of bare sand dunes. Now I almost feel as if I had watched him doing it. The little stone statue of John McLaren, hidden somewhere in the Park, which I came across only once, is indeed a misrepresentation. It need not be there. Golden Gate Park is the memorial to John McLaren. He died at ninety-three, but Golden Gate Park will keep him alive for ever. I cannot help marvelling at the early men of San Francisco, but I marvel at John McLaren *literally*.

My friend, Gladys Brooks, wife of Van Wyck Brooks and author of

Gramercy Park, Boston and Return, and other books, once repeated
to me what her teacher, Professor Charles Sargent of Harvard Arboretum told her:

> . . . The work, therefore, of the true landscape maker is essentially
> unselfish; he can hardly hope to witness its completion, and his
> only delight is that of conception and of watching its growth as
> far as he may; the latter activity, akin to parental responsibility,
> is commingled with pain. . . . It may be seen, then, that no other
> form of art creation deserves more reverent care, more protection
> from thoughtless or mischievous hands, than that of such a master
> whose canvas is the earth and whose pigments are the objects
> themselves that the painter aims to counterfeit—the turf, the
> trees, the grass, the flowers, the rocks, the water, under the chang-
> ing skies.

Those acres of sand-dunes had been the canvas of earth for John
McLaren, out of which he had created a masterpiece in Golden Gate
Park. Whenever I re-visualize what I saw there, I marvel at him afresh.

IX

Smiling Unconditionally

THERE ARE FEW THINGS in the world so enviable as flowers: they are always smiling and they smile *unconditionally*. In the human world there are natural smiles, forced smiles, false or pretentious smiles, and even a very costly smile like Mona Lisa's. They are subject to one condition or another. But flowers smile without reservation, and on all kinds of people without any bias against race or faith. Flowers, I can safely say, have no enemy in the world; they receive no harsh words from any man, good or bad. "Everywhere about us are they glowing"—as the American poet, Longfellow, wrote.

Flowers may suffer from malnutrition, frost, hail, tempest, and torrent, but fortunately in San Francisco and its neighbourhood these globe-trotters are seldom encountered: I have met flowers smiling unconditionally everywhere in this part of the world.

It would be futile for me to speculate what kinds of flowers grew there before the Bay region became a great metropolis. But the blue lupines and the California poppies must surely have grown all over the peninsula and hillsides. I do not remember having seen lupines growing wild in central China where I was born, while the lupines I found in England were all garden plants. As the San Francisco area has been inhabited for more than a hundred years, every little piece of land is utilized, cultivated and set in order, and it is rare to find anything quite wild now. But I was fortunate to be in San Francisco one April, and once on the way up to Mount Tamalpais I saw a shaft of sunlight catch the top branches of some tall redwoods in Muir Woods and masses of blue lupines growing on the slope of the hill as our car passed. An ethereal vapour like a thin blue veil hid all the smiling faces from me: yet the mingling of radiance and mist in the flash of blue as we swept by gave an enchanting effect. I asked my friend if he could stop the car somewhere for me to have a better look at the wild lupines, but it was impossible, for there was a constant stream of cars coming and going on this winding hill-road.

California poppies cannot be seen in masses on the peninsula, for almost every accessible inch of land is occupied with human habitations. Any big open space is either a golf-course or a well-kept park where wild poppies are not allowed to flourish. However, I once found a sheet of them round the foot of Mount Diablo. The masses of tiny orange flowers knit together like a most beautifully woven French Gobelin tapestry. My curiosity led me to examine the tiny poppies at close quarters and they all seemed to smile hilariously at the bright sun that shines so steadily in the area of Mount Diablo.

Poppies

There is an interesting legend about the red-skinned Costanoans, who were the early occupants of the Bay region. There were two lovely twin daughters of a chief, who were very fond of flowers. One day a divine maiden, wearing a garland of poppies, the emblem of the Spirit of the Land, appeared from nowhere and warned the two young girls that they should be prepared for an attack from an arch enemy of their father across the Bay. They were given for protection *a magic iris*, each petal of which possessed the power to grant their wish in time of need. Then she vanished into the sky.

The two sisters kept the secret from their father but remained on a hill the whole night carefully watching the Bay water and the land beyond. As soon as the light of dawn penetrated the pitch darkness they saw dense white smoke rolling along from the other side of the Bay. The invaders were indeed on the march. So the sisters tore off one petal from the magic iris and wished for a great mass of fog to arise in order to blind the eyes of the invaders. Immediately thick fog rose up to engulf the hill and the two sisters. Then they tore the second petal off and wished for a great storm to wreck the enemy's boats, and also the third petal to wish that all the invaders should be turned into animals. Everything happened as they wished. The invaders were turned into sea lions who swam through the Golden Gate towards the rocks under the cliffs. The sea lions we see now on the seal-rocks are said to be their descendants. The two sisters were eventually transformed into the Twin Peaks. They are there still, engulfed in thick fog from time to time. But the divine maiden never appeared again, as far as we know, nor could many wild poppies be gathered to make her garland. Why are the wild poppies regarded as the emblem of the Spirit of the land, now the State Flower of California? There must have been masses of them growing profusely all over the San Francisco peninsula before the Gold Rush days.

Daffodils do not grow wild in San Francisco, yet they contribute a special occasion to the City, particularly along Maiden Lane, the shortest thoroughfare of all streets. I learned this by accident. One morning I went to have a look at the shop designed by Frank Lloyd Wright, and was surprised to see the whole lane filled with daffodils —rows and rows of them strung across the houses on both sides. Bright sunshine flooded the street and made every petal shine like gold. An unforgettable sight. Someone explained that this was the annual Daffodil Festival of San Francisco. On my further enquiring, I was told that one April there had been a glut of daffodils: the Maiden Lane merchants had bought more than they were able to sell. They could not discard the whole surplus, so they decided to invite the City to a party on the street, which was forthwith closed to traffic. That day they even arranged for bands to play; there was loud singing and plenty of cheerful noise and even weeping as the huge throng crowded into this very short thoroughfare. Since then it has become an annual festival. No definite date is set, as it must depend on when the daffodils reach profusion. When I was there, there was no great excitement—the street looked normal except for the flowers above our heads and inside the shop-windows, smiling at the sun and at everyone indiscriminately.

The Morris gift-shop that Frank Lloyd Wright had designed did not seem to be taking part in the festival, for the building has no window facing the street but an arched entrance which reminds me of the main entrance to a Chinese or Japanese Buddhist monastery. Wright never gave a thought to the environment for his design; rather he always intended his architecture to dominate its surroundings.

Many have told me that San Franciscans have a great love for flowers, more so than those of other cities. I think it is merely because they are favored by Nature: The mild climate of San Francisco encourages the growth of all kinds of plants, so that there is an abundance of flowers blooming at almost all times of the year. Nearly every house has a garden of some sort. I have seen blooming in profusion rhododendrons, azaleas, camellias, magnolias, peonies, roses, cyclamen and many others that are familiar to me. I cannot help recalling the following words from Ernest H. Wilson's book, *China, Mother of Gardens*:

> China is, indeed, the Mother of Gardens, for of the countries to which our gardens are most deeply indebted she holds the foremost place. From the bursting into blossom of Forsythias, and Yulan Magnolias in the early spring to the Peonies and Roses in summer and the Chrysanthemums in the autumn, China's contributions to the floral wealth of gardens is in evidence. To China the flower lover owes the parents of the modern Rose, be they Tea or Hybrid Tea, Rambler or Polyantha; likewise his greenhouse Azaleas and Primroses, and the fruit grower, his Peaches, Oranges, Lemons and Grapefruit. It is safe to say that there is no garden in this country or in Europe that is without its Chinese representatives and those rank among the finest of tree, shrub, herb and vine.

Ernest Wilson was Keeper of the Arnold Arboretum of Harvard University for many years and had spent twelve years (1899-1911) collecting plants in China. Many of his finds were named *Wilsoni* after him.

The flowers being sold on the flower-stands in San Francisco streets may be no different from those in any other city, but the flower-stands are always there and are more conspicuous than elsewhere, no matter what time of the year one arrives in San Francisco. The English flower-selling girls sit with their flower-baskets on the steps of the Eros statue in Piccadilly Circus, like Eliza Doolittle, only on the warm days of Spring and Summer. Most of the San Francisco flower-stands are round Geary, Post, and Powell Streets, not far from Union Square. But the flower-sellers are all men: "My Fair Lady" could never have been created in San Francisco!

Flower seller

Though Market Street is the main thoroughfare of San Francisco, Union Square is the centre of the fashionable area like London's Piccadilly Circus, for around here there are many Department Stores and many smartly-dressed women, old and young, in a shopping mood. It is no wonder that the flower-sellers have set up their stands nearby. No matter how cold or how hot the weather may be, women will not refrain from visiting the Department Stores. And where women go, men will follow. A Berkeley professor once told me that his reason for living in San Francisco rather than Berkeley was in order to be able to see properly dressed women, unlike the skinny ones in hot places clothed in straw, or the ugly bundles in cold Northern cities, wrapped up as if in hospital bandages. A member of the famous San Francisco Spinsters Club also explains that she likes to live in San Francisco simply because she need not have a different wardrobe for winter and summer. Besides, she need not bother to change so often. I wonder if this can really be true? I remember seeing one of Dior's fashion parades in Paris where morning wear, luncheon wear, afternoon wear and evening gowns were displayed in turn. Have the San Francisco women no interest in these different kinds of apparel? This should not be true. Life is full of interesting odds and ends, as confused as masses of various flowers put together on the flower-stands near Union Square.

It is hardly possible not to pay attention to the flower-displays in San Francisco. Every Department Store near Union Square is even more flower-conscious than its counterpart in New York. The City of Paris concentrates on flowers in pure white colors for their display. And San Francisco Macy's seems to have a new flower-display each month of the year. Once I was most intrigued there by a surrealist design achieved by an arrangement of the bizarre flowers called "bird-of-paradise." This plant has a quite extraordinary type of blossom, unlike any I have ever set eyes on. Its boat-shaped leaf-yet-not-quite-a-leaf, out of which sticks a blue "tongue" and several brown-red petals with sharp points, looks more like a Kandinsky expressionist painting than anything else.

I have visited the San Francisco Macy's more often than any of the other Department Stores. Its monthly flower show is one of the reasons, and my friendship with Frederick Atkinson, Vice-president of all Macy's is another. Frederick, living with his charming scholar-wife, Joyce, in New York, often comes to see to business in the San Francisco store. Frederick was a Colonel in the Air Force Transportation during the Second World War; he is now a Brigadier-General in the same, which with its two hundred and ten thousand men serves the American forces stationed all over five continents. He flew several times over the Humps of the Himalayas from K'un-ming to Chung-king in 1944 and saw something of China. His ability to control so

Birds of Paradise

many men is in keeping with his experience in the management of Macy's personnel in all its branches. Once when we met in New York, he told me about the adventurous New England sea-captain Rowland H. Macy, who had tried his luck in California as a store-keeper over a hundred years ago.

When the news of the discovery of gold in California reached New England, Rowland Macy decided that it was time to try a new venture. Leaving his family behind, he and his brother Charles B. Macy sailed in March, 1849, on the brig *Dr. Hitchcock* and arrived in San Francisco a hazardous four and a half months later, having voyaged there by way of Panama. With two partners acquired in the new country they opened a dry goods and provisions store at Maryville, forty miles north of Sacramento, under the name of Macy & Co. . . . Somewhere the young man [Rowland Macy] from Nantucket picked up some big ideas for business. Is it too much to suggest that he got them in the big California gold rush?

I wondered who actually started the first Department Store in the western world and when. The French, the English, and the German might each claim this invention, but the United States has many more and much larger ones. Perhaps Captain Rowland Macy was indeed the first person to conceive the idea. While in California in 1849 who knows whether Macy was not inspired by stories of the "floating Department Store," as I now call it, which operated outside San Francisco Bay and along that part of the Pacific for almost two hundred and fifty years from 1565 to 1815. This was the Manila Galleons from the Philippines bringing to Mexico almost every kind of goods from the Far East, particularly from China. Mr. William Lytle Shurz in his book *The Manila Galleons* gives a catalogue of the rich and varied wares that were brought to Manila by the Chinese in the sixteenth century and then carried in the Manila Galleons to Mexico:

> Raw silk in bundles, of the fineness of two strands, and other silk of coarser quality; fine untwisted silk, white and of all colors, wound in small skeins; quantities of velvets, some plain and some embroidered in all sorts of figures, colors and fashions, others with body of gold and embroidered with gold; woven stuffs and brocades, of gold and silver upon silk of various colors and patterns; quantities of gold and silver thread in skeins; damasks, satins, taffetas, and other cloths of all colors; linen made from grass, called *lencesuelo;* and white cotton cloth of different kinds and quantities. They also bring musk, benzoin and ivory; many bed ornaments, hangings, coverlets and tapestries of embroidered velvet; damask and gorvaran tapestries of different shades; tablecloths, cushions and carpets; horse-trappings of the same stuffs, and embroidered with glass beads and seed-pearls; also pearls and rubies, sapphires and crystals; metal basins, copper kettles and other copper and cast-iron pots; quantities of all sorts of nails, sheet-iron, tin and lead; and saltpetre and gunpowder. They supply the Spaniards with wheat flour; preserves made of orange, peach, pear, nutmeg and ginger, and other fruits of China; salt pork and other salt meats; live fowls of good breed and many fine capons; quantities of fresh fruits and oranges of all kinds; excellent chestnuts, walnuts, and *chicueyes* (both green and dried, a delicious fruit); quantities of fine thread of all kinds, needles and knick-knacks; little boxes and writing cases; beds, tables, chairs, and gilded benches, painted in many figures and patterns. They bring domestic buffaloes; geese that resemble swans; horses, some mules and asses; even caged birds, some of which talk, while others sing, and they make them play innumerable tricks. The Chinese furnish numberless other

gewgaws and ornaments of little value and worth, which are esteemed among the Spaniards; fine crockery of all kinds; *canganes,* or cloth of Kaga, and black and blue robes; *tacley,* which are beads of all kinds; strings of cornelians and other beads, and precious stones of all colors; pepper and other spices; and rarities, which, did I refer to them all, I would never finish, nor have sufficient paper for it.

Though neither San Francisco Macy's nor any other modern Department Store has yet offered horses, mules and asses for sale, could I say that the Chinese actually started the Department Store in the sixteenth century?

Though the Macy's of today may not have such an exotic selection of livestock goods for sale, its monthly flower-display is unique and remains for me a memorable feature of the City. With flowers all the way and at all times San Francisco naturally infects everyone, visitors and natives, with buoyancy and lightness of heart. With flowers so easily available, flower-arrangement competitions twice annually have become popular events. My friend, Rudolph Schaeffer, is regarded as a pioneer in this field, for he is the founder of the Rudolph Schaeffer School of Design and has been its Director for more than forty years. He took me to see one of these competitions and I was quite impressed by the variety and ingenuity of the exhibits. A few interesting arrangements with flowers and driftwood or dry twigs and branches struck me as unusual, and the semi-tropical and tropical plants attracted me particularly. They contributed special notes, color and line to the show, strengthening my belief in art with local flavor and color as a branch that ought to be developed. I also enjoyed Mrs. Obato's ingenious use of Japanese arrangements for San Francisco flowers.

Juanita Lawson knows that I have great interest in flowers, though no botanist or horticulturist. She made arrangements with Mr. Walter Joseph to take me to see the San Francisco flower market. I had to be up early, at about five-thirty in the morning. When we reached the market an hour later, the pavements were wet as if there had been rain the night before. In fact no rain had fallen, but the thick early-morning mist was wrapping the city in damp gray moisture, a strange

Rudolph Schaeffer and his School of Design

yet familiar sight to me, beautiful yet unsettling. All the city shapes, the lines of buildings and roads, became obscured and even distorted behind the masking mist. The minute particles of the substance touched my face and produced a soothing, cooling sensation.

Before we left the car, Mr. Joseph told me something about the San Francisco flower market. It is one of the few that does big business with all parts of the United States. Los Angeles has a similar one, but San Francisco's is more famous. Nearly all kinds of flowers suitable for marketing can grow in the area, with a few exceptions such as Christmas holly, which is sent from Oregon, for the Bay region has the most enviable climate, neither too hot nor too cold. Some flowers bloom earlier in Los Angeles, for Spring comes earlier there and is always warm. But whereas Los Angeles grows flowers in quantity, San Francisco has the quality.

The market entrance was roped off and guarded by a man in uniform until the time for opening at seven a.m. Before then only retailers and commissioned personnel could enter. We were among the favored. I found the market divided into three sections: Chinese,

Japanese, and White. We walked through the Japanese section first, then the other two. To my mind the flowers in the Japanese section were better displayed and healthier than in the others, which did not surprise me, as the Japanese are famous as gardeners and flower-arrangers. Later I was introduced to a number of flower-sellers and was shown how they kept the flowers in temperature-controlled rooms. When passing through Fifth Street, a big shop was pointed out to me, which specializes in dealing with heathers and acacias such as mimosa. Mr. Joseph said that these were great favorites with people in the East, meaning New Englanders and New Yorkers. Nobody wanted them in San Francisco, for they are too plentiful there. San Francisco's

Wm. Zappetttini Company is one of three great centers in the States for America's Cut-Flower industry, the other two being Los Angeles and Dallas. Zappettini's have a great reputation for the packing and shipping of flowers: they invented the "Petal-Perfect" method which they have been using for the last twenty years or so. A young member of the family showed me how they were packed in the Petal-Perfect box. He also explained that the firm had just invented a kind of plastic which can keep flowers cool in the ice-box without their becoming too wet. The process can be repeated so that flowers can be used on several occasions. They were also experimenting with a kind of paper, black on one side and silver on the other, to protect flowers from heat. The young Zappettini also showed me the warehouses and explained how the flowers were shipped to all parts of the various States as well as to Canada. He also pointed out a huge map on the wall with two kinds of pins—white for retailers and pink for flower-organizations—all over America and Canada.

Through the kindness of Mr. Joseph I gained an unusual insight into business dealings in the United States, which are somewhat different from what I have seen in Europe. In examining the devices for keeping flowers fresh and packing them for long journeys I was reminded of something I wrote in a thin book of ten color-reproductions of Chinese paintings, one of which is a branch of lichihs, the famous Chinese fruit. I described a legend about the notorious beauty Yang Kuei-fei, a great favorite of the Emperor Ming-huang, who lived in Ch'ang-an, the Capital of T'ang dynasty, and took a fancy to eat some fresh lichih which grew in Szechuan Province some thousands of miles away. The Emperor ordered stations to be set up at intervals all along the route and arranged for relays of horsemen to bring fresh lichih to Ch'ang-an in less than seven days. History records that many riders and horses became exhausted and died on the way, so that the lady might have a single taste of the fresh fruit. That was more than a thousand years ago. The present jet-flights would make nothing of such a request.

Although machinery has helped enormously in expediting fresh flowers to all parts of America and Canada, the actual picking, sorting, and wrapping at Zappettini's was all done by hand. The men and women worked with the greatest care and delicacy, yet were swift and efficient. It seemed that no matter how fine and ingenious a machine might be, it could not take the place of those flower-sorters and wrappers. Man is still the center of most activities. I was told that out of all flowers the Mexican and other South American orchids are the most attractive, the most expensive, yet the most in demand. They are large with long petals in brilliant violet, purple, and pink and white with delicate yellow-powdered stamens. The second most popular flower in the flower markets of America is the China aster. It is easy to grow, not too delicate to handle, and has a wide range of colors. It suits all types of vases and fits in all kinds of homes, and above all is not expensive.

The bulk of the people working in this wholesale flower market are women. Each of them chattered while they worked: all seemed buoyant, light-hearted; they sang and joked as well. I could not follow much of their talk, but one let fall a hint that she thought of her work as a vocation rather than just a job. "The flowers I am wrapping and packing into the boxes," she remarked, "are of no great value, but in a home, office, or hospital, they exercise a delicate influence on those who see them . . . patients are cheered, the stern face of the boss beams, the lover's feeling is heightened . . ."

This is the mission of flowers. Everything that sells has its function, but flowers function invisibly. I think it is their unconditional smile that has made them so universally beloved. I feel satisfied to have found in San Francisco a great center of *"smile* suppliers"!

X

Downing Exaltingly

IN THE DAYS OF THE "Manila Galleons," which lasted from 1565 to
1815, the Spaniards who took half the treasures of China from the
Philippines to New Spain, their Mexico, used to think of the expanse
of the Pacific as a "Spanish Lake." Prior to that the Californian Indians, particularly those living on Mount Tamalpais, called the ocean
"Sundown Sea." I suppose because from their habitations they could
watch the sun setting over the sea. Yet the morning and evening sea-
fog, so thick and so white, that usually covers a vast area round the
Golden Gate, must often have hidden it from them.

Whenever I took a good walk along the Ocean Beach, it was very
often gray, windy, even stormy, and chilly. But one sunny afternoon,
I came out of the Fleishacker Zoo and after crossing Sloat Boulevard
noticed the name "Sunset Boulevard." Why is the thoroughfare so
named? I turned on to it and then to the left, to the Great Highway
and the Ocean Beach. The sun was shining brightly, the air quite still,
and the ocean's many-faceted waves rolled unhurriedly along one after
another to the shore and disappeared. Though warm it was not hot,
for the ocean breeze kept coming to make personal contact with me.
The rather pleasant smell of the sea air soon reached my nose and I
reflected that I was luckier than Mark Twain, who describes in "Concerning the answer to that Conundrum" (*Californian*, October 1,
1864) how he went with an invalid to see a whale that was stranded
on the beach at that time. Neither of them liked the smell of the whale.
From the description, I thought I might be just on the spot where the
whale had lain. That was almost a hundred years ago. Within the

Dragon Boat at Ocean Beach

hundred years, San Francisco seems to have undergone more changes than almost any other city in the world. For the past thirty years or so I have travelled in as many lands as I could manage. To me Rome is the only city in the world that has covered the entire history of man's activity, playing a prominent part in each era without a break until the present. There are cities older than Rome, but they are either in ruins or lost in oblivion or have not participated in historical events so long and consistently. Human impact on the whole of recorded history can be understood as one walks step by step in Rome. Rome is an overwhelming city for a man who cannot help realizing how minute he is. It is another kind of human impact within the comparatively short period of a hundred years that San Francisco displays to me; its intense and incessant development is revealed hour by hour. In this respect and, in direct contrast to Rome, San Francisco is unique. No other city has seen so many happenings concerning almost every aspect of human activity within so short a period. The Cliff House which Mark Twain and his invalid companion came to see was not the one that I was viewing at that moment. It has been rebuilt for the third or fourth time. When Mark Twain saw a sign marked "Chicken Shooting" he and his friend sat down and waited. Eventually they went on, for his companion thought "maybe the chicken was not going to shoot that day." I had not known of "Chicken Shooting" as a form of human activity. There must have been such a thing, though it was puzzling even to Mark Twain. He goes on to describe how after having seen the stranded whale they drove slowly, of course in a Hackney carriage, in the open country and then crossed the aqueduct of the Spring Valley Water Company. As far as I can remember there is not any open country until the glimpse of Half Moon Bay. I cannot locate where the Spring Valley Water Company was, nor can anyone tell me. The Sunset district was so named in about 1887 by an ambitious real estate developer hoping to start a community along the eastern edge of the dunes. But why "Sunset"?

Presently I reached the ocean side and saw the Dutch and Murphy windmills guarding the entrance to Golden Gate Park from the Great Highway along the Ocean Beach. They were in use for years and to the amazement of all, Golden Gate Park continued to grow new and more plants. Now they have become obsolete and will soon be dismantled and gone for ever. Friends tell me that in the old days San Franciscans often took their children to watch the rotation of the huge windmills. The present generation and the following ones may not know they ever existed—change comes so quickly here.

Just before I turned to gaze at the expanse of the ocean, three young horsewomen in bright yellow, green, and red sweaters came trotting along the horse track, giggling all the way. They added a flash of color to the scene. There were quite a number of people, old and young, lying on the sand in different poses, some walking and some standing by the shore, only a very few swimming. "The ocean water is cold," somebody said. Those few swimming looked so brave yet so effortlessly mobile. They seemed to be hypnotically directed by the waves; they were clearly in sight when the waves lifted them up and vanished when the waves receded. The ocean according to its name is peaceful; its shore did not seem to be so. The surf rolled in with force as if on purpose to prevent anyone standing still in the water. In the distance the waves looked like molehills: nearer the shore they came as masses of small volcanoes spouting white foam instead of black and red-hot lava. Watching their incessant movement and voluminous foam, I remembered the following Polynesian chant translated by my friend, the late J. Frank Stimson, half brother of Van Wyck Brooks, who had lived in Tahiti since the nineteen twenties:

White gleams her side in a smother o' foam.
　Blow the winds, blow!
Swing high—swing low, seething go!
Foaming, O!

Lapping by ripples near to shore,
　Blow the winds, blow!
Swing high—swing low, seething go!
　Ride the waves, O!
Slapped lightly, O!

These lines described the waves before me most appropriately, I felt.

However, if I ignored the breakers on its borders the wide expanse of the immense water surface looked utterly flat, infinite, immobile and ageless. Suddenly my thoughts returned to an article, which I recently read, on "Man begins to explore inner space." I had not realized before that we men live on only one-third of the earth's surface. All the rest is occupied by the oceans, three hundred million cubic miles of water. The article says: "Biologists have long been studying the life in the sea, but knowledge of life at great depths is sorely lacking." There must be millions and billions of other lives inside the oceans— far more numerous than we men. If we take the mammals and birds, which are also living on one-third of the earth's surface, into consideration, we human beings are a minority among all the living creatures on earth. Have we managed to solve any of our human problems, such as intricate entanglements, unnecessary quarrels, unexpected hunger from famine and drought? Have the other creatures living in the depths of the oceans ever tried probing into our men's way of life? Why do we know so little about them?

While I continued my walk along the sands, I could not free my mind of thoughts about the inmates of the great deeps. Most of them are termed *fish* of various species, like men of different races. According to the Chinese ancient book, *Li Chi* or Book of Rites, there are seven types of human passion: happiness, anger, sadness, fear, love, hate, and desire. I began to wonder if fish also experienced seven fish passions. Suddenly the following poem, written by an unknown poet of the Han period, (220 B.C. - 220 A.D.) about a fish which was stranded on the shore when the tide receded, came to my mind:

相 作 何 枯
教 書 時 魚
慎 與 悔 過
出 魴 復 河
入 鯉 及 法

A grounded fish, now crossing the river, weeps:
"When can I stop repenting of what I did?"
He writes a letter to the bream and the tench
Advising them to be wary of moving in
                and out of the water.

This poet seems to suggest that the fish not only have different passions but also understand how to conduct their life by sound advice. I also recalled the following famous Chinese joke:

> A river-fish became a sworn brother to an ocean-fish and managed to make long trips to the ocean to meet him now and then. One day he asked his sworn brother why the latter never paid him a visit in his humble dwelling, where they might have some amusement together. To this the ocean-fish replied that he would come; the river-fish, after reaching home, announced the coming visit of the ocean-fish and asked all his relations to go and greet the guest in the lagoon. The ocean-fish did come; but no sooner had he swum to the entrance into the lagoon than he turned back. The river-fish did not know what was the matter and swam after the ocean-fish for an explanation: The answer was: "The water in your honourable domain does not agree with me; it is really too poor in quality."

The Han poem suggests to me that fish appreciate injustice and grieve over careless conduct. The joke, centuries old, illustrates the different ways of life in ocean and river comparable with the distinction between the inhabitants of Nob Hill and those South of the Slot in the old San Franciscan days. There is bias, unreasonableness and false arrogance even in the fish world, it appears! How petty and tiresome life can be!

At this I left the shore and turned into one of the buildings beside Cliff House on the east end of Ocean Beach. It was like a sort of museum with many curiosities on show. Quite a number of visitors were walking round and there were young children jumping and chattering loudly, too. I was about to leave immediately, when a group of people surrounding one of the showcases with intense interest induced me to move over. I found there were two astonishingly lifelike figures. They were carved out of wood in minute detail and with precise imitation of reality by a Japanese artist and sculptor, Ito Hamashi in the eighteen-seventies; one represented his mother and the other himself almost nude. They were brought to San Francisco more than sixty years ago and survived the great fire and earthquake of 1906. The people surrounding the cases exclaimed in turn: "Oh, look at the hair; it's so real" or "See the veins and muscles in the arms and chest; they seem to be moving," etc. Someone read a notice aloud: "Ito posed before adjustable mirrors and used more than two thousand separate pieces of wood, which dove-tailed and glued together. . . . The hair is from his own body. . . ." The last sentence drove me away as quickly as possible. Yet images of these lifelike figures kept swimming before my eyes until my head ached. I did not know why this should be, for I have gazed at many famous ancient Greek sculptures of the most lifelike figures, and felt nothing but awe. I must admit that Ito's skill and craftsmanship are far superior to that of Madame Tussaud's wax-figures exhibited in London. All the same, I think it was fortunate for Madame Tussaud that she was not able to acquire Ito's services. What made Ito use his talent in such a manner? It seems that in eighteenth-century Japan realistic and lifelike wood-carving must have already been in vogue. An instance appears in the following story written by the famous Japanese dramatist, Chikamatsu Monzaemon (1653-1725), and translated by my friend, Professor Donald Keene of Columbia University:

There is a story of a certain court lady who had a lover. The two loved each other very passionately, but the lady lived far deep in the women's palace, and the man could not visit her quarters.

She could see him therefore only very rarely, from between the cracks of her screen of state at the court. She longed for him so desperately that she had a wooden image carved of the man. Its appearance was not like that of an ordinary doll, but did not differ in any particle from the man. It goes without saying that the color of his complexion was perfectly rendered; even the pores of his skin were delineated. The openings in his ears and nostrils were fashioned, and there was discrepancy even in the number of teeth in the mouth. Since it was made with the man posing beside it, the only difference between the man and this doll was the presence in one, and the absence in the other, of a soul. However, when the lady drew the doll close to her and looked at it, the exactness of the reproduction of the living man chilled her, and she felt unpleasant and rather frightened. Court lady that she was, her love was also chilled, and as she found it distressing to have the doll by her side, she soon threw it away.

I do not want to see Ito's sculpture any more. As soon as I came out of the building, I was immediately confronted with another group of people, chiefly young girls, rubbing in turn the naked tummy of a wooden Guardian from a Japanese Buddhist Temple—"for luck." I smiled to myself and wondered if the young ladies would also want to rub for luck the naked tummy of the skillfully-carved, lifelike Ito Hamashi if he was placed in the Buddhist guardian's position instead. No lady would care to rub a stranger's tummy even if there were luck to be gained, I think!

There must be somewhere I could get my dusty head cleansed. Slowly I strolled on to Sutro Park. There were only two or three people in sight, though it was still bright daylight. Situated on the slope of a steep cliff, it breathes the atmosphere of a well-planned landscape garden in Europe, yet it is not quite European on account of its natural setting, and also the varieties of plants and trees. Succulent grasses tinged with red grow freely there and cling to the cliff rocks, producing an exotic effect. The glowing fire-bushes caught directly in the bright sunlight reminded me of some special festivities of my younger days in China when many large red candles would be burning all together, while their spiky leaves suggested un-Chinese but beautifully designed candlesticks of emerald. I sat down on one

Rub tummy for luck

of the few scattered cement benches, gazing all round in solitude and with refreshment. I was on the highest point of the park, with an open view towards the vastness of the Pacific Ocean. The throngs with whom I had mingled a moment ago far down below could neither be heard nor seen any more. I drew a deep breath and began to examine my surroundings. There was a structure nearby, something like an old fortress but with low parapets and not made of stone. The bench where I sat was not in good condition. There were signs of dilapidation here and there in the park. It could have been considered an old ruin in the European sense of the word, but it was laid out only some sixty-odd years ago. The founder was Adolph Sutro, born in Prussia, who came to seek his fortune here in the gold-rush days. He was a mining engineer and reached California in 1851 to try his luck in the gold fields. He soon made a name. To begin with, he sold cigars. Instead of joining everyone in digging for gold, he tried to use his engineering knowledge to work out a plan for a tunnel four miles long beneath Virginia City from the Comstock Lode to the Carson River in order to drain the water out of Comstock Hill which contained pockets of gold of inconceivable value. At first, none of the owners of

Comstock mines would heed Sutro's fantastic idea, and he could not undertake the project alone. However, he got his way eventually and his tunnel was built to the benefit of all the miners. Naturally money rolled in and he soon became the wealthiest property owner in Virginia City. Later he sold all he owned in Virginia City and bought the apparently useless sand dunes in San Francisco. Many people, including most of his friends, sneered at his folly, but in a short while the sand dunes turned to gold for Sutro too, to everyone's amazement. It is said that Sutro was stout, handsome and dark-haired, always wore a formal frock coat and had an unusual love for rare books. He bought the first Cliff House in 1883. In 1894 he became Mayor of San Francisco. A fire destroyed Cliff House that year. Sutro not only rebuilt Cliff House but also built the well-known Sutro Baths, the world's largest indoor swimming pool, near by. He built a mansion with a great library to house his collection of rare books. Sutro Park, or Sutro Heights, in which I had been walking, was formerly the garden attached to this house. There is no trace of the Sutro Mansion to be found now, nor of the great library, and little of the much talked-about maze of statues of beautiful ladies which used to stand in the gardens. Five or six statues are still left on their pedestals, but all are dilapidated. From a distance they looked like statues brought over from the ruins of Greece or Rome. Actually they were all made of plaster and cement. Parts of them have long been blown off or damaged by storm. Indeed, Sutro must have been a most controversial sort of man, and a most extraordinary one, too! He could have easily collected many fine specimens of ancient sculptures from Europe and shipped them over to ornament his garden. He took pleasure in the plaster statues during his own lifetime and did not care what happened to them later. He seems to have conceived the idea of making a mockery of life!

Suddenly one of the tall plaster ladies with only one arm, who had looked so sad and pathetic in her gray dirt a moment ago, turned bright and cheerful with a pinkish hue all over her face and body. Could she have penetrated my thought and felt a blush? No, it was the sun, *downing* and *downing* slowly but surely! There was an intoxicating tint on the tip of every needle and leaf of the firs, cypresses and

Sutro Garden

pines that lined both sides of a footpath leading to the edge of the cliff. Usually the massive clusters of cypress and pine needles blend with the evening mist to form a dark-green-and-blue canopy, with the strong, rugged trunks of the trees for the supporting pillars. Through the gaps, towards the ocean, the sky is usually a cloudless blue or mist-clad gray, which gives me a feeling of serenity and exaltation as I walk along. Now the purplish hue over the trees with the violet sky between the trunks suggests a good hope for feeling not only serene but uplifted while I walk step by step there. The gradual appearance of the whole round, red disc of the downing-sun makes me hold my breath with an undescribable sensation within me. The bright red sky and the sun just under the dark purple leaves against the almost black tree-trunks are a beautiful sight. I halt my steps now and then in meditation.

Presently I have again reached the highest point of the park, with an open view towards the ocean as before. Yet there is a great difference. A reddish hue floats all around me as if everything in Nature, not men alone, were enjoying a little drink of wine. The myriad waves, so big and forceful when I was near them, are now like dazzling fragments of gold and silver tumbling together towards me. There must have been some heavenly being far, far away beyond the horizon, pushing along the gold and silver to the shore, for he or she knew that there was no more of these precious metals to be dug up from the land around San Francisco. There is an exquisite miracle of transparency about the waves. Far from being fierce and formidable, they now look so gentle, easy-going, never-rushing and with no sign of weariness. The whole atmosphere is uncannily peaceful. Perhaps this is why it is named The Pacific. All my insoluble questions over the lives in the deep ocean and my inexplicable thoughts about the plaster statues are cast aside by the ocean-spell at the moment of sun-down. I watch the sun when it becomes a solid golden ball as if standing still there hovering motionlessly. In a moment it has sunk a little nearer to the horizon line. In addition, it becomes bigger and brassy in color instead of gold. In another moment it downs a little more and grows larger still. It is now neither gold nor brass but a red glazed porcelain dish of perfect shape but unusual size of the K'ang Hsi period. From moment to moment it grows bigger and bigger in bright scarlet, not quite the ox-blood type of Chinese porcelain, but most exquisite in form, making my fingers itch to handle it as I have handled quite a few famous pieces in the past. Actually it is not a piece of ceramic but a lovable lively being; it is not masculine but feminine. It is understandable that according to an ancient legend of the Japanese, the Sun appears as a Goddess instead of a God as in the stories of many other ancient peoples. To me a gentle but serene-looking lady does seem untouchable and even formidable from a distance. But face to face, she gives warmth and becomes exalting after a few good drinks. Being exalting and flushed, the face actually looks bigger than when it was calm and serene. The exaltingly scarlet face of the Goddess of the downing-sun now appears only half above the horizon, still shyly excited before she shuts her boudoir on me. Her exalting warmth still lingers in the air for a while. Then all is dark and chilly. I then trace my steps back to where I was staying.

Lying in bed, the scene that I just witnessed comes vividly again before my eyes, from the beginning till the end. I then compose a poem in Chinese, translated as follows:

曹觀日落廬山後　今見落日大洋邊

太平洋面闊無際　一線蒼茫接遠天

上有金圓之古鏡　似下不下空中旋

欲與海洋互親嘴　形碎隨波來我前

我乃報之以微笑　萬里飛紅忽赧然

轉眼西沉形反大　波光倩影益嬋娟

浮空四野皆分彩　捉浪紫鷗狂更顛

豈僅人間歌燕爾　乾坤亦自喜姻緣

半露半遮羊留戀　我欣我慰我參禪

Once I watched the sun-downing behind Mount Lu;
Now I see the downing-sun beside the ocean shore.
The great Pacific, wide and boundless,
In one hazy line touches the distant sky.
Above is an ancient mirror, round and golden;
It is sinking yet not sinking, spinning in space.
It longs to kiss the ocean waters;
Its broken reflection is borne to me on
    the waves.
I return it a gentle smile.
A shy blush suddenly spreads over thousands
    of miles.
Presently it sinks to the west, transformed in size;
A fresh red covers its full face—
    lovelier still.
The whole of space, on every side, shares
    the brilliance;

The wave-catching gulls in purple swoop
    and dart more wildly.
Does only the human world sing for the
    newly-weds?
The universe also enjoys a happy union.
Partly she shows her face, partly hides
    and partly lingers;
I rejoice, I am content, I am lost
    in dreams.

XI

Eating Customarily

WATER-FRONTS attract me as much as hilltops. San Francisco has both. I always try to give them an equal share of my time whenever I stay in the city. Embarcadero gets its due, too, from its share of North Beach, Baker's Beach, and Ocean Beach. On many an occasion I rode the cable car to Fisherman's Wharf and then walked along the Embarcadero to Market Street. Once I did the other way round. I seldom managed to see much of the Ferry Building, known as the "Symbol of San Francisco," for it is a traffic center and no one stops by unless he is waiting for the crossing-the-Bay buses. It is an elegant structure, modelled after Seville's Giralda Tower in the style of a Moorish minaret, I was told. It is true to its name at night, when it becomes a beacon strikingly illuminated in different colors and can be seen best from a distance. But when I stood inside it, I felt there was a kind of emptiness and superfluity about the building, for the bus-users, though numerous during the rush-hours, never seemed to fill it to capacity. During the gold-rush days of the eighteen-fifties and sixties, before this building was erected, all the men and the few women would wait around here for the arrival of the steamers on what was called "Steamer Day." It was here that between 1873 and 1877 from two-and-a-half to five-and-a-half million passengers used the ferry-boats between San Francisco and Oakland. Now the Bay Bridge together with other bridges carries all the traffic, and the ferry-boats are there no more. Will the Ferry Building remain as the "Symbol of San Francisco" for ever, I wonder?

Being born a Chinese it is only natural that anything—big or small —connected with my native country should draw my attention. In connection with the Embarcadero I learnt the origin of the curious word "Shanghaied." Before the Embarcadero became a well-constructed street and before all the piers were built along the waterfront,

there used to be many ships coming and going from Meiggs' wharf. Most of the ships were privately owned and run, and some of the captains very mean and even brutal in their treatment of their crew. Once on board the captain became the dictator, and the voyage to Southeastern Asia or the whaling cruise usually lasted three years, three years of hard labor in prison. Many ships were called hell-ships and were always short of crew. However, a special type of profession sprang up in the San Francisco of the eighteen-sixties. Members of this profession found ways of rounding up drunkards in the clubs on the Barbary Coast to provide a constant supply of crew at a certain amount of profit to themselves. I was greatly interested in one of the professionals who was called Shanghai Kelly. How did he get his Christian name "Shanghai" and how could the word "Shanghai" be used for a Christian name? Had Kelly been in Shanghai in those early days? It did not sound like a nickname. Apparently he had a way of becoming friendly with lonely men who came for gold and though they did not find any, stayed on in San Francisco, which was then chiefly a man's city. One day Shanghai Kelly hired a boat and announced a birthday party with free liquor for all his friends. Almost a hundred came, and each one was soon doped with whisky. Kelly then ordered the tug to put out towards three crewless ships in the Bay, each of which he supplied with enough sailors in exchange for the expected reward.

When the birthday party guests woke up, they were all on the high seas. In other words, they were all "shanghaied." What friendly ways this Kelly had! And what a good thing this special type of profession is non-existent in San Francisco now. Has it been completely wiped out of every port in the human world? The word "shanghaied" is still in use, though in a wider sense.

I took a walk one morning along the Embarcadero, with no special object in view. Aimlessly my eyes strayed, vaguely my mind pondered, and jay-walkingly my legs strolled. Nowhere could be quieter, as if there had never been any boat anchored by any one of the set of piers before. Very few people were about on the road. I did not even meet a longshoreman. I amused myself by reading the numbers of the separate piers. Suddenly I was tickled to notice a number missing between two piers, twelve and fourteen. This reminded me of my first visit to New York when I spent almost a whole day riding up and down the sky-scrapers in Wall Street in order to see if there was a thirteenth floor. None! I was told that this state of affairs was not due to the superstition of the architect or the contractor but no one would like to rent such an ominous number!

Presently I reached Fisherman's Wharf. The noise, color and activities there suggest many similarities with a Chinese country market, Bagdad's bazaars, London's Caledonian market, Paris' Marché aux Puces or even New York's Coney Island. But none of them has such a very attractive setting as Fisherman's Wharf on the Bay water-front. Fisherman's Wharf must have originated in a cluster of fishing-boats and fishermen who settled in this quarter in the early days after the gold rush, or at least when the gold mines were nearing exhaustion. So some of the men began to make gold out of fishes instead. One of the outstanding sights is still the clusters of masts of the fishing boats. But the most striking sight of all are the piles of large crabs with brilliant orange shells being cooked, and many still steaming beside huge boiling hot cauldrons here and there. After several visits I found nothing specially mysterious about Fisherman's Wharf, yet I felt there was some great mystery in existence behind those masses of hot steam rising up from the cauldrons. The usually fat man who attended to the sale of the crabs, occasionally lifting his hand to chop some object with a large knife, and the slender figure of a young girl in bright green or yellow jumper standing by watching, her pinkish face and arms together with the white overall of the salesman and the red crab-shells, all veiled behind the gray steam, revealed to me a mysteriously beautiful combination—rough, gentle, large, small, visible, invisible, real yet unreal, and vividly colorful! This is to me a typical picture of San Francisco life in one of its aspects.

I wonder why the crab is the most prominent sea-food for sale on Fisherman's Wharf, and why so many of the fishing boats clustering round the wharf are engaged in crabbing? In an essay on crabs by Dr. Robert Gurney, I read the following passage.

> The crabs *brachyura* may be regarded as lobsters which have had their thorax pulled out sideways and the abdomen reduced and tucked in under the thorax. There is no doubt that the ancestors of the crabs were long-tailed *crustacea* like lobsters, but the new invention proved so successful that there are now more genera and species of crab than of any other groups of decapod *crustacea*. As in commerce, so in nature, success has led to imitation, and there are some impostors looking like crabs which have really no claim to entry into the "Who's Who" of crabdom, although they may have acquired the name in common parlance.

He goes on to discuss the different types of crab, such as the hermit crab, the river crab, the ribber crab, the stone crab, the sponge crab, the fiddler crab, the land crab and the fresh-water crab. What interested me particularly was his discovery of the "Who's Who" of Crabdom and also of "those who acquired the name of crab in common parlance." I wonder if an entry in this "Who's Who" needs any specific qualifications beside being a real crab? Are those who acquired the name of crab in common parlance considered as social outcasts by the real crabs? I do hope no zoologist can discover a racial quarrel actually existing in Crabdom!

The crab-sellers of San Francisco's Fishermen's Wharf offer a sharp contrast to my mind from the lobster-seller in Bar Harbor and all the coastal towns of the State of Maine. There every lobster is kept alive as long as possible and there is no sign of any being cooked on the spot.

It is the general belief that a lobster should be eaten straight after being cooked, for it tastes best then. Does not this belief extend to crabs? Or perhaps crabs cannot live out of the sea for long? The most puzzling point for me is that *Crabdom* seems to lie in the bottom of the Pacific around the west coast covering San Francisco while *Lobsterdom* (if any) is in that part of the Atlantic covering the New England States. The Chinese proverb "Pai wen pu yu yi chien" or "Hearing (about a thing) a hundred times is not better than seeing it once" proves true. Had I not been in both places I should not have realised the existence of these separate kingdoms, Crabdom and Lobsterdom!

I must admit that I have become something of an addict for freshly-cooked lobsters in New England, particularly in Maine. Each time I had a dish of lobster, the picture of a friend of mine, Wendell S. Hadlock, Director of the William A. Farnsworth Museum at Rockland, holding up some live lobsters to show me before driving me to his home, would come vividly to my mind. The deliberate death of the live lobsters on my account did not seem to bother me at the time, for the taste was beyond description. Later I remembered my younger days at home, how my grandmother would always repeat to me the saying of Confucius, "A gentleman will keep away from the kitchen," whenever I went to see the cook. She said that if I saw how the food was prepared I would then not like to eat it. My grandmother was an ardent Buddhist believer and never liked killing any live thing for food. When young I felt greatly moved by this Confucian saying. Now it seems to me that Confucius was trying to cover something up after all. He must have liked eating good things just as I enjoy the freshly-cooked lobsters in New England. Besides, I have not been able to have my own cook for many years, so I have a good excuse for not being a strict Confucian!

A few years ago when living in Boston, I read about an interesting contest: Massachusetts Governor Herter had issued a challenge to his five fellow New England Governors when he proclaimed Bay State Lobsters as "the tastiest, the most tender, the most delectable in all New England—nay in all the world!" Four of the other State Governors made similar boasts; only Vermont's Governor, Lee E. Emerson, kept silent. Six plates, each containing lobster meat but with no indication of where each came from, were placed in front of the six Governors and their wives to taste. All twelve judges were unanimous about one plate which tasted the best. The lobster meat came from Vermont! It interested me at the time that Vermont should have won the contest for it has no seacoast. However, this is the same sort of contest we used to have in China with tea. I wonder if a San Francisco Mayor ever proclaimed the Bay City crabs as the best in all the West coastal cities and in all the world? Perhaps no other coastal city dare compete with Fisherman's Wharf crabs.

The color of the cooked crab-shell, brown or orangey, though pleasing to the eyes, is not as startling and brilliant as the crimson red of the cooked lobster-shell, particularly when it is freshly taken out of the cooking pot. A certain Chinese poet of the Ming dynasty (1368-1644) once composed a rather ironical line saying that only shrimps (and lobsters) seemed to enjoy death, changing to a brilliant red gown from the drab dark gray of their lifetime. The official robe of the Ming dynasty is red and this poet never passed his civil service examination to earn himself a position in the government. So he consoled himself with this sly remark!

There are many eating houses one beside the other, covering almost the whole of Fisherman's Wharf. Most have Italian names. I was told that there is a large Italian community in San Francisco, whose fathers and grandfathers came to make their fortune there like many others in the gold rush days. Fresh new Italian blood still comes in. Many fishermen are Italian, and I found them speaking Italian together when I strolled on the wooden piers around the lagoon, where many fishing boats were anchored. Some fishing nets were airing on a cord stretched between two poles. Two elderly fishermen were sitting on the ground mending a net. I noticed a number of round cases made of iron-wire and cords piled on the bow of each boat, which are apparently used for crabbing.

Suddenly a circle of birds, chiefly seagulls, appeared in the air above the lagoon, and a little bunch of onlookers began to move along towards the end of the pier where I stood. The squeaking noise rang in my ears long before the arrival of the gulls. Some distant crying drew my eyes towards the entrance to the lagoon, where it met the open Bay, and I saw many more birds circling above the tall masts of two fishing boats as if escorting them home to anchor. Seagulls have long been regarded as the fishermen's friends. To us the squeaking noise of the gulls may sound a little monotonous, yet for the fishermen on the open ocean even this could help to break the vast-scaled monotony of the sky, clouds, and sea. A sea-fisherman's life far away from the land is unknown to the majority of the Chinese, for we have never been a sea-faring people despite the fact that China has such a long coast line covering several thousand miles. Until very recently we have had no merchant marine and even now it is hardly worth mentioning. The precarious life of sea-fishermen, full of anxiety and dangers, with the unpredictable weather, has never been described by any of our writers in the long history of Chinese literature. This is something that my fellow-countrymen of the future could learn from the West. Sea-faring has been in the blood of the Westerners since the ancient Greeks and Egyptians, and also in that of the Japanese as islanders. To us it is still quite alien. . . . Presently the two boats were anchored. The four or five fishermen on each boat looked at ease, smiling and joking as if to tell us that they had not done too badly. The gulls now squeaked louder, more wildly and continuously; they were also diving swiftly to catch the fish being thrown to them. The flash of movement with which they made their catches always deceived my eye, for in the next moment I saw them flapping their wings rhythmically as if nothing had happened. The seagulls have a great sense of sport: The fish-thrower can be young or old and the fish may be thrown high or low, but the gulls will not allow any fish to fall back into the sea. Their eyesight must be extremely sharp and their minds concentrated and alert. They even seem able to adjust the speed of their flight in an instant, as if measuring the distance between them and the fish. Though they created a great commotion in the air just above the lagoon, which now looked quite congested, none of them showed any spitefulness to any other. This is sportsmanship indeed!

To my amazement I noticed a few darker and bigger birds flying together in the midst of a large flock of seagulls. They were brown pelicans. Whenever I see pelicans I wonder why they should have been given such an oversized, pouched beak and heavy rounded wings. They look so clumsy and uncomfortable while walking, like aged patients who have just got out of bed. Why should nature have created such an unbirdly-looking body for the pelican? I was interested now in seeing pelicans in flight, flapping and gliding in as leisurely and swift a manner as the seagulls, though they needed a little more room above the lagoon. They were good sportsmen too. The interesting difference was that the pelicans never showed any intensity and eagerness in their manner of snatching the fish; there were no outstretched necks nor beady eyes; instead, they flew with necks drawn in as if they could not care less whether they caught a fish or not. They looked perfectly at ease. When they knew they were near the fish, they simply opened their beak and the fish fell into their pouch, as if they were spooning it up.

Sometimes I noticed a pelican purposely letting smaller fish be snatched by the seagulls. Their eyes seemed able to distinguish between big and small booty. I saw one of them catch a good-sized fish which stuck across its pouched beak so that it had to alight on a wooden post near some boats to stretch its neck upwards and make the fish slip down its throat. Did it get any taste of fish? As I wondered about this, a well-known Chinese joke came into my mind suddenly, but first I must remind you that we Chinese, by tradition and under Confucius' principles, place scholars and any learned persons at the top of the social ranks in the community, while merchants are placed at the bottom. On the other hand, the scholars are usually bookworms, never knowing how to make money or how to feed themselves properly. They are inclined to be sour, pedantic and thin, while merchants would be well-fed, hearty and prosperous-looking. One evening a big tiger, after having roamed on the mountains the whole day, came back to his den complaining loudly of hunger. His wife and other relations retorted: "What, didn't you meet any men all this time you were out?" The answer was: "I did, but I didn't eat them." "Why not?" "Well," came the reply, "the first I met was a frowzy priest whom I couldn't stomach. Then I encountered a second who happened to be a B.A. with all the flavour of a literary pedant, and I didn't like eating sour food. The third one was a superannuated scholar of some Academy, whom I didn't eat either." "Why not?" again asked his wife. "Because I was afraid I might easily break my teeth on him," the tiger remarked.

I chuckled to see so many well-fed persons all around the lagoon, and thought what a feast that tiger would have had!

All the seagulls and pelicans changed direction and flew out into the open Bay, as soon as no more fish were thrown to them. I moved towards the two young boys who had been feeding birds and asked how they could spare so many fish to feed the birds. The ten-year old answered me quickly, saying that he, and his brother aged fifteen, liked to come here after school to watch the fishing-boats come back. After the fishermen had sorted their catch, they would throw the rest on the bank for the birds, so he and his brother picked them up one by one and threw them to the birds for fun. The elder brother was now clinging by his arms round the railings and bending down towards a fishing-boat just coming in down below. He turned his head from time to time to give his young brother an angry look as if annoyed at his talkativeness. Eventually the younger one moved close to this brother's side and also watched the fishing-boat down below, though he had to go up a step higher on the railing. I shared their interest in watching three stout fishermen counting and sorting and placing their catch into bags, and enjoyed as well seeing the two brothers gazing at the procedure so intently and patiently. The fish-packing had nearly ended when the bigger boy cried: "Mister, Mister, give me a fish, a big fish, my mother likes fish!" None of the fishermen took any notice of him. But he went on and on begging, while his young brother was fidgeting up and down on the railings all the time. The begging words then became low and sorrowful. The three fishermen began talking together but in Italian, unintelligible to my ears. Eventually the eldest fisherman who had white hair and a white mustache threw a good-sized fish up to the boy, who caught it as if performing like a seagull. Immediately the young brother cried: "Me, me Mister, I want a fish. Mister, give me a fish, too . . ." Up came another fish into the hands of the little fellow as well. Both laughed happily, the elder brother threaded each fish on a string and off they ran, in the direction of the Aquatic Museum.

I walked on slowly behind them. I could still hear their laughter. Their two figures, sometimes bending and sometimes running, silhouetted against the bright sunset, still revealed their happy mood.

Seagulls at Fisherman's Wharf

Now they stopped and spoke to someone on the road, lifting up their fish to show their luck, I supposed. They soon stopped again to talk to another passer-by and again displayed their fish. By the time this had happened once more, I had caught up with them. They were trying to sell the fish! I saw this third person taking out his wallet and giving two dollar notes to the boys. He looked as happy as the youngsters. I smiled and turned my face towards the open Bay water, greeting the sea breeze. Oh, life! This is life, full of wonders, full of uncertainties, and full of unexpected happenings.

The sun was about to disturb the slumber of the lovely maiden on the slope of Mount Tamalpais. Someone was unrolling the white-fog bedcover slowly from the Golden Gate. Something inside me demanded dinner, and since there was no eating place in that district I walked back towards the Bay and chose a window-table in a busy

Italian restaurant. It did not seem very different from any other restaurant in the downtown area of the city except for the many gift-shops surrounding it and the clusters of masts of fishing boats in the lagoon that I looked out on. Something on the menu struck me as odd; it was "Boston clam chowder" and "New York clam chowder." Why not San Francisco clam chowder? My Boston friends never accept New York clam chowder as the real thing. In Boston I saw no New York clam chowder on any menu. Perhaps San Franciscans are wiser on this point. However, I have no preference for either clam chowder. Besides, there were several dishes of crab-meat and I chose one, thinking it should be better on Fisherman's Wharf than anywhere else. I saw no such claim as "the tastiest, the most tender, the most delectable" for the crab-meat, and it proved to be unnecessary. Once when I was taken to lunch at Saint Francis Hotel by William Hogan of the *San Francisco Chronicle* and also chose a dish of crab-meat, my friend thought I was keen on trying the Bay City crabs. I replied that "any dish is tastier in the company of a good friend; the dish only gets its share."

There is also a Fisherman's Wharf in Honolulu. Dean Shunzo Sakamaki of the Summer Session asked Dr. Snyder, President of the University of Hawaii, and a number of other professors including myself to lunch there in the only restaurant built in the shape of a big fishing boat. The atmosphere was much quieter there than at Fisherman's Wharf. There was neither Honolulu clam chowder nor any crab dish. The conversation centered on fishing, in which I could not take part. Apparently Dr. Snyder is an experienced fisherman.

Talking about crab dishes, Bob Farlow once introduced me to one of soft-shell crabs which he recommended highly. I had never tasted this before, either in England or any where else in Europe, and found it quite as tasty as he had promised. Later an English friend told me that the Act of 1877 made it illegal to sell soft-shelled crabs, which is evidently why I had not met it before.

Eating a whole freshly-cooked lobster or crab, though some small forks are usually provided, involves some action with the fingers from time to time, which in turn involves "table manners." This brings to my mind many little problems concerning Chinese eating manners. Whenever I gave a dinner party in a Chinese restaurant some of my guests might ask how they should hold the chop-sticks or a bowl or a plate. Some, who had either been in China or seen Chinese eating rice by raising the bowl close to the mouth and shovelling the rice in, would give a comic display. I always felt it was a pity that none of them could have taken part in a Chinese old-fashioned banquet. We Chinese have two definite styles of eating: formal eating and eating for pleasure. At a banquet it is all formality and good manners; at other times we just enjoy ourselves, and then there is no question of etiquette. That is why some of the typically Chinese restaurants in San Francisco have a number of partitioned rooms, unlike the modern fashionable restaurant with many tables neatly arranged all together. Within these partitions, one can enjoy a meal with one's friends, and eat as unconventionally as one likes without being criticized. Unfortunately this kind of typical Chinese restaurant with partitioned rooms is beginning to disappear even in San Francisco.

It was on Fisherman's Wharf that I had a good discussion with an American friend about eating manners or not. When it came to choosing a restaurant he insisted on giving me a change! Neither Italian dishes, nor Chinese cuisine this time; he wanted me to try the Japanese sukiyaki at a Japanese restaurant which was drawing more and more people to Fisherman's Wharf. We entered and went up a few steps. A girl in Japanese dress greeted us and enquired where we would like to eat. The characteristic Japanese restaurant contains a tatami, a little higher than the floor, with bamboo mats spread for seats and a low table set in the center. Two tables were already occupied by American families and even a young five- or six-year-old had learned to take off his shoes and sit with legs crossed. We preferred to sit by a table. The main item for dinner was of course sukiyaki, which consisted of many sliced meats and chopped vegetables boiling in a dish in the center of the table. Apart from this, many small dishes of various Japanese delicacies were brought in. I had to be excused from eating raw fish. My American friend had not been to the Far East, and thought the Chinese and Japanese were the same sort of people fond of similar dishes, including raw fish. I joked that I had just been watching the seagulls and pelicans swallowing raw fish and had had my fill. Later our conversation came round to oysters. "They

"He can't swallow!"

should always be eaten raw," remarked my friend. "I know," I replied, "not only raw but alive. But I do not eat oysters," though I added that many of my compatriots love them. I remembered the words of Mrs. Fanny de Bary, wife of the head of the Department of Chinese and Japanese at Columbia University, who told me that her mother was an expert on oyster-eating, and always says "eating oysters the moment they are brought to the table is one minute too late." This means that oysters should be eaten just as the shells are opened; in other words, standing at the fishmonger's counter. I pointed out that the Japanese would not eat oysters at all, at that rate, for they could not eat standing. We laughed more than we actually ate. The continuously boiling soup needed more water from time to time and adding meat and vegetables kept our chopsticks very busy. My friend had much to say and many enquiries to make about Oriental customs. Finally our conversation centered on ways of eating.

Before the dinner was over I told my friend about an American scholar who won honors at Oxford University. I joined the party given in his honor. He made this most likable after-dinner speech: "Having just finished my devoted studies for the necessary degree, I must tell you of a secondary study which I have made. It concerns ways of eating. I have come to the conclusion that there are three distinct ways of eating in this world. The English eater is an architect, who first cuts up the meat and then piles it up on the fork together with vegetables as if building before eating and at last puts the finished work into his mouth. The American eater is a mathematician, who uses his knife to cut up everything on the dish into small pieces and then changes the fork from his left hand into his right hand to eat the small pieces one by one, as if counting all the time. The third type of eaters are the French and the Chinese. They are just eaters!"

"Where do the Japanese come in?" my friend asked, but I could not tell him.

On Fisherman's Wharf in San Francisco one can make a good study of eating manners.

XII

Contrasting Simultaneously

COLOR IS in the mind of the beholder. The commonly-accepted terms "red," "blue," "yellow," "black," and so forth are only an ap-proximation. A happy young girl who is madly in love will have a much more intense feeling for the red of a red rose than a gentle middle-aged lady whose life has been comfortable and smooth in all its aspects. The red rose will seem colorless or perhaps even black to the eye of the mother who has just lost her child. "Red" may be experi-enced identically by two pairs of eyes under identical conditions. Yet it alters when it is laid beside another color, say, green or yellow. The color becomes modified in the first place by the presence of another color, and then seems to change places with the other by the optical activity of the eyes. That is what I understand to be colors contrasting simultaneously and that is what I have found so interesting in the colors of San Francisco.

Many have remarked that San Francisco is a white city. George Sterling in one of his poems described it as "The cool, gray city." Both descriptions are correct, but they do not distinguish San Francisco from many another city.

The general impression it gives is of whiteness, for most of the houses are painted white. Quite recently I paid Athens a visit in the height of summer. My first sight of this ancient city of mankind from the top of the Acropolis reminded me much of the modern city of San Francisco beside the Pacific. Owing to its economic recovery and prosperity after the Second World War, Athens seems to draw more visitors than many other historical places. Tall buildings have sprung up like young bamboo shoots in the Chinese countryside, and many more are under construction. All of them are painted white, blazing in the scorching white sun of the Greek summer. As I sat on the stone edge of the Parthenon, I realized that Athens was built some distance inland and that the sea air from the Aegean hardly disturbs the deep azure sky that hangs above this ancient land. With such a spotless indigo as background, the city of Athens with its whitewashed houses of all sorts becomes whiter and brighter.

Though the San Francisco houses are white and clean, they never stand under a scorching sun which keeps one's eyelids semi-closed, nor have they a spotless indigo sky behind them to enhance their whiteness. In fact, San Francisco stands by the Bay with the Pacific Ocean close at hand. The bracing sea air has always acted as Nature's hand to mold the mists and clouds into ever-changing forms. Such infinitely varied forms, big or small, dense or loose, make a game of gliding over the city's houses, sometimes lingering for a while, sometimes rushing from one side to the other, and sometimes drifting to and fro. They prevent the city from wearing a monotonous whiteness. They cast shadows of varying density, and their not-always-white color juxtaposes with that of the buildings. Besides, San Francisco has long replaced her sand-dunes by a luxuriance of plants and trees, providing much green to contrast simultaneously with the white or gray. The result is often that the gray or whitish color appears tinged with red through the influence of the complementary green, and the green appears brighter —more yellow, perhaps. Therefore, I can hardly agree with George Sterling's description of San Francisco as simply "the gray city," unless one stays near the tip of the peninsula, where one meets sea-fog almost every morning, particularly during the summer months.

George Sterling, as I have read, was a poet, a sorrowful man at heart, who perhaps had a preference for gray or who saw things gray all the time during his stay in San Francisco. He ended his own life in 1918 by drinking a vial of poison in his room in the Bohemian Club, having waited in vain for his friend, H. L. Mencken, whom he admired more than anyone else in America. I do not know what to say about Mencken, for I know very little of his work. But "fame" able to cause another's death is something new to me. Mencken may not have promised to come to George Sterling's party from Los Angeles, yet one should be careful in enjoying one's "fame." The sincere passion that Sterling possessed for his fellow-being whom he admired so much is very rare nowadays.

George Sterling did not *always* see San Francisco as "the cool, gray city." The following lines illustrate his keen observation of the city he loved so well:

> At the end of our streets is sunrise;
> At the end of our streets are spars;
> At the end of our streets is sunset;
> At the end of our streets are stars.

With the constant alternation of sunrise and sunset over San Francisco houses, the city is full of warmth. Through the simultaneous contrast of the colored spars and the sparkling stars the city cannot be gray for long. The lines are a wonderfully apt description. Actually no one can easily see to the end of any of San Francisco's streets; yet one is uncannily deceived into thinking one does when facing the sea, the hills, the trees, houses and even clouds, directly ahead. When I came to San Francisco for the first time I enjoyed the surprises which kept cropping up one after another each time I thought I was nearing the end of the street.

I had an experience of watching the sunrise from the top of Mount Tamalpais before five o'clock one morning, but San Francisco was too far away to be clearly visible from where I was standing. But from the footpath on the east side of Golden Gate Bridge I saw the city under the sunset in its unbelievable colors. I could not find my way there on foot, so a friend took me out by car one afternoon on his way to Sausalito. It was one of the rare afternoons when the sun shone around Golden Gate Bridge; there was neither strong wind nor fog. I strolled on slowly towards Marin County, gazing all around and trying to locate what I had seen previously, high up on the tower of the bridge. Reaching the end of the footpath, I moved on to an open promontory and joined a group of people who had left their cars to have a look at the city for a moment. Involuntarily I agreed with them "how white the city looks" in the distance under the bright sun. Returning to the footpath I lingered on awhile at each step and even the fast-moving cars behind me were not able to rush me away.

Nobody else was walking along the footpath. I felt I owned the full length of the Golden Gate for the time being and was actually in command of the whole harbor. The City lay remote, yet not so remote as it had seemed from the top of Mount Tamalpais. The whitewashed mass of houses, some distinctively tall and many low, looking like a number of irregularly-shaped doorsteps assembled together, grew less white than they were an hour ago. The sunbeams were not white either, for the sun had been gradually sinking. There were large patches of blue up in the sky and various streaks of red and pink floating on like a shoal of red goldfish swimming in different lanes. Some of them soon took on the shape of red porpoises and dolphins jumping one after another through the dense balls of yellowish cloud which were ringed with bright golden lines. All this threw some simultaneously-contrasted colors over the City. The Coit Tower, the skyscrapers on the hills together with the rest of the houses, all changed from white into solid gold. According to the rules of the simultaneous contrast of colors, the whitish clouds appeared tinged with orange from the influence of the complementary blue patches of the sky, and at the same time the whitewashed buildings seemed to be tinged with yellow from the rays of the setting sun, through the influence of the complementary red and pink streaks up in the clouds. There were thousands of silver lines moving towards me on the surface of the Bay water. Many of the skyscrapers' vertical lines of windows were reflected against the sun and became bright silvery stripes. Gradually the surroundings of the city turned a more and more brilliant red, while no more blue patches were visible in the sky directly above. It was a most unforgettable sight for me. It was not like a beauty in uncontrollable ecstasy, but rather a beauty in serenity and grace. The whole of the scene reminded me of the brilliant red sari in Indian silk fringed with golden threads in intricate designs worn by Mrs. Bina Chaudhuri, and the sparkling of her gold earrings and other gold ornaments together with her bright eyes, one evening when Rudolph Schaeffer and I had dinner at her house not far from the San Francisco Conservatory of Music. Curiously enough, it also proved what Dr. Haridas Chaudhuri expounded in his book *The Rhythm of Truth*—the concept of truth as creative harmony— in which he showed how unity and diversity intermingle in the concrete texture of reality. That reality is embodied in San Francisco and it may explain why Dr. Chaudhuri has been so successful in running his ashram in the City. His followers have increased in number each year since I met him. Dr. Chaudhuri is President of the Cultural Integration Fellowship of San Francisco. He and Mrs. Chaudhuri had two lovely children, Rita and Aushim, when I saw them for the first time in 1953. Good friendship has no boundary on the globe. I felt happy after having seen the serene beauty of San Francisco under the sunset as well as refreshing my memory of my friends, the Chaudhuris.

To have seen the City and its surroundings from high up in the air was another piece of good fortune. One night as I was leaving an interesting party given by Mr. and Mrs. A. J. Murphy in Sacramento, Steve William approached to ask if I would like to see the devastating forest fire that was raging through the Sierra Nevada and causing millions of dollars' damage. "If you would," he continued, "I'll come to pick you up at six-thirty tomorrow morning." I agreed with a laugh, but thought he must be joking. As they were getting into their car, Willa and Charlie Inks lowered their heads to say "good-bye" to me remarking, "Take a camera with you and you will get some good shots from the air." I laughed again, not sure what they were talking about. My host and hostess, Bob and Thelma Morris, made no comment before we retired, and I thought that to take a plane in the early hours of the morning without having made any arrangements for tickets was wholly impracticable and I cast the matter aside. However, I was awake very early next morning and was about to dress when the doorbell rang. Steve William was there and Jack Murphy too. They rushed me to the car, saying that we would be back in an hour for breakfast. I felt quite bewildered as we drove off, but asked no questions. Presently I was told to get out in front of a large garage-like structure. Steve pushed a button to raise the door and then with Murphy's help pulled out his private aeroplane! No sooner had they put the winged monster in position than I was told to get into one of the two back seats as I had often been told to do in a friend's car. Before Steve took his seat, he spoke to a young lady who had come to get her plane out from the garage next to Steve's, and who was going to give her son a ride. Then Steve drove the plane a little distance to a place where he asked the boys to refuel as if stopping at a gas station. Shortly we three were high up in the air over Lake Tahoe and soon saw where the masses of whitish smoke lay clustered together like balls of cloud far down below us. My mind continued to be numb; I was neither thinking of anything nor able to think, while I looked round in amazement, sometimes straight ahead, sometimes downwards. A few high peaks of the Sierras were pointed out to me, but their names did not stay long in my head. I have seen the Sierras from the highway and they always look very remote and far above the human world. Perhaps Steve did not fly his plane so very high, for I could see the wide expanse of rocky mountains quite clearly down below—all rocks, with dark patches of trees scattered about. Presently our plane headed straight forwards and then slid downwards to where the dense smoke was blowing, tossed about by the strong wind. Steve tried to locate where the big forest fire was continuing to spread by maneuvering the plane this way and that, tipping first one wing and then the other. Moving up and down as well as circling round, he eventually pointed out to me some red flames looking like sparklers directly below us. The burned area full of bare tree-trunks was most extensive, and the fire was still raging furiously and continually shooting up in new places. No matter how advanced scentific studies have become, there is still no means of stopping such a fire. Steve had a good word to say about the early American Indians. When the Indians lived in these areas, they used to burn down the dry grass round the roots of trees almost every year, so that the fresh grass never grew too tall. Even if a fire started unexpectedly, it seldom spread far. Now the Indians have vanished and the modern Americans cluster together in the towns and cities they have built, letting the dry grass pile up and the new growth flourish. When a fire starts unnoticed, it soon spreads and becomes uncontrollable.

While flying, Steve was fully occupied: at one moment he would kindly explain to me about the fire and the land around the Sierras and at another he would pick up the microphone to conduct business with his secretary before he came down to earth. I asked him how far we were from San Francisco. By way of reply he said, "We can go over there if you would like to see it." Before I could answer, he had asked Murphy to take over piloting while he conducted some more business from the air. The extensive land area of the State of California was soon revealed to me down below. It seemed to take about twenty minutes before I spotted the Bay region. It was a very clear and bright morning and not a single strip of cloud came to veil the view, nor did I see any other plane over San Francisco while we were there. Murphy flew the plane fairly low and made a circle or two. At first I was not particularly attracted by the idea of seeing a city from the air, for many airphotographs I have seen looked like embossed maps without any aesthetic quality. But as our plane flew over rather low, the effect of the simultaneously contrasting colors of San Francisco was far more interesting than I could have imagined. The summer brown hills along the San Rafael and Richmond sides of the Bay, the dark green clusters on Presidio, Sutro Forest, and Golden Gate Park as well as the Berkeley Hills, the deep blue Bay water together with the whitewashed buildings in different intensities all contributed their hues and modified one another, producing a colorful whole of unusual beauty. The new housing developments as I saw them from the air, in parallel rows of whitish lines, laid in various directions, unconsciously imitated the early American Indian pottery patterns. The outstanding color was the red of Golden Gate Bridge. Influenced by the complementary green from the hills on both sides, and the violet tinge of the sky and the water, the Bridge looked even redder and brighter from the air. The San Rafael-Richmond Bridge, seen from above, becomes merely one long curved line; the Bay Bridge a short line with a big swelling in the middle as if a rattlesnake had just swallowed a large sheep which had stuck half-way; both of these bridges could be overlooked from the air, but the red Golden Gate Bridge will never be. I have often wondered who was the one to suggest using Chinese vermilion to paint the bars and towers of Golden Gate Bridge. The effect of spatial depth can be obtained by the function of different colors: cool colors such as blue, gray, and black tend to recede, while warm colors such as red, yellow, and orange advance. The red of the Golden Gate Bridge comes upwards and forwards from its surroundings. It creates a sight and a symbol for the Bay Region as a whole.

Murphy tipped the plane to one side and then to the other when flying over Golden Gate Bridge in order to let me see it from every possible angle. Had I been standing on the top of the east tower of the Bridge at that moment, I would have thought Murphy was doing an air-display over my head. Or I might have been scared of being whipped into the water. However, in a wink of my eye, a big curved sweep lifted the plane high up again to return to Sacramento half an hour later than scheduled. Steve had to rush to his office. Murphy took me to a near-by airport restaurant for breakfast, where I learned that he and Steve had been flying their own planes for two years or so. Steve was to fly his plane alone to Alaska for a deal next morning and hoped to be back the following afternoon. I would like to suggest to modern medical scientists to give up trying to invent new wonder drugs to prolong human life, for life in our modern era is already prolonged by our ability to do so many things in one day, each of which might have taken days or months to do in the past. Apart from my new experience of flying in a private four-seater plane so unexpectedly, I had enjoyed an unexpected view which showed the simultaneously-contrasting effect of the San Francisco colors from the air.

Though the effect of spatial depth and temperature can be conveyed by different colors, light can enhance such effects by accentuating and intensifying them. This is particularly so in San Francisco. Unlike the islands of the State of Hawaii or those in the South Seas, where one gets, after a longer stay, a monotonous feeling from the uniformity of the cloudless blue sky and blazing sunshine day after day, San Francisco sky is neither very blue nor is it ever cloudless. The bright sun seems to have gone through a modifier and to have come out shining over San Francisco purer and fresher, allowing the human eye to gaze around in perfect ease. The sunlight there is neither too strong as if bent on burning everything up, nor too feeble like the moonlight keeping everything dreamy and cool. Each color is left completely free to contrast simultaneously with others. San Francisco displays these effects more fully than any other place I have seen.

Unlike the foggy atmosphere of London, where fog accumulates far from the sea, infused with the chimney smoke of many coal-fires, so that it can envelop the whole city in darkness, San Francisco fog, coming direct from the near-by sea, is clean and fresh. It never spreads far enough to engulf the whole city; there is always sunshine somewhere. Mission Street is the border line, I am told. On the south side of Mission it is sunny almost every day, while on the east side the sea-fog invades the area for long periods. I have always found it interesting to watch the sunshine welcoming with a beaming smile the approach of the fog which moves forward with stealth—shyly and hesitantly. Presently they embrace with great affection and kiss lingeringly, like two young lovers who have been parted for a long time. Eventually the sun becomes soft and loses all his energetic glory. This seems to give me a proof of the ancient Chinese philosopher Lao Tzu's principle; he advocated harmony between Nature and man, for he thought every living thing and creature in Nature possesses feelings as poignant, passionate, and loving as man. San Francisco sun and fog are perfect lovers.

There is a good point to be noted about these perfect lovers of San Francisco. The San Francisco sun projects great warmth but never in excess, for the fog driven forward by the sea air constantly modulates his heated affection. The union of sun and fog unconciously affects the colors and objects with which they come into contact. In due course those human beings who happen to live in San Francisco for a long time receive a similar influence. I have accepted much affection from many in San Francisco but never in great excess.

The twilight and the myriads of electric lights do their share in producing another simultaneous contrast of San Francisco evening colors. I do not know if the San Francisco twilight lasts longer than in other places, but I have seen it lingering for a long while even after most of the street-lights and the lights inside the tall buildings have been turned on. Even the sharp steel and glass buildings are softened by the power of the San Francisco twilight. I have enjoyed the effect from the many thoroughfares over the ridges of the hills. In the twilight, the hard-working day becomes drowsy. People in San Francisco work as hard as those in other cities, but San Francisco's softening twilight should prevent high blood-pressure in anyone. Late one afternoon, I was walking down Hyde Street from Russian Hill. Suddenly I noticed that one of the five towers on the Bay Bridge had turned a glossy red. I hesitated a while, remembering that the Bay Bridge was not painted red like the Golden Gate Bridge but silver. Perhaps it was being repainted and had had an undercoat of red? I looked again and found the tower glowing brilliantly as if from neon-lights within. When I turned my head I saw a brilliant red sunset, filling the sky and casting its reflection on the bridge tower. A beautiful sight. I decided that this was a good reason for the Bay Bridge to have been painted silver: it provides various color effects under the sunset and the different lights and colors of the day.

Gradually the day's eyelids close and San Francisco shows another juxtaposition of colored and black substances that gives rise to a contrast of tones. Those myriads of electric lights, which could be easily overlooked in twilight, now become more luminous and heightened. San Francisco then enters a state of trance and a dream world. The lights of San Francisco spread and scatter far and wide, and at the same time seem to form a pattern of gold-nuggets, large and small, pinned on a huge shroud of Nanking jet-black satin. The pattern looks most intriguing, differing from one angle to another. The view through glasses from the Top of the Mark creates a dreamy feeling which would become still more enhanced if silence could be imposed on every visitor.

A number of friends have taken me to see the views from their windows, but none impressed me more than the first one I had from John Howell's house in Berkeley in March 1953. Through Karl Küp of New York Public Library, I went to see Mr. John Howell at the John Howell Bookshop in Post Street. His first words were: "Karl Küp is a very good friend of my son, Warren. Any friend of Warren is my friend. Karl is my friend. Any friend of Karl Küp's is also my friend!" An interesting piece of logic not very different from what my grandfather used to say. He then suggested taking me for lunch to the Bohemian Club which is only round the corner from his bookshop. In the Bohemian Club he showed me the room where George Sterling had stayed and had killed himself. When he showed me some relics of the author of *Treasure Island* he had a great deal to say about Robert Louis Stevenson, who spent two years in a San Francisco rooming-house before he became a celebrity. Stevenson used to come to the Club for meals and was very fond of Portsmouth Square and its environs. There is a Bronze Galleon, mounted on granite and backed with tall trees, commemorating R.L.S. in that Square. The Square was actually then the nucleus of San Francisco City. In 1846 it was a potato patch belonging to Candelario Miramonte and later became the

Portsmouth Square

Spanish and Mexican Plaza. The members of the Bohemian Club played an important part in the early literary work of the City and of the whole West Coast. John Howell himself used to write plays for the High Jinks of the Club and also acted in them. He promised to take me to see the Club's camp in July, for the Club members would spend two or three weeks in their camp at Russian River and play High Jinks. It is a most exclusive camp; even wives are not allowed there. Before I said "Thanks and good-bye" to him, John Howell gave me a copy of the book, *Sketches of the Sixties*, by Bret Harte and Mark Twain, which he edited and published in 1927, and also urged me to come to his house for dinner when Karl Küp was back. Karl makes several trips a year to different places to find rare books for the New York Public Library. John Howell deals chiefly with old and rare books, and is an authority in this field. His own collection of various editions of the Bible from the ancient days—ninety-eight items altogether—is well-known.

When Karl returned to San Francisco five weeks later, I went to Berkeley for dinner with the Howells as arranged. We met first at the book shop. Karl was already there, discussing books with Warren. He was born in Holland and must have had a good home education in the European social etiquette of the nineteen-tens. His constant visits to Europe where he mingles with many noted connoisseurs of rare books and art collectors in high society have molded him into quite a rare and outstanding personality, even among the party-goers in New York. He dresses meticulously, neatly. What I have always liked to watch is the way Karl raises his right hand in the air and brings it rhythmically down to turn the pages of some rare book, held in his left hand, as if he were conducting a symphony.

Presently the door flew open and there entered a sparkling, charming young girl whom both Karl and Warren called Antonia. Her eyes flashed all round and Karl immediately became her cavalier. Warren took the wheel to motor us to his parents' house.

Antonia also came from Holland and had a great deal to say to Karl. Amid laughter the short journey to Berkeley was soon over pleasantly. There was good light outside and Mrs. John Howell left the rest to do what they liked, while she took me to see her garden where she and her pupils sometimes performed *A Midsummer Night's Dream* and other pieces. She came from New Zealand and her family was connected with the Ruskin family of London. Trained as a teacher of drama, she has always been interested in theatrical work and acting. John Howell accompanied us and also mentioned that he once took part in *A Merchant of Venice,* which was played in the living room of his house. Before we went inside the house again, John Howell whispered to me that he hoped something would be decided soon. "You know," continued he, "Warren is an unusual young man—seldom talking and not quick to make up his mind." I nodded as if I fully understood what he

Birds at Lake Merritt in Oakland.

meant. When I visited him at Post Street for the first time, Warren was not there. John Howell expressed the wish that Warren would get married and settle down soon. How like any other parent anywhere on the globe! I thought at the time.

Dinner was ready on the table. Karl was the one to give eloquent descriptions of the dishes; we all approved them as we ate. With good food and wine, Antonia and Karl enlivened the gathering with sparkling repartée and stimulating talk. Later on, while the two ladies and gentlemen were engaged in conversation on personal matters, John Howell rose to tell me that he had something particular to show me, which the rest knew well. He led me to a room with a huge window along the whole side of one wall. He opened part of the window and the fresh Bay air entered to clear my head and eyes. Then I was told to move up to it and just to gaze. The whole of San Francisco lay before me! I had seen the lit-up city before—once from Mount Tamalpais, from where it looked small and vague in the distance, and again from the front terrace of the Legion of Honor in Lincoln Park, but there I could only see a part. Now the whole glittering city was in full view; the myriad lights seemed to be alive, some moving forward and some receding, through the ethereal Bay air. Their gentle and graceful activities were thrown into prominence by the great dark stretch of the Bay water between the lights of Berkeley directly underneath the window and those over on the other side. Without the various static lights of the Berkeley streets close by, the lights of San Francisco on the opposite side of the water would not have seemed so lively and even brighter by comparison and contrast of tone. The gentle and graceful movements of the lights were enhanced by the wind that moved the Bay air.

I do not always care to look at the colored lights that flood the Campanile tower of the Ferry Building, for they are artificial and of commercial significance. But now the various color from the Ferry Building complemented the lights nearby and also those some distance away. They did not stand still either, nor did they keep the same hue all the while. They were not like the conventional curved rainbow but formed a ball-like mass of rainbow colors combining and separating over and over again. It was all mystery and magic, unreal yet real.

Sunrise from Mount Tamalpais.

Instinctively I began to hum something. John Howell thought I was speaking to him and moved a step nearer. I explained that the view in front of my eyes reminded me of a well-known poem written some thousand years ago, which could have been written here. In the golden age of Chinese culture, the T'ang dynasty, the Emperor Hsuan-Tsung (ninth century) enjoyed a long reign of peace and prosperity. Being artistic and musical himself, he used to compose some special pieces of music for his most beloved lady, Yang Kwei-fei, to dance to with other court-ladies. It must have been on a hot summer evening that a great feast was arranged to take place on a high terrace in the Palace grounds when the Emperor appeared with his ladies and ministers as well as some famous artists and poets. Soon the feast began to the accompaniment of music and dancing. Maybe in the middle of this feast or afterwards, the most famous poet of the time and of all times in China, Li Po, composed the following poem:

疑　萬　霓　如
是　家　虹　夢
銀　燈　光　笙
河　火　裡　歌
落　連　影　上
九　霄　纖　紫
天　漢　纖　煙

Dream-like music and song rise up with the purple mist;
Within the rainbow lights are the movements of shadows,
　　　so graceful and elegant.
Glittering lights from a myriad houses join with the firmament;
I almost believe the Silver River* has fallen down from Heaven.

* Silver River is the Chinese for Milky Way.

What I had been humming was as follows:

> Yü meng sheng-ko shan . . . tzu-yen;
> Ni-hung kuang-li ying . . . chien-chien.
> Wan-chia teng-huo lien . . . hsiao-han;
> Yi-shih Yin-ho lo . . . chiu-t'ien.

"Well," John Howell exclaimed, "that's it!"

Now John Howell is not with us any longer, but he had the happiness of seeing Warren and Antonia married.

XIII

Embracing Wholly

BESIDES CONFUCIUS there are two other major Chinese philosophers: Lao Tzu, an older contemporary of Confucius, and Mo Tzu, who lived in north China about three hundred years later, from 479 to 381 B.C. Confucius advocated the moral law of man and his principle centers on "Jen," the goodness that binds human relationships. Lao Tzu, whose principles and teachings are contained in a small treatise of five thousand words entitled *Tao Te Ching*, advocated the eternal law of Nature which inspires harmony between Nature and man: Nature's creatures and man were to enjoy their rightful places in the rhythmic life of the universe. Mo Tzu seems to me a little more down-to-earth, for he advocated "Chien Ai," interpreted by many translators as "Universal Love" or "All-embracing Love." In other words, one's love should not be confined within a limited circle as Confucianism seems to advocate, for such a limitation gives rise to enmity and conflict between the various groups, and this in turn may lead to war. On the whole, Confucianism lays its chief emphasis on man; Taoism on Nature and man; and Moism on all created things.

I do not think I am qualified to discuss Chinese philosophies, yet I somehow feel that all the three great Chinese philosophies are adhered to in the City of San Francisco, though it would be difficult to say exactly how and where. "Do nothing and all things are done": that is the keynote of Lao Tzu's teaching. Therefore, "no teaching but teaching is everywhere," might be an extension, I suppose. At any rate, I feel that something had taught me something in San Francisco each time I returned.

As San Francisco is more open to the air than many other great cities, there must be more feathered beings around here. At least, it is easier to watch the flight of birds on the way up to the hills, for the buildings in San Francisco offer little obstruction to the view. San Francisco is so built and situated that one can oversee great distances far and wide; this is one of its most attractive characteristics.

San Francisco seems to have all the feathered beings I have encountered in other cities. The starling, for instance, is one, but when they come to roost in the evening on the eaves of houses they do not seem to chatter so busily here. The pigeon is another. It is probably the only feathered being who enjoys the company of humans and loves to be in the midst of throngs as if displaying its right to take part in man's activities. It delights them to waddle along in front of the passer-by, or to display their antics in front of people idling on a public bench. Their attitude conveys the sense of a popular Chinese phrase "Wu hsing wu shih," or "I do as I please." The pigeons' persistence in being with men may be the reason for their survival in such numbers; they have learned the hard way of living. In the ancient days of China from the tenth to the first century B.C. the pigeon was chosen as a symbolic bird to be carved in jade and mounted on a rod as a gift from the Emperor (Son of Heaven) to those of his subjects who had lived to the age of eighty. It was a symbol of health, for the pigeon can digest almost anything.

Somehow I find something different about the habits of the San Francisco pigeons. They do not have to cluster round Union Square, for there are many open spaces and parks for them to roam in. They seem to lead a more civilized life than their fellow-beings elsewhere; at least they have learned to take advantage of the modern device called rain-birds, just like human beings. It is a common sight in San Francisco to see hoses turned on through the rain-birds to water the plants and lawns outside houses and in the parks. I often saw pigeons purposely walking or flying underneath the water spray for a refreshing shower. Their enjoyment can easily be observed in the forward-and-backward movements of their heads when they leave the water spray. I often enjoyed watching them going through this performance on the lawn in front of the old structure of the Palace of Fine Arts.

California quail can be frequently seen in San Francisco parks but not in the cities of the New England States. I first observed them in Reno when the Morrises took me to spend a night with Charles and

Pigeons having their shower bath

Lura Inks there in 1953. While Charles was showing his dexterity in grilling juicy steaks for breakfast, I sat by the door watching five or six California quail idly pecking the grass around the flower-bed in the garden. Unlike the pigeons, whose scurrying walk indicates greed, the quail moved with deliberation and occasionally curved their bodies in graceful poses. They are handsome birds and their attitudes highly paintable for my brush. The swaying of the tiny tuft on their heads added to the grace of their eating movements; they looked this way and that like a well-trained Chinese lady whose eyes express her appreciation of the food to the hostess before she gently dips her chop-sticks into the dishes, not thrusting them in like a glutton. The white spots around the quail's eye and among the plumage stand out as a beautiful design against a fresh green lawn.

I have observed that the California quail who live in San Francisco have better road manners than many human beings. On several occasions I saw a number of them, say eight or nine, standing together under a rhododendron bush by the main thoroughfare in Golden Gate Park, and waiting patiently for the many cars to pass by. As soon as they realized the road was clear for a moment, one took the lead and all the rest followed across in a line without any fuss. Once or twice I saw a driver stop his car to let the quail cross the road. And the quail seemingly appreciated the courtesy, for they ran over faster than ever. This reminded me of seeing a tall London policeman stop the traffic to let a mother duck lead her young family of ten or eleven in a long line across the road to St. James' Park.

California quail crossing the road

In China we have a common saying: "chu chu wu ya yi pan hei"— "A blackbird is black everywhere," meaning that a dark-hearted person can be found anywhere, and that his nature cannot be altered. Literally, it is true that the blackbird is black everywhere in China. I began to doubt the saying when I saw a white blackbird in Dublin, Ireland, until I was told that this one was an albino. A common saying is only a generalization and I have found that not all blackbirds have black wings, some have them spotted with red.

The clearest impression I had of the red-wing blackbirds was when walking by Lake Merced. One morning early I had set out to explore Golden Gate Park. After a few hours of strolling I found that I had come out of the park and reached a wide-stretching golf course. Fine-shaped cypresses with black clusters of foliage at the top stood out beautifully against the fresh green of well-mown fairways on which the players in their brightly colored sweaters formed a pattern. Presently I sat down on a bench to watch a group of youngsters trying to build up a fire and cook a meal in the picnic ground by the side of Lake Merced. They were having great fun. Then I walked along the lake-shore. To my surprise a flock of blackbirds flew out of some tall reeds. They were not common blackbirds but had a bright red spot on each wing. They flew over the deep blue water of the lake towards the other side where three or four tall, whitewashed buildings rose behind some distant trees. The color scheme was alluring. I said to myself: "this would make an interesting painting." The flash of the birds along the opposite shore reminded me of the scattered lights of single, small fishing-boats on Lake Kan-t'ang of my native city, where I used to stroll before dusk in my younger days.

I cannot say whether pelicans exist along the China coast, but I do not remember seeing any there. I have seen white pelicans in Europe but only in the zoological gardens, where they aroused even more sympathy in me than the elephants in their limited paddocks. The pelicans are so ill-shapen, and seem to have such trouble in stretching their large wings, and their beadlike eyes express a tolerant sorrow as if saying "I have to put up with it." But in San Francisco I have seen pelicans moving and flying at ease in their natural state. I have read that the pelican is descended from a species of bird whose bones have been found in Oligocene deposits thirty or forty million years old, and that they were known to the Greeks and the Romans who gave them the name "pelecan." But the Spaniards and Portuguese call them "alcatraz." Did the young commander, Don Juan Manuel de Ayala, on his ship *San Carlos* see so many pelicans or "alcatraz" perched on the rock "Alcatraz" in 1776 that he first gave it this name? Today we cannot see any "alcatraz" on Alcatraz; perhaps they are all white pelicans which have been enclosed within a high-walled paddock. But there are many *brown* pelicans to be seen along the Bay-shore. These birds with the peculiar pouch under their beak and a wing-span of seven feet or so on a rather small body, always look awkward as they take off from the ground, but when they are in flight they have a fine, easy movement. I always enjoy watching the flight of the larger birds. The eagle or hawk circling high in the air is a graceful sight, but its outstretched neck suggests an anxious eye, hungry for prey. Seagulls also have a graceful movement when they fly high; swift when they fly low and betray their greediness. The pelican in flight rests its long beak on its folded neck, carrying its head well back on its shoulders. This gives them an air of "flying for flying's sake." I became very fond of watching pelicans in flight. Unlike the eagle or hawk, which fly alone, and the seagulls, flying in confusion, the pelicans are disciplined social birds and often fly in a long line of five or six, evenly spaced. I have often found them trying to catch fish with seagulls in Fisherman's Wharf. Once I watched a number of them flying quite close to where I was standing on Telegraph Hill, with the sunset light on Bay Bridge behind as a backcloth—an interesting, impressive sight!

"Mammal" sounds better than "beast"—at least to me. I do not know what kinds of mammals inhabited the peninsula of San Francisco before it was discovered by man and eventually developed into the great metropolis of the west coast. To be sure, the few rocks, known as Seal Rocks, that face Cliff House, must have been the seat of the Seal Family since time immemorial. Who first saw and gave these rocks their name? It may also have been the young Spanish commander Manuel de Ayala. These seal rocks have not suffered human interference like the alcatraz one, yet they have had a little annoyance now and then from man, strangely enough from my good-natured and kind friend, Professor Choh-Hao Li. Professor Li has been for years Director of the Hormone Research Laboratory, University of California, Berkeley-San Francisco, and his work is well known in the fields of biochemistry and medicine. He seldom mentions his research to me, but one day he explained to me that the seals of the Seal Rock should be called California sea lions, a distinctive species, and that he had been conducting some experiments on them. I was glad to hear that no invasion had ever occurred on the Seal Rock, but felt puzzled as to why Professor Li and his colleagues should be experimenting on California sea lions, for they are not zoologists. In a subsequent letter Professor Li explained:

It is quite a surprise for me to learn that you are interested in my brief comment on the experiment we carried out with the pituitary glands of the Californian sea lion. Our reasons for these studies were chiefly concerned with the identity of growth hormone in the sea lion's pituitary with other mammalian hormones, including man. The method we employed was the immunchemical technique. The results showed that the growth hormone in the sea lion's pituitary is not the same as that in man and in other animal species. Unfortunately, we have not been able to obtain a sufficient quantity of the sea lion pituitaries to continue our studies and identify the chemical nature of the growth hormone in this species.

He also sent me one of his articles entitled "Anterior Pituitary Hormones," and urged me to read the section on "metabolic hormones." I read and re-read it but had to give up eventually. Francis Bacon said "Reading maketh a full man," but this sort of reading only makes me frustrated. In my younger days my greatest ambition was to be able to read and to read more and more. When I grew up I ran into difficulties in trying to read books not written in Chinese. Now I manage to read some English books, but thousands of publications printed in English are beyond my ability to understand, though I can recognize most of the words: my friend's article is one of them. But at least I can see that the seals on Seal Rock near San Francisco have contributed something to the sum of human knowledge. Professor Li did mention that he could not get a sufficient quantity of the sea lion pituitaries for further experiments. As sea lions can live inside the water, I at first hesitated to think of them as mammals. But science tells me that seals and sea lions are aquatic carnivorous mammals, with limbs developed into flippers and adapted for swimming, and having elongated bodies covered with thick fur or bristles and terminated by a short tail.

One kind of mammal on the peninsula—the raccoon—I know well. I was told that they are known as the bear-faced rascals, native to the Americas, getting away with just about everything. They are night-workers, robbing nests, raiding garbage pails, and making themselves completely at home in other mammals' dens. They keep pace with modern civilization, for they know how to twist door-knobs and to open refrigerators. My friends, the Lawsons said that the raccoons had found Mount Tamalpais their paradise, seldom caring to go down to the lowland of the Bay. I must say that they are good-looking fellows and highly paintable, with their cunning eyes, pointed snouts and ringed black and tawny tails against the green foliage or fall colors of any tree.

Curiously enough the mammal called *panda,* a Nepalese word, which is found in the south-eastern Himalayas, belongs to the raccoon family and looks exactly like the raccoons except that their fur is redder in color. The Italian Jesuit, Giuseppe Castiglione, who went to China as a missionary in 1715 and became a Manchu court painter of distinction till his death in 1766, left among sixty-two paintings in the Palace Collection, one of a Himalayan raccoon on a peach tree. This Himalayan raccoon was given the new name of *lesser panda* after the recent discovery of the *giant pandas* in the high mountains of Szechuan Province in China. The original meaning of the Nepalese word "panda" is "bear-cat." Actually the lesser panda is more like a cat, while the giant panda is more like a bear. The giant panda was first spotted on the high mountains of western China by a French Jesuit at the beginning of the present century, and live specimens were brought to Europe and America in 1938 and 1939. Unfortunately none of them lived more than five years outside China. They were newly-discovered mammals and their nature and their food, chiefly bamboo shoots and young stems, needed further study by western zoologists. As they are rare mammals, near extinction, none of them is allowed to be sent out of China any more, though one arrived at the London Zoo two years ago by a special arrangement.

When the first three giant pandas came to the London Zoo in 1938 one of them was a baby of a few months old who at once created a great sensation, for the creature's comic color scheme—two black ears, two black rings round the eyes and four black legs with the rest white—and unusual antics won the heart of everyone who saw her in person or through the news reels in the movies. She was called *Ming* and children loved to go and cuddle her in the Zoo. When grown up, a giant panda weighs over four hundred pounds; though they are vegetarians, their powerful paws with sharp claws can do harm unintentionally. But the baby *Ming* was playful and her image soon took the place of the traditional teddy-bear in English households as a favorite toy. She was featured in films and music. I was lucky to have been in London at the time and had the opportunity to paint these Chinese fellow-creatures in the Chinese traditional manner on silk and paper. I went constantly to the Zoo and was privileged as a Fellow of the London Zoo to spend evenings with *Ming* to study her night activities. Afterwards I produced a book for children entitled *Chinpao and the Giant Pandas,* in which one of my paintings on silk of a giant panda was reproduced in color. This painting prompted the Director of New York Zoological Gardens, Dr. John Tee-van, to write me saying that he had read the book and liked the illustrations, and this was the beginning of a good friendship.

While *Ming,* the baby giant panda, enjoyed her popularity and glory in England, two young giant pandas of the Bronx Zoo did likewise throughout the United States of America. Because of their safe arrival from Chungking, then the wartime capital of China, under the care of Dr. John Tee-van, the amicable director earned a new title—"The Panda Nurse."

The Panda nurse and the two youngsters under his care had an unexpected connection with San Francisco. The day after their ship left the coast of China, the Japanese attack upon Pearl Harbor occurred, so the voyage home was made by a circuitous route to avoid meeting Japanese warships. They stopped at Tagaytay outside Manila and at some other islands and then flew in to San Francisco for a rest before proceeding to New York. Before their arrival, I can well imagine the staff and management of the St. Francis Hotel—how embarrassed and busy they were preparing accommodations for the unusual guests and their nurse. They were given a spacious suite, almost a whole floor to roam in, high up in the building. John grinned when he described what a wonderful time his two youngsters had in the big bathroom, turning on the water taps and splashing the water over the floor. They made occasional appearances downstairs in the hall to meet an enthusiastic crowd who had gathered for a glimpse of these novel visitors. The panda nurse always beamed with pleasure when he told this story, and he would often repeat it. Cuddly pandas are now one of the most popular toys in the American toy-world.

Most of the animals seen in San Francisco today are not native to the area. Perhaps owing to its geographical situation and favorable climate many creatures have been brought to live in San Francisco from other

Dr. John Tee-Van, the Panda Nurse

parts of the world, though not all remained. For instance, there was a
time when bull-fights were important annual events and many fresh
bulls were brought over from Mexico and Spain, but they have long
disappeared without descendants. The unusual appearance of a mammal dubbed "The Noblest Brute" has contributed something to the
history of the city, I think. It was the dromedary. In the eighteen-fifties,
problems of the American wild west must have exercised the brains of
the authorities in Washington, D.C., before the advance of modern
science. Army transportation and supply gave them a big headache.
One brainy officer, Major Henry C. Wayne, suggested using camels for
the purpose. This was logical, for much of the wild west was a sandy
desert. After it had been investigated by the War Department and
backed by the Secretary of War, Jefferson Davis, Congress decided to
finance the project. A few officers went abroad to buy a contingent of
dromedaries and seventy-six were shipped to Texas. They were used

to transport supplies between California and Arizona. Despite many difficulties and obstacles they did their job and were praised as "the Noblest Brutes" by Commissioner E. F. Beale, who used them to take the place of wagons on the roads from Fort Defiance, New Mexico, and

Passing by the San Francisco Historical Society

Los Angeles. Unfortunately, while the country was in the throes of the Civil War these animals received no proper care; they became home-sick and miserable. The attempt to build up a camel express line between California and Arizona gradually broke down and thirty-five of the above-mentioned noble brutes were driven to a place near San Francisco Bay for auction. Most of them were then used to carry salt and other supplies to the silver mines in Nevada. Later on the camel craze spread; a Mr. Otto Esche decided to import Mongolian Bactrian camels, which have two humps, to run a Camel Express between San Francisco and Salt Lake City. Many died on their way from Mongolia to San Francisco, but some fifteen arrived. This project, however proved impracticable, and the camels became exhibition pieces. Soon San Franciscans lost interest in them and they were sold again or turned loose to become wild in the desert. For a time they were occasionally spotted in the wilds of Nevada and Arizona, but they did not long survive the climate and the game hunters, particularly the hungry Indians.

The camel is not often seen south of the Yellow River in China. In Peking where I stayed for a while some thirty years ago, a camel

caravan would occasionally enter the city from Mongolia to unload
Mongolian products and to take back other goods from the capital.
Each time, the youngsters would gather round to have a good look.
I can remember a herb merchant taking a camel with a full load on its
back to trade from town to town south of the Yangtse River. I still have
a vivid memory of seeing this huge mammal for the first time in my
home town of Kiukiang as a young boy of eight. Last summer I was
travelling on a cruise from Athens to Crete via Istanbul and some
islands. When we landed at Pygamus I followed the passengers on to a
bus to explore the scenery. On our way someone spotted four camels
and shouted for the bus-driver to stop. About thirty of us jumped down
at once to take pictures of these "noblest brutes," who were nibbling

A show

grass by the roadside with heavy loads on their backs. It was interesting
to see the astonished faces of the young members in the group while the
cameras clicked busily. It helped me to imagine the stir when some
Bactrian camels were put on exhibition in 1854 at the Bush Street
Music Hall in San Francisco.

Neither donkeys nor elephants are to be seen as a rule in San Francisco except in the Fleishhacker Zoo, but on one of my visits to the city
I was astonished to meet a great number of elephants and a good few

donkeys in Market Street. For a few days I had been noticing an unusual display of elephant toys of all shapes and sizes in the shop-
windows. There were donkey toys as well, although it was nowhere
near Christmas. One morning as I was walking in Market Street, I
found it even more crowded than usual, and the whole street was
decorated with elephant emblems among numerous American flags.
Soon the sound of bands was heard and a long procession began to
march by. Any parade or procession interests me little now, for I have
seen far too many of them in New York. Any important occasion becomes a commercial one in America. In the procession along Market
Street I noticed that almost everyone had an elephant emblem in his
buttonhole, big or small. Someone near me explained: "They are all
elephants!" These words seemed to play a trick on me, and I immediately saw the figures in the procession swelling and their eyes becoming
smaller in proportion. It was the G.O.P. Convention, which was being
held in San Francisco that year. To my enquiries nobody could explain
why the Republican Party chooses an elephant and the Democratic a
donkey as their symbol. One joked to me that the elephant always looks
well-fed and solid in the belly rather than in the head, while the
donkey has an alias, that is, "ass." All this is beyond my comprehension.

I learned that the procession was going to Cow Palace. This name be-
mused me still further. America, I thought, has never been a kingdom
with a monarch and nobles; no such building as "Palace" or "Castle"
was ever needed on the soil of the United States. I decided to see what
sort of place this Cow Palace was. A self-titled near-elephant introduced me there. I did not stay for the Convention, being neither
elephant nor ass, but I learnt that the Palace was built for livestock
shows in the Bay area. It is a most spacious structure able to hold
thousands and thousands of mammals. How unique San Francisco is in
having a Cow Palace!

There must surely have been many deer and bears roaming on the
San Francisco Peninsula before the city became the great metropolis
of the West. Though I have seen many of them in Yosemite and other
areas surrounding the Bay, they are no longer to be seen in this densely
inhabited spot. The species of bear found in California is the "grizzly,"
and some legends about them are connected with the Bay Area of the

gold-rush days. It is said that the gold prospectors, when they had time for sport, used to chain a ferocious grizzly to a stake and then loose a maddened bull to attack it with charging horns, while in turn the grizzly would sink its sharp teeth into the bull and rip him to shreds. This so-called sport must have been derived from the Spanish bull-fights, and a gold-collector rather than a gold-miner must have invented it. Another legend concerns a Massachusetts shoemaker, John Capen Adams, who came to California to capture, train, and exhibit wild animals, particularly the grizzly bear. He earned the name "Grizzly Adams," for he rode grizzlies, wrestled with them and sometimes fought them hand to hand for shows in San Francisco.

There are many deer in Golden Gate Park but they are kept inside a very big enclosure, shared with a number of bison. I always regard the bison, commonly called *"buffalo,"* as a typical American mammal, though it is said to be the descendant of immigrants from Asia. Bison used to roam North America in great numbers some two thousand years ago, but so far no rock paintings depicting bison have been found such as are to be seen in China. Before Columbus' days there were many American Indian legends concerning this mammal, for it meant much to their way of life. Only recently I learned that Buffalo Bill won his nickname as a hunter for the Kansas Pacific Railroad. He is said to have killed four thousand one hundred and twenty bison in eighteen months, quite unaided. Bison are now almost extinct and can only be seen in special reservations.

The skunk seems to be exclusively American. I heard much about it in New England, and was even driven away by one without having seen it; and I once met a fellow walking on the great highway beach with a skunk on a leash. It was the owner's pet, like a small dog. I must admit that this mammal has a very *unmusical* name, and though it is common in America it does not appear in any European Zoo. Rarity does not necessarily make something precious, contrary to the general Chinese belief. It has been said that the skunk has the unenviable reputation of being literally in worse odor than any other known mammal. The possession of the horrid effluvium is a most valuable means of defense, for there is no enemy that will dare to attack him who has the power of overwhelming his foes with so offensive an odor that they are unable to shake off the pollution for many hours. When the skunk is alarmed, he raises his bushy tail in a perpendicular attitude, turns his back on the enemy, and ejects the nauseous liquid with some force.

A pet skunk

Secure with this means of defense, he appears remarkably quiet and gentle of demeanor, and has more than once enticed an unwary passer-by to approach him and attempt to seize so playful and attractive a creature. Why did Nature devise such a creature if he can be so unpleasant and even mischievous and destructive to his fellow mammals? This is Nature's mockery. I am happy to think that somebody has succeeded in turning the skunk into a pet, and that San Francisco extends her all-embracing kindness to include a skunk to be seen along the highway beach!

Unlike the skunk, the Koala or Australian bear has been sought by every Zoo authority for exhibition, but with little success. During my twenty-odd years' stay in England I heard and read much about this creature and also saw many photographs of it but never a live one. I was told that years ago a couple of koalas were brought over from Australia to the London Zoo, but they did not live long, since they missed their special diet of gum-tree leaves, as well as disliking the damp English weather.

When I came to the Bay area for the first time in 1953, I was surprised to see so many eucalyptus or gum-trees growing abundantly in San Francisco, but it did not occur to me to connect them with koala bears. However, Grace Chen remembered reading about an Australian present of two koalas to San Francisco City and at her suggestion Shih-hsiang Chen drove us to the Fleishhacker Zoo to see them. After a while we found the quarter where they were kept. The sun had already set and we seemed to have arrived at the right moment, for koalas are nocturnal in habits. There were three of them up a good-sized eucalyptus, busy eating the young leaves, buds, and twigs, within a large wired enclosure. Their quaint expression with the tufts of long hair on their ears and their little eyes above the soft, hairless muzzle are adorable, while their climbing and eating antics, always with a few leaves at the corner of their mouth, standing out against the darkish sky, made my hand itch to paint them. A special keeper was standing by to tend them. He took the youngest one out on his shoulder, enticing it with a branch of the eucalyptus. The baby made no fuss at the change of position and began to eat perfectly at ease. At times he moved closer to the keeper's head and put a forepaw on it. Grace went to exchange a few words with the keeper, who seemed delighted to discuss his charges. "This little guy was born right in this Zoo, the only one ever bred outside Australia in the whole big world," he told us with great pride. He went on to relate how the father and mother koala came to the Zoo and how the little one was brought forth to be the first San Francisco citizen of Australian ancestry. He was the nurse in sole charge of the family. "This little guy is worth half a million dollars!" he boasted. The koala is a very gentle creature and usually suffers capture without offering much resistance, or seeming to trouble about captivity. In this he is quite the opposite of the skunk. Indeed, San Francisco is a unique city as far as mammals are concerned.

XIV

Living Pre-assignedly

CAN ONE lead one's life as pre-assignedly as one imagines? Many exceptional cases can be found anywhere, and San Francisco perhaps furnishes more than other places, for she numbers such striking and extraordinary characters among her pioneers. I feel that I, too, like many an early settler and gold-digger, have been wandering accidentally, not pre-assignedly. Life is a riddle. Many came to dig for gold but not all found it. Of those who struck gold, a good many unfortunately were eaten up by it. Life is a mockery, too. Many thought happiness could be attained by satisfying their needs. What do they mean by this? Material necessities or emotional ones? There is hardly any answer.

Before the gold was discovered, there were very few native-born San Franciscans of any note. Sam Brannan, who came to San Francisco in 1846, was of East Anglian ancestry. He created a Mormon Battalion with the Sandwich Island (now State of Hawaii) rifles, became the first lawyer and first millionaire, but died penniless. He was one of the first to be described as "fabulous," an adjective still used to describe Americans as Europeans see them nowadays. John Augustus Sutter, in whose millrace was discovered the gold which started the gold-rush, came from Sweden. Adolph Sutro, whose name remains to the present day in Sutro Heights, came from Prussia as a mining engineer, built the Sutro Tunnel, earned the title of the King of the Comstock, became the mayor of the city and designed the Sutro Baths, the world's largest indoor swimming tank, near Cliff House. John McLaren came from Scotland to turn the wild sand dunes into a beautifully-wooded Golden Gate Park. Andrew Smith Hallidie, a Londoner, invented the Cable Railway System and built the first cable car for San Francisco. The German engineer, J. B. Strauss, designed and directed the building of the Golden Gate Bridge. Rudyard Kipling was not as fortunate as Robert Louis Stevenson in earning fame for his writing in San Francisco when he came with empty pockets and the manuscript of his story *The Light That Failed*; it was not accepted by the editor-in-chief of the foremost Western newspaper. Neither Stevenson nor Kipling stayed long; Oscar Wilde was better received in a crowded Platt's Hall in Montgomery Street to deliver his delicate aphorisms. Dr. Sun Yat-sen, founder of the Chinese Republic, had a temporary office in the Montgomery Block for his revolutionary work. All these were strangers who arrived accidentally in San Francisco, and yet left the mark of their personality on the City.

George Gordon, a Yorkshireman, is another figure who contributed much to San Francisco in her early days. The story is told that he went one night with one of his neighbors, Bramwell Brontë, brother of the famed Brontë sisters, to a local inn and had a few more drinks than usual. When he woke up, he realized that he had gone through a marriage ceremony with the inn's attractive barmaid. He thought she loved him and took the marriage gallantly as a gentleman should. However, his future was doomed in mid-nineteenth-century Victorian England; he could not introduce the barmaid to his relatives and friends as his wife, so he took her to San Francisco to start a new life. Mrs. Gordon soon disclosed her plot to make him drunk and marry her in order that she might lead the comfortable life of an English country squire's wife. She demanded to go back to England. At the same time it came to the knowledge of Mr. Gordon that his wife was an incurable alcoholic. He never yielded to his wife's demand, but to distract himself from domestic bitterness, he set up in the sugar business and made his way into the social life of the City community. He quickly made a substantial fortune and had his wife well-cared for at the hands of a trusted butler. Later a girl was born in the family, who immediately became the idol of Mr. Gordon. Unfortunately he did not realize that his wife was secretly planning revenge by putting whisky into the child's drinks. The little one was already an addict before she reached seventeen. When the father discovered this, he sent the girl to a boarding school, but the indulgent mother smuggled bottles of whisky in her daughter's laundry. At her father's plea the daughter tried to stop drinking but could not break the habit. Eventually she married a ship's surgeon, also an alcoholic, who drank himself to death as did his young wife soon after when she was still in her early twenties. Mr. Gordon had already died of a broken heart. Mrs. Gordon was not brave enough to return to England by herself. Instead, as a rich man's widow, she sent for her brother from Yorkshire to keep her company and they both soon died of alcoholism. The whole chronicle of the Gordon family in San Francisco was full of tragedy. Had they lived in the overcrowded metropolis of today what happened to them might have been easily overlooked by the rest of the city. But Mr. Gordon was a noted personality in society at the time, respected by all who knew him. The family scandal—every movement of his wife and daughter was watched and noted; stories went round quickly with distortion and exaggeration. They spread far and wide, even crossing the Atlantic and resulting in a novel entitled *The Daughter of the Vine*, published in 1899, long after Gordon's death. George Gordon was unquestionably an English gentleman and bore all his pain within his own heart, and did much to contribute to the building up of San Francisco as a fine city. With the substantial fortune he made out of the sugar business he planned a real estate development. On a few level acres between Third Street and the sharp slope of Rincon Hill he designed an oval-shaped English garden, with many flowers and trees, chiefly eucalyptus, round his Victorian-style mansion house. He named the quarter South Park and divided the land into sixty-four lots for sale to San Francisco's wealthiest men. Soon a fine stone mansion went up on each lot. That was the beginning of the Victorian architecture in the city; hardly any of the houses are still standing nowadays. No one can tell me whether George Gordon was the first to introduce the eucalyptus tree to San Francisco, but it was he who imported English sparrows from London and listened to their quarrelsome noise in his garden to forget his own sore heart. So the present San Franciscan sparrows may trace their family tree back to England!

In Marin County I was once driven through Fairfax, a town under the shade of Mount Tamalpais, with its main street lined on both sides by tall royal palms. Fairfax has many beautiful-looking houses with gardens and thick-foliaged trees—a very pleasant place to live in, I thought. I was told that the town had been named after "Lord"

Charley Fairfax. Sometimes he was known as Charley "The Baron" Fairfax. Charley Fairfax, though not born in England, was of true English blue-blood, being a son of one of the First Families of Virginia, in line of succession to the ancient Fairfax barony in England. But Charley never bothered about that. He was born a gentleman of leisure like many of aristocratic lineage in England, but his father owned a large estate in Virginia and probably could afford for Charley to be a gentleman of even more leisure and more pleasure than his counterparts on the other side of the Atlantic. Charley loved reading, unlike most of the Virginian gentlemen of affairs at the time. He was friendly to everyone, even making friends with his family's slaves, and was not happy under the strict Victorian etiquette at home. Against his parents' wish he sailed for San Francisco. He had not come to join the gold-rush, never amassed wealth, and in fact, was always in debt. On his arrival, his amiable manner of a jolly-good-fellow Englishman won the heart of society overnight. From what I have read, and proved by personal contacts, the English seem to have earned a great reputation, from the mid-nineteenth century till the Munich episode of 1938, for being sociable, pleasant and good companions the world over. Repeatedly I was told that the early Virginians were more English than the English themselves. This I readily believed when I read that Charley Fairfax was immediately known as "The Baron" and that everybody loved him and addressed him as "Lord" Charley. He had a soft, kind voice and a pair of lovable, gentle eyes that pleased every girl he met. As a young man at home he learned that a gentleman should not refuse a drink and was always willing to take a glass with a ready smile. He loved his drink and drank heavily. With his many friends he was quickly elected clerk of the Supreme Court of California with a salary of thirty thousand dollars a year—very good pay some hundred years ago. He then married a beautiful and wealthy wife. Yet he often had hardly money enough to buy a drink or a lunch after spending generously on his friends.

This lovable person never dreamt of having an enemy. Unexpectedly he encountered one who had been his deputy in the Supreme Court and who challenged him in most offensive language for an alleged injustice. A thoroughbred gentleman like Lord Charley could not stand this: he caught the challenger by the throat and threw him down. When his assailant came upon him with a sword he met the thrusts with his bare hands. His shoulder was pierced and Charley fell to the ground. He then drew a gun from his vest but soon dropped it, murmuring "What's the use? You are a cowardly murderer. You have killed me. But you have a wife and small children. On this account I will spare your life." He was carried home, dying, as it was thought.

This event must have caused a great stir in the city at the time, and a big crowd came to stand by his door, weeping, like those who clustered outside Buckingham Palace when they learned of their late King's critical illness. I am sure there must have been big headlines in the English papers, partly because Charley Fairfax was in the line of succession for the ancient Fairfax barony but also because the news-reporters would have seized this opportunity to strengthen an already deeply-rooted conception of the wild, fantastic life of San Francisco then. However, "Lord" Charley Fairfax recovered and lived a good many more years; he died in Baltimore, Maryland, in 1869. It was he who discovered the hidden valley at the foot of Mount Tamalpais and loved it enough to have a house built there around which eventually grew the pleasant town of Fairfax.

A few years after my own visit to Fairfax I spent a week-end in Charlottesville and had a talk about "Lord" Charley with my good friend Frank Berkeley of the University of Virginia. Since then I received many letters from him with all sorts of information about this *de jure* Lord. I am very grateful to Frank for them and also for a photograph of Charley from which I made a line sketch. I feel strongly that the type of true gentleman which Lord Charley represents deserves our admiration, for it is so rare in the modern world. It seems to me that many people today do not even know what it is (or was) to be gentle and courteous.

Unlike any other emperor in the history of all the nations in the world, Emperor Norton was neither a ruler by hereditary right nor a victor in many battles. In the first place, San Francisco was neither a separate country in the eighteen-fifties nor the capital of the United States of America. Emperor Norton had no crown, no throne, no palace, no cabinet ministers, no armed forces, and hardly anything an emperor should have but a name. Nevertheless, he reigned in his own way for twenty-seven years and everyone in San Francisco respected his royal title. He was known as a kind, democratic emperor and would make his daily round through the San Francisco streets with two body-guards, Bummer and Lazarus, his faithful dogs. On his way he greeted and talked to anyone who had time for him. A printer whom he knew well printed a large number of cash certificates of different denomina-tions under the title, Norton I, Emperor of the United States and Protector of Mexico; they were honored by all shopkeepers in the city and accepted whenever the emperor used them. It is said, they were never refused except once when he made one of his usual trips to Sacramento, capital city of the State of California, to attend a session of the Legislature and to give advice to the Legislators. A newly-em-ployed waiter in the dining-car did not recognize him and refused to take his cash certificate. Upon this particular occasion he actually roared with anger and declared as he pounded the table that he would revoke the railroad's franchise. The train-conductor soon dashed in to apologize and the next day he received a railroad pass, valid on all trains, from the head office of the Central Pacific Railroad Company. The State authority of California and the legislators seemed to have found nothing odd or improper in providing a regular seat in the visit-ing gallery of the Senate for the emperor of the United States and they even listened amiably to his advice. Everything always went well with Emperor Norton. He always wore a uniform, probably designed by himself, a combination of the American army and navy regalia of the time, with a high beaver hat which had a brass clasp round three brightly-colored feathers in the front. But he had no empress to take care of his laundry; the executive session of the San Francisco Board of Supervisers passed an act in the city charter to provide Emperor Norton I with thirty dollars a year to buy uniforms as long as he lived. The money was assessed against the city taxpayers. He ate at the free-lunch counter in any restaurant, visited the markets and the wharves, the banks and exchanges, and also passed candy to children on his walks. Men in the street always greeted him, bowing. Entire audiences would rise to their feet when he made his entry to the theatre in the evening. Most of the time he busied himself writing documents and issuing proclamations, which the San Francisco newspapers always printed in full. He also sent telegrams to many monarchs of European countries on diplomatic matters to Queen Victoria of England, the Tsar of Russia, and the German Kaiser. He even felt responsible for a successful negotiation to end the Franco-Prussian war. Once he cabled President Abraham Lincoln, ordering him to marry the widowed Queen Victoria in order to maintain Western civilization by promoting mutual understanding between the two English-speaking nations. He received a reply from the President's secretary promising "careful consideration to the command." Emperor Norton went on living up to his name till his end in 1880. He dropped dead in front of old St. Mary's Church. Two days later, ten thousand San Franciscans filed past the royal rosewood casket as Emperor Norton lay in state at Lockhart and Porter's funeral parlor in O'Farrell Street. Thirty thousand people followed the funeral cortege to the grave that had been prepared for the sovereign in the family burial ground of Joseph G. Eastland, a San Francisco pioneer. On that day flags were flown at half-mast in the whole city. And the funeral expenses were provided by the rich Pacific Club, now the Pacific Union. Fifty-six years later in 1936, when the city development forced the transfer of Emperor Norton's remains from the old Masonic Cemetery to Woodlawn Cemetery, hundreds of wreaths were placed on his new tombstone by the San Francisco civic leaders and other members of the public. The San Francisco Municipal Band played dirges, while a three-volley salute was fired over his grave by members of an infantry battalion!

How fantastic and how unreal, I thought, when I read several accounts about this amazing San Francisco figure. But his life-story was real; it was a fact and not a fairy tale.

Joshua A. Norton was born about 1815 in the British Isles. He left London to open a shop in San Francisco in 1849 with a capital of forty thousand dollars, and hung a wooden board over his door, "J. A. Norton, Merchant." He was good at business dealings and soon increased his fortune to two hundred and fifty thousand dollars. Not content, he wanted to make even larger profits, but he met with bad luck and was finally ruined. However, he was an honest man and paid

Emperor Norton and his two courtiers

his debts as well as he could before he disappeared. In 1857, he came back to San Francisco under the delusion that he was a monarch.

The older residents of San Francisco still talk about Norton and newcomers hear and read about him. As far as I can make out, he may have been a prophet seeing things long ahead of his time. It is said that he went to see the President of the city's most representative bank with a check for three million dollars which he wanted to be used for building a bridge over San Francisco Bay. He was politely received but his suggestion was considered absurd. Now the Bay Bridge carries a heavier load of cars than any other in the Bay area. In the eighteen-sixties Norton suggested at Christmas time that a lighted Christmas tree should be placed in Union Square for all to enjoy. His idea was approved by the city and complied with, but regarded as crazy. Nowadays every open square in any city of America has a huge, well-lit Christmas tree and Park Avenue of New York has one in every block center.

Many more outstanding characters appeared on the San Francisco scene in the later part of the nineteenth century, but none to my mind contributed more than Norton to making San Francisco a distinctive city in the world. Even the story of the bandit-poet, Black Hart, who robbed twenty-seven Wells Fargo stage-coaches from 1877 to 1883 and left a poem behind each time, has less novelty than Norton's: I have read many such tales in Chinese story books. Perhaps I have tried to make too much of this eccentric character, but I feel that Norton's life-story had a remarkable significance in the human history of San Francisco. The city from its early, rough and eventful days was composed of lonely individuals whose heart always secretly cried for help and friendship, though on the surface they appeared harsh and self-seeking. Whenever they found a chance to relieve their feeling of loneliness they would extend a helping hand and try to gain friendship. Despite all bitterness and savageness, they all joined hands to work for the common good, for they instinctively knew that one could not live for happiness alone while many others were unhappy. Norton's twenty-seven-year "reign," acknowledged by all at the time, is unmistakable evidence for the tolerance and mutual helpfulness of the people of San Francisco. Only in San Francisco I heard of the practice of having a free-lunch counter in bars or restaurants for those who might drop in for a meal without a penny in their pocket. Though little use is made of them now—perhaps they are no longer necessary—the generous spirit behind them is still apparent in the city. Many things begin by accident. Any discovery, any invention, even any law starts with an accident. Though one's birthplace is an accident, many now feel fortunate to have been born in San Francisco.

XV

Edging Invariably

P ETER B OODBERG is a "character" in the San Francisco Bay area.
Nowadays few people there earn the reputation of being a "character,"
for the area is populated to saturation point and everyone is almost too
busy to notice his fellows, whereas in the gold-rush days someone who
came to San Francisco might earn fame overnight. Perhaps "character"
is not the right word to describe Peter Boodberg. If so I apologize, but
I can find no better English equivalent for the Chinese term "chi jen"
or "uncommon person."

Peter Boodberg is in every way a gentleman and scholar. He is of
medium build, rather short, has a full-moon face and walks with the
sort of gait one can see if waiting at the entrance to the English House
of Lords. As a matter of fact, he is not specially distinguishable in a
crowd, for he has no beard and wears no strange clothes. In a crowd no
one would realise that he was born in Russia and can speak ten or more
languages: Russian, Hebrew, Arabic, Greek, and Chinese in addition
to English, French, German, Spanish and Italian, or that he had been
Professor of Asian philology at the University of California for years.
I met him first outside the Asiatic Library at Durand Hall, when I
called on Shih-hsiang Chen, Professor of Chinese Literature at the
same institution. His ready smiling face and genial manner attracted
me quickly and still hold me.

Later on he gave me a few mimeographed copies of his "Cedules
from a Berkeley Workshop in Asiatic Philology." I became interested
in his philological point of view for translating Chinese, particularly
Chinese poetry. He says:

> "Most students of Chinese prosody would readily agree that a
> disciplined inquiry into the principles of stylistic paralellelism is
> propaedeutical to all translation work, for in Chinese, a language

innocent of morphology, clarity of thought, and intelligibility of syntactical relations are often dependent on rigid adherence to word-order patterns, particularly so in the poetic style with its paucity of kommatic particles. Yet few translations reflect adequately the more intricate cases of parallelistic construction, and fewer still show an awareness of what may be called crypto-parallelism."

Again, he writes:

"Of all European languages, English enjoys the greatest commensurability with Chinese in its morphology and syntax. This gives English translators an enormous advantage over their continental confreres, but—by the same token—places them under heavier obligation to exercise their resources in diction and taxis so as to achieve the closest possible approximation to the original, a goal frequently beyond the powers of those whose tongue is burdened with the impedimenta, i.e., grammatical distinctions alien to Chinese, such as gender, desinence, and a strict differentiation between verbal and nominal forms. This obligation is, unfortunately, ignored by most translators who persist in encumbering their versions with supernumerary syntactical paraphernalia."

When I read these papers I realized that Peter Boodberg was an expert philologist.

One afternoon Shih-hsiang came to fetch me out to Cliff House where Peter and Mrs. Boodberg were expecting us for dinner. Shih-hsiang had been trying for some time to arrange this meeting. There are many facilities in our modern way of living, yet we, the men of this era, seem to have become more isolated and individualistic than our forebears. The exercise of "friendship" has altered; now it may mean only an exchange of words through the telephone. I think "friendship" in its real sense is a precious concept, marking the importance of social life in the history of mankind. Its disappearance would have an irreparable effect on the integrity of our human relations. Concentration on material gain has done great harm to the essence of the word "friendship"; the ever-increasing preoccupations of modern life lead to its being ignored completely. However, I was brought up on Confucius' principles, which are based on the obligations of human relationships, and I value friendship more than anything else in life.

I had often passed Cliff House and admired its situation, which commands a wonderful view over the Pacific Ocean. I had learnt that the original house, standing on this site built by Adolph Sutro and burned down after having withstood the earthquake of 1906, had been used as a center for entertaining the American Presidents Hayes, Grant, McKinley, Roosevelt and Taft as well as being a rendezvous for theatrical and literary lights such as Sarah Bernhardt, Adelina Patti, Mark Twain and Bret Harte. The present building must have its famous visitors too.

No sooner had we sat down than the Boodbergs entered. After we had exchanged greetings and begun to talk, I noticed Peter Boodberg's gaze lingering on the movement of the waves as they followed each other towards the shore. He observed that the shadow of each wave moved ahead of the wave itself. "The waves chase their own shadows." What a poetic notion! We discussed the Chinese terms "po-kuang," the rays of the wave, and "lang-ying," the shadow of the wave. While the sun shone brightly on the whitecaps, so that they seemed to be made of silver, and being of uniform size they might have been molded on masses of wheel-counters, like candy bars from a colossal factory far away on the horizon, a darkish shadow was cast underneath each of them. When the whitecap moved forward, its shadow jumped ahead and continued on and on, always ahead. All the silvery whitecaps moved towards us incessantly but disappeared as soon as they neared the cliff. They were gone, yet they still came on towards us. At times they looked less like candy bars than silver-rimmed military caps, worn perhaps by cadets from Annapolis, marching along with their bodies packed together in the deep sea-blue of their uniform, not hurrying, but as if in a procession which had gone on for centuries.

Shih-hsiang displayed his expertness in choosing food, mostly seafood. I enjoyed a dish of shrimps, which were very fresh and cooked to the right tenderness. In general sea-food is simpler to cook than meat, but the timing is important. Mrs. Boodberg expressed her preference for prawns rather than lobsters. She, like Peter, was born in Russia. I do not know whether lobsters are found in the cold Russian waters,

A mirage-like scene from Twin Peaks.

but Japanese lobsters have always been an expensive item among Peking and Shanghai dishes. Lobsters are plentiful along the South China coast and the Cantonese have a special way of cooking them; "Lobster in Cantonese style" is a good Chinese dish and I like it. I think a whole cooked lobster lying in the center of a big dish surrounded by the fresh green leaves and watery white stem of a lettuce is one of the most attractive arrangements on any dinner table in the western world. The crimson color of the lobster's shell and claws is so striking. I have read in a Chinese book called *Cheng Tzu T'ung* that the natives of South China sometimes put a light inside the shell of the largest lobster they can find to make it look like a fiery dragon. A modern electric bulb could achieve a still more startling effect, and huge plastic lobsters have already been produced by the gadget-minded Americans. However, when a natural object is replaced by a realistic replica it immediately becomes less interesting.

"Look at the lovely sky, what a wonderful color!" Mrs. Boodberg suddenly made us all turn to the huge window we were sitting by. The sun had been sinking towards the horizon for some time. Half of the sky was brilliant red and almost all the rest was rosy. The brilliant red was just the color of the lobster shell I had been thinking about. The wave-caps were no longer of silver but transformed into gold. Perhaps a new regiment in gold-rimmed caps was on the march. But this time it was not such a large troop, for many of the gold-caps grew dim under the dark shadows of clouds; they were scattered on the ocean and far apart. Presently there seemed to be only a few walking on the vast sea, flashing their flood-torches about. And how feeble those torch-lights were on the wide darkish expanse! I had the curious impression that the waves were *walking* on the Pacific, in contrast to the people of the West coast who are so rarely seen taking walks on the land.

Peter Boodberg did not agree with me that people along the west coast have no idea of walking. The luxury of two or three cars per family is a recent phenomenon, he said. Had the Texans not struck so much oil the event might have been different. Shih-hsiang interrupted to say that I was too fond of walking and gave him a headache whenever he stopped his car; I was always slipping off for a walk. Peter Boodberg smiled as if to say that that was nothing. He told us how he

Sunset over the Pacific from Sutro Garden.

used to walk miles and miles for days on end. He once walked from Lake Tahoe to Salt Lake City, about seven hundred miles. It took him a month to reach his destination. The land covered in his walk was largely American desert country, where the villages were often twenty and thirty miles apart, and he had to plan carefully where to stop for rest and water, etc. On the whole he preferred to walk at night, for in the daytime the heat was too great in Arizona and Utah. He talked about the Mormons, their beliefs and way of life. He found them a fine people with high principles. He also told us an anecdote about his exploration of Bryce Canyon. One evening he set off to examine the Bryce Canyon rock-formations. When it was getting dark and rather late he had to clamber up some crags to get back on to the road. As he reached the top, a small rock gave way and he fell some distance and lost consciousness. Early next morning he was roused by two highway patrol men. They pushed him into their car without allowing him a word of protest. They showed him their official cards as Highway Patrol Men: "Were you the young man who fell down the Canyon," they asked, and without even waiting for an answer, they drove away at high speed. He could not believe that falling down the Canyon was a crime, and tried to expostulate. The officials told him brusquely to shut up. He kept mum. After a while he was told to get out of the car —he was free to go anywhere he wanted. Both the officials smiled and laughed, saying it was all a joke: they had come to rescue him and were glad to find him unhurt. They urged him to continue his journey, but he protested that he had no money. Thereupon they presented him with a complimentary railroad ticket paid by the county authority. We had a good laugh over the story. I never thought highway patrol men could show such a sense of humor. That was only some twenty-seven years ago. I asked Peter what had induced him to attempt such a walk as seven hundred miles in thirty days. "Just to see a very good friend," was the reply! His friend was not a good letter-writer, nor could Peter afford the fares for trains and buses at that time. So he just set out to walk and did not care how long it would take. What a strong feeling of friendship, and what a spirit! And how rare to find such friendship and such spirit nowadays!

Peter Boodberg has a preference for walking at night; he gains wonderful experiences and meets unusual characters in this way. One evening he was walking in the country. When darkness had already fallen, a car drew up beside him and the door was opened for him to get in. The driver was a farmer—a very silent farmer. No matter what Peter said to him he just drove on in silence. As they passed through a village, Peter offered to treat the farmer to a meal in return for the lift, but the driver neither spoke nor stopped. He just drove on. Eventually the car was brought to a standstill and they had some food. The farmer was a big eater and even took some pieces that Peter had left on his plate. Still not a word passed between them. Peter left a quarter for the tip but the farmer picked it up and put it into his pocket still saying nothing. Then they got into the car again and moved on. Suddenly the car came to a stop and the door was flung open to let Peter out. The farmer got out, smiled, took the quarter out of his pocket, threw it to Peter and said: "Boy, don't waste your money that way again." Before he had recovered from his surprise enough to say "thank you" the farmer had vanished. With a quarter and a dime in his pocket he now read a signpost on the road which told him that he was a hundred and twenty miles from where he had started. He managed to get a loaf of bread in a small village and stayed there until dawn.

Another time Peter walked back to San Francisco from Carmel. "That was only a hundred and twenty miles," he said. It took him nine days. He was quite fatigued when he reached San Francisco at dark on the last day. He sheltered under the porch of a big house and began to feel drowsy. Yet he had to keep on the alert, for thirty years ago the streets of San Francisco were not so peaceful as they are today. Once he was wakened by a soft murmur, "Who are you? Who are you?" He roused himself and prepared for any emergency but made no reply. No more was heard and he fell asleep. Again he woke up with a start to hear the same question and felt alarmed but again nothing happened, and this was repeated several times. Eventually a large bird flapped over his head and flew away. He realized that it was a San Francisco owl, whose cry had sounded like "Who are you? Who are you?" After that he slept soundly until dawn.

Before leaving Cliff House, Mrs. Boodberg remarked that whenever they returned to San Francisco after a tour in Europe she felt she was coming to the land's-end of Western civilization. Beyond San Francisco's coast was another civilization—the Chinese—and she longed to get to it again. I exclaimed how wonderful it was to think that we were sitting right on *the edge of Western civilization!* At the same time I felt nostalgic, for I had passed over the Pacific some twenty-seven years ago and had not crossed it since. Confucius once remarked: "Well, the principle of Tao, the Correct Way, is not prevailing; I shall set myself adrift on a raft on the sea!" Confucius was born at a time when China was in a chaotic state with the feudal lords vying for power with one another. He went to them one by one and tried to persuade them to adopt his principles of government, but none paid him any heed. So he sighed and wished he could drift away from his ungrateful country. Of course he did not go away but instead taught and compiled the famous Chinese classics. If he had carried out his threat and managed to drift on a raft out to sea, he would probably have landed on the coast of Japan, for his birthplace was on the Shangtung peninsula in the north China sea. Suppose again an *if,* only an *if,* his raft had not stopped at the Japanese coast but had drifted on and on westward, he could have landed in this very bay. Then he might have started his teaching here and promoted Chinese civilization in Western America as he had done in north China. San Francisco would then have become the *beginning point of Eastern civilization* instead of the edge of the Western. The origin of mankind was an accident. The history of mankind is full of accidents. Our Shih-hsiang, the Boodbergs and a so-called dumb-walking man gathering at Cliff House was a negligible accident among accidents, yet one that helped me to discover that Peter Boodberg was a "chi jen."

XVI

Feeling Nostalgically

WHILE I STILL LIVED IN China I never gave much thought to what China looked like or what sort of a country it was. Such thoughts only arose after I had left her. The day that the French boat on which a young son of my cousin's and I were travelling left Shanghai for the South Seas and the Indian Ocean, we were facing, for the first time, totally un-Chinese faces and also un-Chinese writing for thirty-three days on end. Neither of us knew a word of French and only a few common useful phrases in English. At the time our heads were full of expectation and we did not bother much about the other passengers. But the first Chinese face, that of a friend of mine who came to meet our train from Marseilles at the Paris station, stirred our feelings so ecstatically that I just loved hearing him talk in Chinese without paying much attention to what he had to say. As soon as I got my young companion settled with someone who would supervise his studies in France, I left for London. That was some twenty-seven years ago. A week later I was taken to Limehouse, London's Chinatown in the East End, for a Chinese dinner. Following my friend through a number of quiet, deserted lanes and streets on a Sunday afternoon, I entered a tiny shop, where only four small tables were laid and only one occupied. Nothing suggested any resemblance to the good restaurants I used to visit in Peking, Shanghai, Nanking, Canton and other places in China. And yet the food in the four small, irregularly-shaped dishes, provided by a mysterious kitchen in the back regions behind a dirty curtain, proved tastier and more delicious to me then than anything cooked anywhere in China. However, at my subsequent visits to the same restaurant in Limehouse I found the food had deteriorated each time, and I stopped going there after a few months. Had the food really become worse? The proprietor, who was also the cook, remained the same. It was actually my personal *feeling* that had changed, for each time the food tasted so different from anything I had eaten in China that it made me feel more nostalgic than ever. "China" began to obsess me.

I first arrived in England in the second half of 1933; the popular comedy, "Chu Chin Chow" was in full swing at the time. Whenever I went out with one or two Chinese friends, particularly in the East End, we would inevitably be followed by a bunch of London children, shouting "Chin Chin Chinaman . . ." At first I felt curious about their reaction but later grew rather tired of it. Occasionally I had to go to the Bank of China on business, but the policeman in the City of London would always direct me to the Bank of Yokohama. Later I found out the reason. The policeman did not really listen to my enquiry, even if my pronunciation of the word "China" had been correct; he just looked at my tidy suit and concluded that I could not have come from Limehouse. In those days all the Chinese in London appeared to be either laundrymen or restaurateurs, who could not afford to wear respectable suits. Those who were better-dressed must be, the policemen thought, Japanese. No news about China appearing in the London daily papers was any good then. The handful of Chinese studying in London, including myself, could not wear a cheerful expression, which gave substance to the belief that my countrymen have emotionless faces.

However, a great change took place when the big International Exhibition of Chinese Art was held at Burlington House, London, in 1935-1936. During the six months the exhibition was open, articles were constantly appearing in the daily newspapers all over England in praise of the great past of the Chinese civilization. Officially or unofficially I ceased to be regarded as a restaurateur or laundryman. Big mansions and noted private collections of Chinese art, particularly Chinese porcelain, were open to my inspection, and at that time I made many good friends including George Eumofopolous, Oscar Raphael, Laurence Binyon, General Sir Neal Malcolm, Mrs. Walter Sedgewick, Sir Reginald Johnston (who was the tutor to the last emperor of the Ch'ing dynasty), Sir William Milner, Sir Herbert Read, and others. I even had five minutes' grace from George Bernard Shaw to make a

sketch of him for my book *The Silent Traveller In London*. During
the second World War China became an ally of the Western countries
and we Chinese living in London were loaded with work; translations,
writing, and lecturing about China. I myself had many requests, for I
wanted to talk solely on Chinese literature and art, not politics. At that
time I sat together with H. G. Wells in a big gathering of the International P.E.N. Club in London when Thornton Wilder flew in to take
part in 1942. "China" became as dear to me as if I could not live without mentioning her each day or each hour.

At the end of the war I was planning to go back to China for good.
But somehow my twelve-year residence in England had accumulated
many associations and friendships which would have been hard to
break altogether. So in 1946 I came to pay New York a visit instead.
After I had postponed my return to my fatherland for the time being,
I tried to push "China" out of my mind. But each time I walked round
Times Square, the shouting of "Tour to Chinatown" or "Chinatown
Tour" kept reminding me of it. Eventually I decided to join the tour
and listened to the guide's description and remarks carefully for almost
two hours. The things I heard from the guide were all beyond my
knowledge and at the end, I began to think that I did not know much
about China any more. I actually wondered whether I had been born
a Chinese!

New York's Chinatown has many better restaurants than the few in
London's Limehouse, which had been almost wiped out by bombs in
the Second World War. During my first visit to New York I dined in
Mott Street on many an occasion, and found the "fortune cookies"—
a New York invention. I was frequently advised to go and see the
Chinatown of San Francisco, which is known as the first and largest
Chinese community outside China. I did not manage to come this way
until 1953. It is true that San Francisco's Chinatown is much bigger,
has more Chinese gift shops and restaurants, and shows more of the
color and smell of China than those in New York, Boston, and Chicago.
Perhaps I myself have changed somewhat after being away from China
longer than most of my fellow countrymen; I have grown older too, so
that nothing, real or unreal, can really astonish me now. I dined in
San Francisco's Chinatown very frequently during the ten visits I have

made to this city so far. I went there chiefly for *eating*—seldom for anything else. I have not once followed any tours there, though I have often been stopped by people asking me to direct them to the Joss House. I tried to locate the original Joss House and was told that it had long gone with the dust and fire. The 1906 earthquake and fire had not spared San Francisco's old Chinatown; a few old-timers, whom I met, lamented the disappearance of the old, glamorous Chinatown of San Francisco. One old China-hand even sent me a copy of the now rare book "Old Chinatown," with pictures by Arnold Genthe and text by Will Irwin, published in 1912. I read about the "The tinkers," "Fish Alley," "No Likee," "A Slave Girl in Holiday Attire," "The Street of Gamblers," "The Opium Fiend," "The Devil's Kitchen by Night," "The Sword Dancer," "The Paper Catcher," "The Fortune Teller," and so on, with interest but certainly no lament for their disappearance. San Francisco's Chinatown at the present day is still a great show place, as attractive as ever, but without the old smell of "Slave Girls, Opium fiend, Devil's kitchen," etc. I met more people coming to dine in San Francisco's Chinatown each time I was there. I think its past laid the foundations of its popularity but its present has improved it, so that it is no longer a mysterious place exposing human ignorance, but a healthy quarter attractive to people with refined appetites. Whether one laments or admires the change, San Francisco's Chinatown has marched on with time alongside the rest of the City.

Change is an inevitable factor in the history of mankind, as I have often expressed. I am sure that China herself must have undergone great changes within the quarter of a century of my absence. How could one stop San Francisco's Chinatown from changing while the speed for change that surrounds it is far faster than in the ancient land of China? Nevertheless, an old custom, though carried out with modifications, still serves as a good reminder of the past and caused me to feel nostalgically. I was fortunate to be in San Francisco in February, 1953, to experience the Chinese New Year Festival once again after twenty-odd years. There were some differences from the events I described as "What a Business!" in my book *A Chinese Childhood*. One of the best things in the traditional Festival has always been the display of lanterns, particularly the show-game of the dragon-lantern playing with the red pearl-ball, which usually went on from the first night of the first month till the fifteenth—the first full-moon night according to the Chinese lunar calendar. Many verses have been written by famous poets for this occasion, but none has become as popular as the little poem attributed to the Sung poetess, Chu Shu-chen:

去年元夜時
花市燈如晝
月上柳梢頭
人約黃昏後

今年元夜時
月與燈依舊
不見去年人
淚濕青衫袖

Last year, in the first full-moon night,
At the flower market, lanterns were as bright as day;
When the moon reached the top-twigs of the willows,
My love promised to meet me after dusk.

This year, in the first full-moon night,
The moon and lanterns are the same as before;
But I do not see the one who was with me last year;
Tears wet the sleeves of my Spring gown.

It is a poem—or rather a song—by a woman restrained through rigid Confucian principles from expressing her lovesickness. From its poignant feeling, we can still imagine what may have been going on during the lantern show on a first full-moon night many hundreds of years ago. The lantern show is a part of the New Year Festival, but when it actually started in China no one knows. We know from records that it was already popular in the seventh century under the T'ang when China had her golden age. Every night during the New Year Festival, every corner of the streets and every open space was filled with people, old and young, out to enjoy the sight of every shape of lantern, every color of dress and every noted beauty of the city. Every child had some sort of lantern in its hand and every home had its main gate wide open, ready to offer gifts to one group of dragon-lantern carriers after another. In the courtyards or halls of larger houses tables were prepared for the lion-dancers to leap up and down on in their swift, nimble display. Fireworks and Chinese drums, gongs and cymbals deafened every ear and covered up all such whispers as those implied in the above poem. I can remember vividly evenings of merry-making during the New Year Festival in my hometown in my younger days.

But, there are no willow trees near Grant Avenue for the lovers to wait under, watching the full moon reaching their topmost twigs. Nor is there any lantern show on the first full-moon night of the year in San Francisco which could be compared with what I experienced in my younger days, for no one can afford to have more than one or two days' holiday for celebration. I read the following announcement in the local paper:

> San Franciscans who know perfectly well that this is 1953 are ready to flock to Chinatown to celebrate the arrival of the year 4651....

> Actually, Chinese New Year's Day would be Saturday, but the Chinese community decided that the advent of the year of Serpent is so important that the occasion demanded a second day of celebration.

A Chinese New Year Parade through Chinatown sounded new and intriguing to me, so I begged to be excused from a New Year's Eve dinner given by a Chinese family, to which I had already been invited.

I must say that I did not come to San Francisco with any idea of taking part in the Chinese New Year Festival. As a matter of fact, the memory of this festival had almost left me after many years' stay in England, for I had more or less become accustomed to the Western Festival of Christmas. With much travel and writing and sketching on hand I had let one Chinese New Year Festival after another go by until this time in San Francisco. Generation after generation of Chinese in

San Francisco have earned the reputation of being faithful to Chinese customs and festivals. Most of my friends who have lived in Berkeley for years have seen the Parade at one time or another. They all thought it was better for me to see it for myself.

I set out for Chinatown by the Californian trolley-bus near dusk on the Saturday. At first I did not notice any signs of celebration except for numerous strings of Chinese lanterns lighted and hanging high on the north-east end of Grant Avenue, which always has well-lit windows, especially along the streets frequented by tourists. On Saturday evenings the shopkeepers there are always busy. When I reached the office of *The Chinese World*—one of the influential Chinese newspapers on the west coast—four huge red Chinese characters meaning "Respectfully Celebrating New Year" were displayed to mark the special occasion. Then someone handed me a program which described twelve hours of entertainment to be presented by the Chinese New Year Festival Committee of San Francisco's Chinatown. It consisted of sports, official opening ceremony, Chinese music, folk songs, lion and Sword dances, Grand Parade, Physical culture exhibition, Chinese art exhibits, stage fashion show, and public street dancing. This all sounded rather different from what I had experienced at New Year Festivals in China. The programme was to begin next day. Fireworks began to go off here and there as I walked on. Many young Chinese children lit their squibs and threw them into the center of the street. American youngsters, boys and girls, did the same with joy and laughter. Then I came upon people busy building a high platform; another group rehearsed drum-beating while others decorated cars and erected a sort of shrine on them for the coming parade.

On Sunday I did not go to the official opening ceremony on Grant Avenue at which the drum corps performed, but wandered about and reached a good spot for watching the Grand Parade long before it was due to begin at seven in the evening. It was a big affair. Spectators poured in from all sides and I was soon pushed back step by step by new arrivals. There were lights and fanciful lanterns hanging over our heads with their red-silk tassels in constant motion. Records of Cantonese music relayed through the loudspeakers were partly drowned amid the bangs of large-size fireworks, while strings of firecrackers went off incessantly. Presently the music heralded the coming of the parade and everyone leaned forward eagerly. The grand marshal of the parade, a veteran Chinese-American, Cpl. Joe Wong, born in China-town, led the parade in a car with two young girls in American Women's Air Force uniform. The appearance of the American Sixth Army Pipers, all blowing Scottish bagpipes, revealed to me an un-expected Chinese-Scottish-American mixture. Then followed a few cars with some army officers in uniform and I heard someone point out the mayor and the City Police Chief. Two of the cars were highly decorated, one carrying Miss Chinatown of 1952, Anne Chow, and the other Miss Hong Kong, Judy C. L. Dann. There were some thirty-eight units taking part in the slow-motion Parade.

Later on two huge animal-heads—dragons, or lions, it was hard to tell which—appeared above the human-sea and reared up in turn with their eyes popping out, as if shouting. "Let's move!" As I watched them, the dragons or lions became so hampered they could not make use of their prowess. They were supposed to be dancing; they hopped about and jumped up and down, but were hemmed in on all sides. Nearly all the houses and shops along Grant Avenue had wide-open doors, with gifts and candies in packages ready for callers, and I noticed Chinese proprietors giving away packets of sweets to the young-sters, American and American-Chinese alike.

It was indeed an experience for me once again after more than twenty years—an experience consisting of many new items, and it was late before I got back to my lodgings that night. Next morning the newspapers told me that the Year of the Serpent had received the largest and best New Year's welcome in Chinatown's history, with an estimated hundred thousand persons joining in the fun. It seems to me that the importance of this special occasion is no longer confined to the Chinese and American-born Chinese inhabitants of Chinatown. The presence of some of the City's high officials in the Parade indicated to me not only the harmony between the different nationalities in the City but also that the booming trade of Chinatown is one of the City's life-lines. Upon reflecting on what I had read about the arrival of Chinese laborers in California since the Burlingame Mission in 1868, I decided that a remarkable change in the attitude of human beings towards one another had developed within the past hundred years in this corner of the world. This change did not come along a well-paved highway.

The first American vessel, *Empress of China,* to start trade relations between America and China left New York for Hong Kong in 1784. Afterwards envoys were exchanged, and missionaries followed. The first three Chinese students to study in the U.S., Wang Shing, Wong Foon, and Yung Wing, arrived at New York on April 12, 1847. No Chinese came to work as laborers until the discovery of gold in California in the latter half of the nineteenth century. At that time south China was suffering a succession of famines which caused much unemployment among manual workers and peasants. In one way or another, though no one knows exactly how, a few managed to come across to the West coast of America. They accepted a meager payment rather than starve to death. Those prospectors who suddenly struck gold and became rich now took advantage of the almost starving southern Chinese and brought large groups of them over as cheap laborers in order to make themselves richer and richer. It must be clearly understood that not a single Chinese came as a gold-rusher, nor did they learn any word of English before they were driven into the lowest corner of a vessel to cross the Pacific. As they had to stick together in order to live at all, how could they later realize that they were infuriating Americans by preferring their own way of life to the American one? All they knew was that the first batch of emigrants had not died of starvation, so the second lot, the third and the fourth rushed to California hoping to survive too. None of them received sufficient pay to better themselves and they had to live in a subhuman manner within a limited area. Being mostly illiterate and having the sole idea of keeping alive, they were not likely to behave like gentlemen or saints. Naturally there were then many reasons for the frequent cry for the removal of the Chinese. Then a "Chinese Massacre" occurred in Los Angeles on October 24, 1871, the result of which was the Chinese Exclusion Act passed by Congress in 1882.

A book called *The Barbary Coast,* which became a best-seller, probably owed some of its popularity to probably two long chapters, one entitled "The Chinese and the Hoodlums" and the second "The

Slaves of Chinatown." They describe how the Chinese were perse-
cuted, discriminated against, robbed, beaten, and frequently murdered
for almost half a century; Chinese laundries and restaurants were
freely set on fire; a favorite pastime of the young hoodlums in San
Francisco was to board street cars or cables on which the Chinese were
riding, tie the yellowmen's queues together, and, if possible, onto the
bars without their knowing it so that when they got out, they might be
dragged along with the cars. Once a Chinese crab-catcher was captured
by a score of rowdies, robbed, beaten with a hickory club, branded in
a dozen places with hot irons, and then had his ears and tongue slit;
another Chinese was burned to death under the old Ford. The authors
of the early volumes of *The Annals of San Francisco* have more to say
on the manners and habits of the Chinese which were very repugnant
to Americans in California. B. B. Lloyd, in his book *Lights and Shades
in San Francisco* gives a vivid picture of how the Chinese lived in those
days. Many times I threw the book aside, not wanting to read any
more; yet I picked it up a moment later to find out if any reason for
such happenings was given. No doubt the reasons existed, for as I have
mentioned, the Chinese laborers were unable to live like gentlemen or
saints. They were simply hopeless and desperate. Being a Chinese myself, I cannot help feeling sympathy for Yung Wing when he says in his
book *My Life in America and China*:

> In my despondency, I often wished I had never been educated, as
> education had unmistakably enlarged my mental and moral hori-
> zon, and revealed to me my responsibilities which the sealed eye of
> ignorance can never see, and the sufferings and wrongs of humani-
> ty to which an uncultivated and callous nature can never be made
> sensitive. The more one knows, the more he suffers and is con-
> sequently less happy; the less one knows, the less he suffers, and
> hence is happier. But this is a low view of life, a cowardly feeling
> and unworthy of a being bearing the impress of divinity.

Though human injustice will still occur here and there throughout the
world, it is being eliminated gradually and human relations among all
peoples are much improved nowadays. I sometimes wish I could have

lived earlier to have witnessed what actually happened in the Chinese quarter of San Francisco after the gold-rush days, though my long queue might have been tied on the cable-cars many a time. On the other hand I am really glad to have been born later and to be living in the present day, for to me the human world is far saner than it used to be. In view of the possible nuclear warfare many will not agree with me that the present era is better than the past. If I am not being too cynical, it seems to me there is a kind of fairness in being killed by a nuclear bomb rather than by some unreasonable human injustice.

Indeed, there are two sides to everything. The Chinese concept of the universe with its *yin* and *yang*, or *negative* and *positive*, principles is always in evidence. But misconceptions frequently result from a one-sided point of view, namely, seeing only the *yin* side or only the *yang* side. The author of *The Barbary Coast* and those of many other early books written about the Chinese residing in San Francisco and elsewhere in America and Europe in the second part of the nineteenth century, with good intentions and otherwise, have described the horrible, lawless way of living and the maltreatment among the Chinese themselves, with clarity and even with sympathy, but none has pointed out that those Chinese were brought over wholesale to a place where no law was quite established yet. Those who loved to see "The Devil's Kitchen," "The Street of Gamblers," "The Girl Slaves," and so on, forgot their own status as human beings. It is recorded that on April 5, 1874 a gigantic mass meeting, attended by more than twenty thousand persons, took place in San Francisco, at which various city and state officials delivered violent harangues against the Chinese. Copies of the resolutions of the meeting and also of the speeches were sent to Congress and President Grant by a special committee. The following were some of the accusations:

> That not one virtuous Chinawoman had been brought to America, and here the Chinese had no wives or children.
> That the Chinese had purchased no real estate.
> That the Chinese ate rice, fish, and vegetables, and that otherwise their diet differed from that of white men.
> That the Chinese were of no benefit to the country.
> That the Six Companies had secretly established judicial tri-

bunals, jails, and prisons, and secretly exercised judicial authority over the Chinese.

That all Chinese laboring men were slaves.

That the Chinese brought no benefits to American bankers and importers.

I am sure that people nowadays, particularly those who love to frequent Chinese restaurants, will have a good laugh over these statements. How could this be? Have we not become saner now? The reports of health inspectors have clearly stated that Chinese kitchens rank among the cleanest. And those who have made investigations into juvenile delinquency have not found a single case in Chinatown. Have we not become more level-headed in our thinking now?

While thinking of the changes that had taken place in San Francisco's Chinatown within the past hundred years, I could not restrain my warm feeling for those early Chinese settlers who actually founded it without knowing what they did themselves. They, the first bunch of Chinese laborers, came with the sole purpose of keeping themselves alive. They had no means of receiving education in their own country, and driven to starvation by famine, they got no help from their selfish Manchu rulers and corrupt officials. They knew very well that they could receive no assistance from their own country if they complained, so they were absolutely prepared for any possible humiliation and even the risk of being cut to pieces so long as they had the *hope* of keeping alive. Above all things, living and merely living was the most precious and sweetest treasure that they hungered for. So they worked and worked in unimaginably rotten conditions. Some even could not fulfill their mere hope of staying alive. But those who managed not only came through all their humiliations to enjoy a natural death but also instilled drops of their exhausted but-not-entirely-dried-up blood into second and third generations. And so Chinatown went on, from its early days as a handful of shacks sprawling down Montgomery Street to the present prosperous-looking street that covers two thirds of Grant Avenue and attracts admiring visitors from all parts of the globe. It is a miraculous achievement. No other nationals have managed to promote their own culture in another land and succeeded in winning the understanding and trust of another race, not as a colony nor by means of government backing with military or missionary force, but simply through sweat, blood, humiliation and hard work. It cannot have entered their thoughts that they could lay claim to spreading Chinese civilization to other lands. Yet Chinese culture in one form or another first became known outside China through their singular, humble, personal presence. Beyond their own ability and hope they have created towns with the startling qualifying word "China," the country where they were born. No other country or human race has managed to create its own towns in a foreign land like that. "Chinatown" bears no political implication or religious design whatsoever: instead it rings happily in people's ears. Is it not a wonderful anecdote in the history of mankind? Is it not also an example to show that men, after all, are friendly and good by nature and that they could live together peacefully if no distinctions of race, creed, faith, color, nation, and politics were forcefully impressed on them? I sincerely hope and even feel sure that in the future, such distinctions will lose their importance and that all men on earth will live together as one people. Though it may take one or two thousand years to reach this sort of state, it will come to that, nevertheless.

Some Americans and Europeans may still remember something about the Tong Wars among the Chinese and also the tales of Dr. Fu Manchu and other detective stories with a sinister Chinese as the hero. Those of a younger generation may still have heard or read some of these stories. The notorious Little Pete, an Americanized young Chinaman of the old days, is still talked about. These are all one-sided stories: while none of those sweating and suffering simple Chinese had their names known to anyone. This is most unfair; perhaps it has been left to me to mention a few of them as follows:

When I came to teach in Columbia University in 1955 under Professor Carrington L. Goodrich, Dean Lung Professor of Chinese, I asked who Dean Lung was. It appeared that he was a Chinese servant, or personal attendant, to General Carpentier, who in 1901 gave a large sum of money to set up the Department for Chinese studies at Columbia in his honor. Horace W. Carpentier had been a former mayor of Oakland, later Brigadier General of the State Militia of California.

Professor Goodrich told me the following interesting story about the two personalities:

Horace W. Carpentier was the son of a cobbler, who lived on Canal Street, when a canal actually existed in that part of Manhattan Island. His father realized his ability, and urged him to get all the education he could. In due course he came to Columbia College and graduated as valedictorian. After graduation he went around the Horn to California in 1849 but did not join the gold rush. Instead he set up a store for those who did, and eventually amassed large wealth. As time went on the building of the transcontinental railroad began, and a large number of Chinese laborers were brought over to do much of the manual work. Carpentier employed a number of them in his expanding business and in his home. One of them was Dean Lung, who later became his personal attendant. Carpentier was a man with a keen sense of values, and more than one man's share of vision. He acquired a townsite in the present downtown Oakland, imported a few "residents" from the redwoods, and in 1852 incorporated the Town of Oakland, with himself in the mayor's chair. The name he selected from the numerous stands of *encinas* (evergreen oaks) that dotted the landscape. Two years later Carpentier incorporated the town as a city, and by that time had acquired the entire Oakland waterfront in exchange for building three tiny wharves and a frame schoolhouse. After a successful career there, Carpentier returned to New York, the city of his birth, and to his alma mater, serving as trustee of Barnard College and of Columbia University, and helping in other ways. In 1901 he wrote to President Low of Columbia University, saying, "For fifty years and more I have been saving something from whisky and tobacco bills, with which *fair interest* would amount perhaps to about the sum of the enclosed check ($100,000.) which I have the pleasure to send you towards the founding of a department of Chinese language, literature, religion, and law; to be known as the Dean Lung Professorship of Chinese." He then described Dean Lung in the following words: "Pagan he may be . . . as Socrates, Lucretius and Epictetus were pagans. . . . But a man of rare integrity, temperate, vigilant, brave and kindly; doing well today the work of today, by birthright and education a follower of Confucius, in conduct a puritan, in faith a Buddhist, and in character a Christian." A little later the Department of Chinese was started with this fund of $100,000 from Carpentier. More astonishing was that Dean Lung took his life savings and sent in a check for $12,000 as his own contribution to the Department.

Mr. Dean Lung

The chief moral in this story is that General Carpentier, who had neither been to China nor showed any interest in other lands, was motivated solely by the practical example of the good conduct of a single man. For the same reason he also gave a considerable legacy to the University of California to buy books on Asia.

General Carpentier

Dean Lung had had some education in China before he joined the group of laborers going to California: he could write and read and knew some of Confucius' teachings and acted accordingly. He entered Carpentier's service in the eighteen-fifties. He cooked, served meals and looked after his personal daily needs in the capacity of a valet. Carpentier's position and busy life in the public eye gave him an irritable temper at times. One day, over some small matter, Carpentier fired Dean Lung and told him to go. The next morning he realized he had no one in the kitchen, but unexpectedly Dean Lung brought him up his breakfast as usual. This surprised him greatly and he sincerely regretted his bad temper of the day before, saying apologetically: "I am so happy to see you still here. I must apologize to you for my bad behavior yesterday. I need you, and at the same time I can assure you that from now on I shall reform my behavior." "Though it is a fact," replied Dean Lung "that you have a bad temper, I think you are after all a good man. Besides, Confucius' teachings do not allow me to leave you suddenly. Confucius said one must do one's duty to the person one is attached to. Therefore I remain here." When General Carpentier returned to New York in 1889 Dean Lung went with him. Afterwards, Carpentier said to his valet: "For all these years of service I am very grateful to you and would like to do anything you wish." Dean Lung replied that Americans did not know anything about the Chinese civilization and its importance, and that he would like the General to do something to rectify this. The result of that talk was the setting up of the Department of Chinese and Japanese at Columbia University. Professor Goodrich joined the Department in 1925 and later became the third holder of The Dean Lung Chair of Chinese. Though the teaching of Chinese started some fifty years earlier in Europe, Columbia University was one of the first few, with Yale, Harvard, and California, to foster the same study in America. Now there are about one hundred or more higher institutions giving courses in Chinese studies. Chinese has been elevated to the same level as other major studies and has also been introduced in some American high schools as one of the modern languages. For over thirty years Professor Goodrich's enthusiasm for his subject has not lessened, and he always pays tribute to Dean Lung's effort. I must admit that even without Dean Lung, Chinese studies would have started in America in one way or another; they had, in fact, already started in Yale. But the amazing thing is that Dean Lung in his humble position as a valet and from his scanty knowledge of Confucius' teachings could have influenced someone so utterly different in upbringing as General Carpentier by his integrity in everyday life. He deserves the utmost admiration. Dean Lung had not been trained to carry out any definite mission, like the Western missionaries

Professor Carrington Goodrich

in China. He acted on his own account, simply, naturally, and unpretentiously. The transliteration of this unusual Chinaman's name should really have been "Ting Lung": "Ting" is one of the most common family-names in China and "Lung," meaning "Dragon," a usual first name like "Tiger," "Unicorn," "Phoenix," often chosen by the Chinese for calling their precious babies. In the mid-nineteenth century very few Americans knew or bothered to find out how to pronounce Chinese names. For convenience, no doubt "Ting" became "Dean," or it is even possible that General Carpentier and his friends might have called him "Dean" for a joke. Thus the name of a humble cook was honored and commemorated in The Dean Lung Chair of Chinese at Columbia.

The next personalities I should like to mention are the Mills China boys. It was through the kindness of Mrs. Steel Little, librarian of Mills College, Oakland, that I came to know them. Through the agency of a mutual friend, Mrs. Edith Cunningham of Boston, a benefactor to Mills College, I was invited to spend a few days at Mills College towards the end of February, 1953, and to give a talk on "How we Chinese artists paint," with a demonstration. Before the talk I was entertained by the entire faculty with a most sumptuous dinner, during which I was told more than once, "it was prepared specially by the Mills China Boys." During my three days at Mills I strolled round every corner of the beautiful College campus, thinking to myself repeatedly how fortunate the girls were who could come to study in such a dignified, tranquil and ideal seat of learning. Mills College was founded in 1852, in Benicia, as a Young Ladies' Seminary, and reached full collegiate standing in 1885, becoming known as the oldest College for women on the West Coast. Mrs. Little managed to find time from her work to show me round the library and Art Building and pointed out to me where Miss Jade Snow Wong, author of *The Fifth Chinese Daughter,* worked and studied. We also went round many other buildings, some in Mediterranean architectural style, some in that of the Spanish Renaissance, and some in a kind of mixture. The latest development of the Californian Modern Style has not made its appearance in this beautiful campus yet. There is a lovely lake called Aliso in which many different types of trees threw their reflection, and where I enjoyed meditating, for the air was always pure there and it was sunny too. Before I left, I felt I must see the Mills China Boys. So I was taken to meet them.

How did Mills come to have China boys in the kitchen and when were they first employed there? I was told that the first "China boys" were brought to the College by Mrs. Mills, probably in 1871 when Mills Hall was finished and occupied. Since then descendants and relations of the first "China boys" have followed without a break till the present day. Mr. Lee Quon succeeded his brother as head of the Mills Hall kitchen about 1940. Directly after the end of the Second World War Lee had the sad news of the death of his wife in China and asked Miss Reynolds, who was then the director of Institution Administration, for leave to return home. Before he left Miss Reynolds told him of her deep appreciation of him and his fine and loyal work for Mills. When she asked if there was anything she could do to express her appreciation Lee answered: "You see always have China boys in Mills kitchen." As a result the College authorities were recommended always to employ men of the Lee Quon family, related to the original Chinese at Mills, in the Mills Hall kitchen, as long as they maintained a desirable standard. Apparently from the first China boys employed

The bells of Mills College

there down to the present ones, they have all worked with integrity, skill, loyalty and devotion. Each head trains the rest in the same way as he was trained by his predecessor and also sees to their personal conduct as if they were at home in China. In fact, they regard Mills College as their home, Mr. Yang told me with a smile. For the eighty-two years from 1871 to 1953, the year of my visit, there had been no friction between the successive directors of the Institution Administration and the three or four generations of China boys. Such a long history of good relations between employer and employee must be rare indeed. I would like to express particular admiration for the China boys, for they were simple folk of China, with little education, but with minds steeped in the traditional Confucian thought. One of Confucius' disciples, Tzu-hsia, said: "if a man withdraws his mind from the love of beauty, and applies it as sincerely to the love of the virtuous; if, in serving his parents, he can exert his utmost strength; if, in serving his prince, he can devote his life; if, in his intercourse with friends, his words are sincere—although men say that he is not a learned man, I will certainly say that he is." I would say the same about the Mills China boys.

The third person whose work in the U.S. I should like to describe here was named Lue Gim Gong, also known in Florida as the Chinese Burbank. Lue left China for America when he was about twelve years old. He boarded a little schooner with a group of adventurous men and left Hong Kong on March 11, 1872; after two long months the party landed, on May 11, at the Golden Gate of San Francisco. There was an Anti-Chinese-cheap-labor fever in the City at the time and the new arrivals felt frustrated and unwelcome. Eventually Lue was drafted together with a hundred and fifty other Chinese to work at the Calvin T. Sampson shoe factory. Later he became an errand boy, but in his heart he longed to be out of doors and in the orchards of New England, for, when a child of four or five, he had been taught by his mother how to pollinate flowers. She would take pollen from one plant and place it upon the pistil of another and cover the plant with a paper bag to keep the wind and insects from carrying off the pollen. A few days later, when the flower had been fertilized, she would pick off the half-dead blossoms so that the plant's full strength might go into one ripening fruit. In this Lue as a boy had helped his mother. By chance he now met a Miss Burlingame who had a sister living in Florida and who was sufficiently interested in him to take him there. Lue spent eighteen years working in the warm climate of Florida, which was so much like that of his native Kuangtung Province of China.

Among all fruits the orange is the most important contribution from China to the West. In his study on citrus fruits Dr. Walter T. Swingle of the United States Department of Agriculture discovered that in 1516 the Portuguese took orange trees from China and brought seeds and saplings to Portugal. When the Portuguese established their empire in South America, they introduced orange trees in Brazil. From Brazil, the orange tree was brought to Florida. Later, other species of orange trees were brought to California direct from the Southern part of China. What is specially interesting is that China not only contributed the orange fruit to the American diet, but also that a man from China actually helped to develop a new type of American orange. This was Lue Gim Gong. In 1911 the American Pomological Society and the United States Department of Agriculture awarded him the Wilder medal for the Lue Gim Gong variety of orange. Florida exhibited a bust of Lue Gim Gong in the 1933 World's Fair at Chicago and proclaimed him a benefactor of Florida's citrus fruit industry. Lue produced the orange which bears his name by cross-pollination of the Harts Late orange with the Mediterranean sweet tree orange. It was found that the orange Lue produced was hardier and more economical to grow than any other known orange. It can be marketed to advantage late in August and September when the other varieties are already out of season and when only the fruit from California is available. Before Lue developed his strain of orange, Florida orange-growers suffered heavy losses because their fruit would prematurely drop to the ground and rot during the rains, which usually begin in June and last for several weeks. Lue's oranges, however, remain on the tree through the heaviest of rain-storms and are known to be edible after two, three, and even four years. This, of course, means that the growers can pick just enough oranges to meet the demand and when there is a dull season, can leave them on the trees until the market comes out of the depression. His oranges are known to retain their juiciness and sweetness for at least two years.

The Lue story refutes the general notion I had gained that it was always Americans who did the impossible; one of my fellow countrymen had actually worked out this wonder. But I must say that if Lue had lived in his own native land till his death he might never have gone further than being a street-peddler or a small nurseryman. It was the amazing, enterprising, try-something-new spirit that floats in the air of the United States which spurred him on. Lue was fortunate to have come to North America, but I am sure that he did not imagine what he would achieve in his life when he came. On the other hand, we must realize how many talented persons have vanished without becoming known. We can only salute the fortunate ones.

The most striking fact about Dean Lung, Lue Gim Gong and the Mills China Boys is that they were all uneducated people, and yet they managed to achieve something of lasting benefit to others. What about us educated ones, who have spent much money and energy on learning? Each time I strolled into San Francisco's Chinatown I could not help admiring that first group of ill-fated fellow countrymen of mine, who stood fast with their indomitable spirit and tireless energy for work, and created a town-within-a-town—a community that has grown and endured. At the same time I despise those, including many of my compatriots, who look down at the town-creators for being uneducated. Some of these youngsters of Chinatown, who felt humble by comparison with their classmates in American schools and refrained from mentioning anything about their uneducated ancestors and parents having been railroad laborers, are mistaken in their ideas. Instead, they ought to feel so proud of their forefathers who sweated and even shed blood to build them their present legacy of a street that covers two-thirds of Grant Avenue. Lately there has been some talk about all the Western countries, even including Russia, joining hands to crush the Chinese. What for? To eliminate all the Chinese from the earth? Such wishful thinking and irresponsible words even from some responsible bodies make me realize that our present era is not yet so sane as it might be. Mere force without sound cause can never be victorious for long. A handful of Chinese managed to stand despite humiliation, against masses of unreasonable odds in San Francisco almost a hundred years ago. My thoughts are centered on those who may have been standing humiliated somewhere for some time now. In San Francisco Chinatown how can I fail to feel nostalgically!

XVII

Mooning Non-Mooniacly

THE WORD "mooning" is not my invention, but I use it in a new sense. If one can say "sunning," why not "mooning"? I love "mooning." Perhaps this is in my blood, for there are many famous Chinese poems on how to enjoy oneself under the moonlight. Unfortunately I could not do much "mooning" during my years in England for the moon showed her face there rather rarely. But I did some mooning in Paris, which I described in a chapter called "A couple of Mooniacs" in *The Silent Traveller in Paris.*

"Mooniac" is my own word, which cannot be found in either the Oxford or the Webster dictionary. In England, it is quite unusual to see a clear moon in the sky: perhaps that accounts for the superstition that moonlight can send people out of their minds, and for the stories of moon-maniacs who dashed out to kill somebody without knowing what they were doing. After some years in England, I went to stay for a time in Paris. When I saw the bright moon in the Parisian sky I dashed outside to walk about and enjoy it as a *"mooniac"* but not a *maniac.* That is how the word came into my Paris book.

In the San Francisco sky the moon emerges as often as she can, it seems to me. Each time I was around the Bay at night I saw the moon. Familiarity makes the difference. Being such a familiar sight, she caused none of the inhabitants to become maniacs, nor turned me into a "mooniac" as I had been in Paris. Mooning frequently in the golden city has been my joy: a particular evening mooning on Telegraph Hill is one of my best memories.

The special evening happened to be the Chinese Moon Festival night. I should have overlooked it, as I have not followed the Chinese lunar calendar for many years, had it not been that a young Chinese lady, the Beauty Queen of Chinatown for that year, came with another representative to ask me if I could tell them more of the legends about the Moon Festival. The City's Chamber of Commerce wanted to stage a special show in order to boost trade in Chinatown. It tickled me to think that a festival custom could help trade. I suggested to them that they should look up the chapter "Up the Pagoda" in my humble book *A Chinese Childhood*.

The Moon Festival is called in Chinese Chung-chiu-chieh or Mid-Autumn Festival and takes place on the fifteenth night of the eighth month according to the lunar calendar, about a month later in the Gregorian Calendar. The day's ceremonies are concluded with an offering of food to the moon as she rises. Every family would have prepared moon cakes from their own recipes, or bought them in the market to give as presents to their friends and relations. I remember seeing a moon cake priced one thousand dollars in a Shanghai Department Store some thirty years ago; it was decorated with precious stones and pearls! But I did not tell this to the Beauty Queen, nor the following Chinese joke I remembered at the time:

> The gifts exchanged at the Mid-Autumn Festival are not necessarily moon cakes. So one of two notorious misers in a certain village painted a small fish on a piece of paper and told his son to present it to the second miser, who was his friend. The gift was greatly appreciated by the recipient, who according to etiquette had to give something in exchange. The recipient's son was therefore sent off to present to the first miser a suitable return gift. When the young boy came back his father asked him if he had done as he was told. The boy answered in the affirmative and explained that he had bowed to Uncle (the father's friend is always known as the son's uncle in China) and said: "My father told me to present you with this moon cake (the boy formed an imaginary shape with the fingers of his two hands) in return for your very substantial gift." The second miser was not pleased at his son's conduct and shouted at him: "Why had you to be so extravagant? I told you to give half a cake—it would have been quite enough," while he extended the thumb and second finger of his right hand to form a half circle. All the villagers dubbed the second miser the champion of the two.

Well, gift or no gift, trade or no trade, I made a note on that special date.

When the day eventually arrived, I took myself to Chinatown for dinner to mark the occasion. I did not notice a difference from any other busy evening there except that a number of shop-windows had four big Chinese characters pasted up: "Chung Chiu Yueh Ping," meaning "Mid-Autumn moon cakes," that they had for sale. I doubted whether most of the visitors were interested in them or understood what they were. The customary type of moon cake made in South China differs somewhat from that in central China where I spent the first fifteen years of my life. There are two kinds, one is filled with meat and other ingredients and is rather greasy, the other with sugary bean-powders and is a little too sweet for me. So I did not sample either of them. After eating a meal, I strolled down the whole street and saw a good many young American-born Chinese children dressed in new clothes and some in the familiar silk-embroidered Chinese jackets and trousers. Apparently their elders still faithfully observed the old customs of China. China's great poet and artist, Wang Wei (701-761) begins a poem with two lines that have become famous; translated literally they run:

獨在異鄉為異客，每逢佳節倍思親

Alone in a strange country, being a stranger,
Each time a happy festival arrives, I doubly
think of my kinsfolk.

This poem, and especially these two lines, have been chanted by many of us on every festival occasion when we were away from home, for more than a thousand years. My first few years in England I too used to recite them but later I did so no more, for nowhere is specially strange to me now. Besides, having got on in years I do not even know where many of my kinsfolk are.

The fancy seized me to walk up Telegraph Hill. Though not really far from Chinatown, it would be a good, solid walk. Of course there is a bus going up there, and I had been taken up in friends' cars many a time, but so far never at night. Slowly and carefully I followed someone's directions to Union Street and then, making a left turn, I reached the foot of the road leading up the hill. Unfortunately that road had been designed solely for motorists: there was no space for pedestrians. That good, solid walk from Chinatown had not taken my breath away, but I was harassed at every step by the speeding cars up and down, for they kept appearing unexpectedly out of the dimness. No one sounded their horn at the turns: of course no motorist dreamt of finding a walker plodding uphill at night. I kept as close as I could to the edge of the road.

On reaching the top at last I drew a deep breath of relief. My body suddenly felt lighter, though luckily, there was no wind there to blow me away. Everything on the hill top seemed more pleasing then than on my many other visits. Even the rather uninteresting Coit Tower had assumed an asking-to-be-liked shape. I relaxed idly on a seat. A few cars came to the compound, made a circle slowly round the new statue of Columbus and then vanished: only a young couple got out of one of them and stood near the short wall for awhile. Night-life is not as popular in the open air as it is indoors with drinking, dancing, and shows going on till dawn.

No pleasant feeling could have been more pleasant than the knowledge that I had managed to walk up Telegraph Hill, and no enjoyment more enjoyable than the feeling that I had worked for it. Despite the intermittent coming and going of cars, I seemed to be in a trance as I leant against the low wall. A strange quietness reigned. My humble presence made no difference to the scene. Even the occasional whisperings inside or outside the cars had a kind of mystery, and enhanced the stillness of the air. I looked first towards the distant Russian Hill with its wide-spreading shoulders on which many tall buildings were neatly arranged on both sides like toys. In each of their windows sparkled tiny lights like fire-works. From the base of the low wall where I stood there seemed to stretch a number of thick cords from which hung countless lanterns at even intervals all along to the remote tops of other hills and beyond. Moving my eyes in a semi-circle I felt I was perched on the top of an enormous Maypole with many long, glittering ribbons. The Bay Bridge wriggled its way across to Berkeley like the longest dragon ever seen in a lantern procession during the Chinese New Year Festival. All the lights arranged in parallel rows looked no larger than candles vibrating ethereally on a deep-blue background. Masses of cars with their lights moved underneath the body of the dragon; it seemed that the people of the Bay region had all come out with lanterns in their hands to witness the merry-making! The movement of the distant cars kept the Bay Bridge shimmering and wriggling all the time while I watched it. I was curious to see whether that very long dragon was going to approach the base of Telegraph Hill. It seemed to be heading straight for the Civic Center of the City.

To my surprise I could see very few lights below Telegraph Hill by the Bay side, yet every building and structure was visible. The series of long piers stretching out into the water along the Embarcadero created a most curious effect, for they looked like well-cut black keys on a cleverly constructed piano of enormous size. How was it that they could reveal themselves so clearly to me in the darkness? Suddenly I noticed the bright, full moon sailing high overhead on the dark-blue silky curtain of the sky. Many scattered little pearls smiled back at her. Now I realized why the lamplights on Russian Hill and along the Bay Bridge looked so small and rather dim. While walking up the hill I had been dazzled by the brightness of the street lamps and had forgotten all about the Moon Festival. According to Chinese traditional belief, the moon on this Mid-Autumn night was brighter and fuller than at any other time of the year. Tonight I bore witness to it. I had not imagined that the moon above San Francisco Bay on this Mid-Autumn night could have shone as bright and round as it had done over my hometown of Kiukiang. In my young days on that Festival night, no matter where my kinsfolk might be, they would all go out to enjoy "mooning" on a local hill. Some of my young cousins used to provide music for the occasion at home by playing the lute or blowing the flute. It seemed appropriate that those huge black piano keys would have been provided for some heavenly musician who would descend to play some melodies by the Bay.

The melodies were inaudible to me yet I felt they were floating in the air. I gazed intently at something invisible yet almost tangible across the Bay. I felt something touch my face more soothingly than the gentle fingers of my long-deceased mother, and more invigorating than a single sip of years-old madeira, and softer than the under-throat fur of a tame rabbit, and cool but not icy chill. It vibrated with hope, shimmered with joy, dazzled with its extreme purity, and lingered affectionately over all living things. It was the ethereal rays of the bright moon far above Telegraph Hill where I was standing. These rays had a cleansing effect on my mind and all my earthly thoughts were carried away without a trace.

Moonlit nights could be damp, chilly, even icy at other times of the year and in some places, but August in San Francisco is quite warm even at night. Up a little height, such as Telegraph Hill, seems to be the right spot for mooning, for the thick sea-fog which comes through the Golden Gate seldom drifts beyond the Presidio. I began to wonder why this little rocky hill should have been called "Telegraph"—such an unpoetic, undistinctive name. I was told that Captain John B. Montgomery was the first to set up a pole on the hill top to fly an American flag. That was in 1846. A little later, Sam Brannan, the noted Mormon firebrand, came through the Golden Gate with the intention of being the first to raise an American flag on the rocky hill and felt frustrated when he saw one already there. He formed a Mormon Battalion, armed with Sandwich Island rifles, and staged a sort of religious war against the Catholic Spanish Californians. Later, against the wish of his own intimate friend, General John Augustus Sutter, he proclaimed to the world the discovery of gold and started the gold mania among a few hundred of his fellow-countrymen and thousands more from other countries across the oceans. He amassed great sums of money and by 1851 owned one-fourth of the city of Sacramento and one-fifth of the city of San Francisco. He was also the first to develop trade with China and he made a fortune out of it. He was regarded as San Francisco's first millionaire, yet he died penniless.

Telegraph Hill witnessed the beginning and end of the Gold Rush. There used to be a signal tower on the hill which announced the approach of any vessel and started a rush of tradesmen, gambling-hall attendants, bartenders and others to the waterfront for all imaginable

Crabs for sale at Fisherman's Wharf.

kinds of business. The coming and going of the ocean steamers was the main life of the city then, and during the gold rush, hundreds of steamers put in at the Bay. The signal tower on Telegraph Hill must have been kept busy. Bret Harte wrote in the eighteen-sixties: "As each succeeding ocean steamer brought fresh faces from the East (New England) , a corresponding change took place in the type and in the manners and morals. When fine clothes appeared upon the streets and men swore less frequently, people began to put locks on their doors and portable property was no longer out at night. As fine houses were built, real estate rose . . ." Telegraph Hill used to be surrounded by huts and tents. Now it is a highly respectable and expensive living quarter.

The Coit Tower on Telegraph Hill showed me another characteristic feature of San Francisco in the latter part of the nineteenth century: everyone then was fire-conscious. The frequent winds blowing through the Golden Gate into the Bay caused much fire and destruction to settlers living carelessly in huts and tents. Even after substantial houses were built fires were still a common occurrence. Many big cities in other parts of the world have suffered from great fires in the past, but none suffered more than San Francisco in 1906. Circumstances mold men's way of thinking, and the early San Franciscans were fire-conscious above all things. Fire Brigades were formed in the city, fire engines became a favorite toy with the youngsters, and membership of a Fire Brigade was considered one of the highest honors. It amused me greatly when I learned that Lillie Hitchock Coit, who later built the Coit Tower in memory of her husband, dashed out in the middle of a friend's wedding ceremony and chased after her favorite engine, Knickerbocker No. 5, in her bridesmaid's dress. She later became an honorary member of the Knickerbocker Fire Company. And so the Coit Tower stands today as a symbol for the fire history of San Francisco; very little else is left anywhere from the disaster of 1906. Only recently I happened to read the obituary of the famous San Francisco-born actress, Edna Wallace Hopper, who never wished to reveal her age as she had managed to remain young-looking over the years. When pressed, she would simply say that she did not know her birth date as her birth certificate had been destroyed in the San Francisco fire of 1906! Thus I realized that even a disaster of such dimensions could be useful to somebody.

New Year's Festival in Chinatown.

As I was pondering about Telegraph Hill and the tales of San Francisco long in the past, the rays of the bright moon had grown clearer and stronger. No more cars swung up to the compound round the Columbus statue. The night had sunk deeper, yet it had created its own activities over the Bay water and the hillside. A few clusters of white clouds appeared on the deep blue sky out of nowhere, and behind the tall eucalyptus trees on my right some mischievous spirit seemed to be hiding to play tricks on me by blowing on the leaves. These leaves turned into countless long slender fingers catching at me to join in their game. Had I become tipsy under the enchanting beams of the moon or was I merely drowsy? The whole atmosphere was profoundly tranquil. Many well-known poems by our great poets of the past came to my mind, for the moon is one of the typical features in Chinese poetry. The following one by Li Po (701-762) described my feeling better than any.

花間一壺酒獨酌無相親
舉杯邀明月對影成三人
月既不解飲影徒隨我身
暫伴月將影行樂須及春
我歌月徘徊我舞影零亂
醒時同交歡醉後各分散
永結無情遊相期邈雲漢

Drinking Alone Under The Moon

With a bottle of wine by me among the flowers;
I drink alone—no company.
I raise my cup to invite the bright moon;
With my shadow we became a party of three.
The moon does not appreciate drinking;
My shadow only follows me about.
For the moment I accompany both the moon and my shadow;
To have pleasure at the height of Spring.
While I sing, the moon moves to and fro;
My shadow confusedly matches my dance.
When we awake we are happy together;
When we are drunk we scatter and part.
I wish to prolong this not-too-passionate
      amusement for ever.
Let us meet again by the Cloudy River on high!

Cloudy River is the Chinese for the Milky Way. There are several English versions of this poem: my rendering endeavours to give the general meaning of each line as faithfully as possible. I hope it will not mislead anyone into thinking of me as a drunkard, as some other versions unjustly represented Li Po. Li Po loved wine. But he could not have written such a poem when he was really drunk. He simply portrayed his enjoyment of the moonlight with some wine. I did not have any wine with me on Telegraph Hill, yet I enjoyed mooning there.

Now I began to make my way down. I did not return to the footpath beside the much twisting motor road but found a side way down many wooden steps. The slope was quite steep but the moon lit up the steps as if escorting me with great care. Now and then I raised my head to look at the moon. All of a sudden something black collided with my right foot, made a quick jump and vanished into the shrubs above me. Immediately a number of similar creatures dashed up in pursuit, making quite a commotion on the wooden steps. One of them was white. I wondered how there could be so many cats on a hill three hundred feet high. Perhaps many of the residents around Telegraph Hill are artists and poets, for they love cats as a rule. I have read many poems in English about cats but few about dogs. Perhaps dogs are a little too compliant for the artistic and poetic temperament. Many find the cat warm in affection, careful in disposition, intelligent, capable of looking after herself, and rather independent, for the cat prefers to be a friend to her owner rather than a faithful servant like the dog. But there are others who say the cat is a selfish animal, seeking her own comfort and indifferent to others, attached only to a locality with little real affection, and even sly and treacherous. While I was thinking of these opposing views, a pair of transparent brown-bead-like eyes shining in the moonlight glared at me from underneath a rose bush. Did she sense my thought angrily or amicably? There was no way of discovering. So I went on down the hill and took a bus back to Lake Street.

Lying in bed I found myself still thinking about the two sides of things. To my great amusement I realized that the full moon I had enjoyed on Telegraph Hill could be some other part of the same moon that I used to see in our garden in my hometown, Kiukiang. China is situated almost directly opposite America on the globe. That part of the moon which I saw in Kiukiang in my younger days could not have been seen by the San Franciscans at the same time. Now this part of the moon I saw on Telegraph Hill might equally be invisible to my home-folk at Kiukiang. This deduction of mine is not based on science, yet it gives me satisfaction that I have found both parts of the same moon equally charming and enchanting to look at, and having a similar hypnotic effect on me. Or the same effect I felt at two different parts of the globe. I must admit that Kiukiang is not as big a city as San Francisco and is not by an Ocean but by the Yangtse River far inland. Nevertheless, its existence was already recorded in the first century of the Christian era and it possesses a famous mountain, Lu-shan, described in poetry since the fourth century and painted by many masters of the past. It is my hometown. No matter how humble one's birthplace may be, one always thinks of it affectionately as one grows older. Kiukiang is also enhanced by the beautiful lake Kan-t'ang as part of its natural setting. The enjoyment I got from mooning over the Bay on Telegraph Hill assuaged my poignant nostalgia for my native Lu-shan and Kan-T'ang. When young I believed the Chinese legends about the moon and when older I felt the legends helped to make the world seem more interesting, but the adventure of the sputnik has shattered them. There are now people wanting to fly to the moon! Modern science has made our human individuality seem unimportant: War in space may eliminate us all. Until that time comes, I would like to enjoy mooning in my own way whenever I can. Mooning on Telegraph Hill helped me to compose the following poem:

天空只有一個月　我卻看到她兩面
九江赤壁舊嬋娟　金門灣上乃新戀
舊識新知同此身　此身幾經人世變
漫誇舊識未模糊　且貪新戀滬史情
一島天仙一島囚　似說人間惡與善
善惡是非已百年　默對金門橋如線
上有唐馬珮巔印女魂　下有急流之史實如閃電
過去現在與未來　史實豈真能再見
挖金金盡月仍圓　清光普照無貴賤
能快心處且忘憂　飛上月宮我不羨
餘生何日可遷鄉　九江金門同眷眷

Up in the sky there is only one full moon;
But I have seen her two faces.
The one I saw at Kiukiang and Red Cliff is my old love;
This one over the Golden Gate Bay is a new love for me.
Both old and new center on this same body of mine;
This body that has known so many changes in the human world.
Though my old love has not been forgotten,
Let me enjoy my new love's charm for awhile:
One island is angelic and the other full of criminals
As if expressing the bad and good of mankind.

But good and bad, right and wrong, have been there
    for a hundred years or more;
Silently I view the Golden Gate Bridge, like a fine thread.
Above it the soul of the Indian Maiden lies on the
    peak of Mount Tamalpais.
Below it the fast flow of history goes by like lightning.
The past, the present and the future—
Can we see history repeated?
The Gold Rush exhausted the gold but there is still a full moon;
Her clear light shines indiscriminately on poor and rich!
Facing a scene so calming to my mind, I can forget sorrow:
I feel no envy of those who want to fly to the moon.
The remaining years of my life can hardly find me back home;
Kiukiang and the Golden Gate share my lingering
    affection equally.

Lillie Hitchcock Coit and her fire engine

XVIII

Learning Unacademically

LIFE MOVES ON slowly, step by step. It can neither be hindered in its progress nor speeded up to reach its destination any faster. Though we can move about far more quickly nowadays than before, at thirty to a hundred miles per hour or even at thousands of miles per hour like the astronauts, it makes no difference to life's journey, along which each of us moves involuntarily. Life is very stubborn and it proceeds neither on land nor water nor air but on a special route of its own. Life's routes differ, yet each of us follows them step by step in the same way. Each stage of life from babyhood, through childhood, youth, manhood, to middle-age and old-age has never been exactly the same for any two people since the first human creature appeared on earth. Unlike the land, the water, or the air, which are all visible and on which one can rely for one's return trip, life's route is invisible, though always present, and has no return track. It is said that one lives and learns. But no sooner have we learned how to live at one stage of our progress, than we move on to the next and cannot practice what we have learned. This seems to me unreasonable and unfair. But how can it be altered?

I have long stepped out of babyhood, childhood, youth, and manhood, and am near the end of middle-age if not on the verge of old-age. Though I know of no way to avert that unreasonableness and unfairness, from time to time I have thought deeply about what I would do if I could be a child or a young man again. Therefore there have been moments in my life when, without any visible or immediate cause, my spirits sank quite low, under the mere pressure of existence, or as one might say, under the pressure of life's stubbornness in insisting on moving on and on without giving me the slightest sympathy. During the past quarter of a century since I came to live outside China, many friends who have come to know me better think of me as having an easy-going nature, able to relax silently and possessing the gift of enjoyment through small, unimportant and insignificant things. Few perhaps can have realized that I have had many moments of unaccountable depression, when I became weary of my very thoughts, taunted by images of my younger and manly days in China that would not leave me—images many and varied, but all poignant and a mixture of joy and sadness. But there is no way for me to become again a baby, a child, a teenager, or a young man living in China, and it would be futile for me to try to stir sympathy in others, for no two people have exactly the same experience. However, I always manage to throw off my unaccountable depression, by not brooding over the past but moving on to keep pace with life. For instance, I know that I did not learn things as academically as I should have done in my college days, and would do so now if I could.

The United States of America of the future will consist only of *academic creatures*. That is my fancy. At least the past few years have shown me that wherever I tread is within or near the campus of one academic institution or another. New York, Boston, Chicago, the Bay Region, etc. seem to be packed with academic institutions of one kind or another. Though China has an age-old tradition of esteeming learning very highly, Peking has only five notable higher institutions. Before I set out to see San Francisco for the first time in 1953, my good friends, Mr. and Mrs. Van Wyck Brooks had me to stay with them at their home in Connecticut for a few days. There I learned that Van Wyck had taught at Stanford University from 1911 to 1913. Modest as ever, he told me repeatedly, as he wrote in one of his books, "Teaching was not my vocation I discovered at Stanford soon, for neither in fact nor by choice was I a scholar, and I was too full of my own thoughts to enter as a teacher should into the minds of students." He was very happy when I decided to come to this country in 1955, but after I accepted a tenure position at Columbia he said with a frown: "Yee, you must not teach. You should write and keep writing." His kindness to me was abundant and overwhelming. I like writing, but writing in a language which is not my mother-tongue has often forced tears out of my eyes, as I tried to express myself well enough to be understood.

Neither am I a scholar, yet I feel that I have the obligation to explain as much as I know about things Chinese, while living outside China. In recent years the progress made in Oriental studies in general and Chinese in particular has been phenomenal in the United States and many noted scholars have mastered our language and produced interesting books from their studies of different periods of Chinese history. It is gratifying to have so many western scholars expounding Chinese thought, history and literature from their cultural background and point of view. Yet it is desirable to have us, native Chinese, to supplement their studies from our first-hand knowledge. That is where my teaching comes in. I must admit that I teach, not as a scholar, but as one who can explain in English what I have learnt through my education and reading in China. I follow Van Wyck's conviction and try not to let my own thoughts enter the minds of my students. "Teaching" can sometimes mean "preaching," and this I have tried to avoid in all my writing and talking. My idea of teaching is to give information or explanations about what one has learned to those who have not yet learned it. Not all things Chinese are good or should be copied, nor would I claim that everything I know is absolutely indisputable. This is the sort of explanation I gave to Van Wyck, but he just smiled at it.

In 1911 Van Wyck was newly maried and young, he told me, and often felt uneasy when he met his students, stout, strong and tall with mustache and beard, as was the fashion in those days. They were all sons of early pioneers and western settlers, retaining a great love of open-air life, and all older than he was. So he had to grow a mustache to give himself a more mature appearance. I told him that I had been in a similar predicament when I became the magistrate and district-governor of my native city at twenty-six. The people with whom I had to deal were mostly of my father's generation and all wore beards. According to the Confucian tradition of those days, older men had an undisputed privilege over younger ones. We have a common saying: "Words from someone whose upper lip has no hair on it cannot be trusted." So I had to grow a beard too. Unfortunately it is not easy for a Chinese to grow a beard quickly. Unlike westerners, there are many Chinese who do not have to shave every morning, let alone twice or three times a day. It took me almost three months to grow a sizable mustache. Before it really looked like something, I was most self-conscious. It was a trying time. I had never thought I would bother about my own looks, yet I had to in that situation.

Van Wyck told me that most of his students enlisted for the First World War and that he heard no more of them. I had now come to see Stanford University after the Second World War as a visitor. When I was just beginning my high-school years I heard of the First World War but very vaguely and without any concern. I little guessed that I would live right through the intensive air-raids over London and become a bombed-out victim in the Second World War. History books describe early wars, one after another, which took place in one corner of the earth or another but never covered so wide an area of the globe as the wars of this present twentieth century. Can we cite this as evidence of human progress? People used to feel proud of themselves if they ever experienced something which occurred very rarely. Shall I take pride in saying that I have lived through two great World Wars?

I would not have thought in this way, had not the name of Lieutenant-General Homer Lea of the Chinese Army come into my mind, after I entered the Stanford campus. Homer Lea was one of the early students there from 1899, and he led an extraordinary life. He proved to be one of those pioneer-descendants, very interested in plotting military strategies over the hills around the campus, and he played formidable games of poker. He might have grown stout and tall, but he had a humpback. His strong body deteriorated after a critical illness, so that his doctor believed that he could only live another three months. That stirred his pioneering spirit to win glory for himself while he could. He went to see Dr. Sun Yat-sen, Founder of the Chinese Republic, and soon established himself as General with sixty thousand Chinese soldiers under him. He beheaded anyone under his control who opposed him. How could this be? This could only have happened in China at the beginning of this century, after Peking had been ransacked by eight Western powers. Later he came back to America to appeal to the overseas Chinese for funds. Furthermore, as Lieutenant-General Homer Lea of the Chinese Army in command of the Second Division, he rounded up a large number of Chinese and drilled them

on empty spaces in San Francisco and Los Angeles. He also led this
Chinese Army on parades, at which he wore a self-designed blue uniform with brass buttons, gold braid, epaulets, and a row of medals.
When Dr. Sun Yat-sen eventually led the Chinese revolution to success
in 1911, Lea rejoined the movement but died soon afterwards. History
does not relate whether he took his San Francisco Army to China. And
so Homer Lea did not die in three months as his doctor had threatened;
he succeeded in winning glory for himself, and San Francisco not only
had an Emperor Norton who came from England but a General of the
Chinese Army with his troops stationed on the spot, who came from
Palo Alto. The Bay Region has an interesting past.

I thought Mary Wright, Professor of history at Stanford University,
would be able to tell me more about Homer Lea from the University
records. But apparently the University did not keep any record of him,
although the life of General Frederick Townsend Ward of the Chinese
Army, who was a Salem man, has been recorded in a book entitled
A God from the West. However, being the Librarian as well, Professor
Wright smiled when I said that Stanford's Hoover Library is known to
house the best and most complete collections of modern Chinese
history and literature in the U.S.A. Mrs. Fang Chao-ying was helping
to catalogue the books there at the time, and it was at the kind invitation of Mr. and Mrs. Fang Chao-ying that I came to spend a day and
night at Palo Alto. Palo Alto first became known as a College city, but
now is growing into a great commercial and residential center along a
big highway. Mr. and Mrs. Fang Chao-ying showed me round the
Hoover Library, then the Stanford Library, the mosaic reproduction
of Leonardo Da Vinci's *Last Supper,* the fascinating fish collection at
Jordan Hall, and also the Art gallery and museum where I was interested to see a portrait by Sir Joshua Reynolds, whose work is seldom
seen outside England, and some Japanese and Chinese objects, ceramics and robes. What impressed me most and still remains in my
mind is the unusual Palm Drive and Campus. I mean "unusual" because I have not so far seen another drive lined with large palms leading to a University Campus, here called the University Quadrangle.
The name reminded me of the College quadrangles of Cambridge or
Oxford in England, but the walls of buff yellow sandstone and the

brilliant red tiles on the roofs in Moorish Romanesque style, gleaming in the bright sun, made a different picture from those buildings in the gray English climate.

Some Chinese like to claim that Stanford University, with its interesting collection of documents on Modern China, was largely built by Chinese contributions. I regard this as a far-fetched story, yet it is interesting to see how it arose. They say that from 1859 to 1872 Leland Stanford made some money out of his holding in the Lincoln Mine of Quartz at Sutter Creek, where many Chinese worked as laborers. He then used the profits for building the Central Pacific Railroad, employing thousands and thousands of Chinese laborers for the construction. Thus he accumulated an enormous fortune, with which later he endowed Stanford University. Therefore the Chinese contribution to it was colossal. What a piece of logic, indeed!

Afterwards, the Fangs took me to a newly-established Chinese Restaurant, named "Peking Duck" after one of Peking's most famous dishes. We tried some of their roast duck: it was absolutely delicious and the very first I had tasted outside China though I had spent twenty-two years in England. The evening talk with the Fangs about our early days in China was poignant but sweet. Next morning I helped to pick many sweet oranges from trees in their courtyard. This made me reflect on the truth of the Chinese proverb "Half an orange tastes as sweet as a whole one." I had only tasted such sweetness of life for one and a half days, but my life so far has been sweet on the whole. Human life does not spare much time for unpleasant recollections. In the afternoon the Fangs drove me back to Berkeley.

Berkeley, like Palo Alto, is also a College city, but does not like being compared with the latter. It is senior in age, of course. Here was the first college founded in the Bay region, and named after the Irish philosopher, Bishop George Berkeley (1685-1753), who crossed the Atlantic to establish an institution for the Indians. To me, Berkeley is always smiling ironically, with half-closed eyes, at her immediate neighbors. She can be engulfed in the Bay fogs or veiled in the sea haze from time to time, gaining a look of seniority like the English Cambridge and Oxford. The University of California dominates Berkeley, directs her expansion and accompanies her even beyond her territory.

Berkeley means the University and vice versa. Only the campus of the University of California has no limit, no boundary, it seems to me. I have come to see San Francisco ten times so far since 1953. Each time I have stayed a few days with friends in Berkeley, and each time I have seen big construction work going on and could not tell whether Berkeley the city or Berkeley the University was building. In England's Oxford gown and town have been quarrelling for centuries. No such idea has ever occurred to me while staying in Berkeley.

Though my living quarters in the Bay region were always in San Francisco, I went to Berkeley more often than anywhere else. Whenever I made the trip, my thoughts went back to an Eating Joint where the late Joseph Henry Jackson and I had dinner together, and he urged me to try to see the lighting up of the Bay Bridge lamps at least once before I left the west coast. I tried to catch the moment, but always missed it. No one can tell when the sea fog will move round the Bay, and I could never find out the exact time for the lights to go up. Just once I caught a glimpse of them, but for less than a minute; everything surrounding us was affected by something intangible, strange and fresh in a flash. Van Wyck Brooks told me that in his Stanford days he knew Professor Bailey Willis, son of one of the early American writers N. P. Willis, and a well-known geologist, who had examined the land and rocks all round the Bay, and had declared that no bridge could be built across it, on account of the gradually sinking bed of the Bay. However, the Bay Bridge is still standing and the heavy load it carries to and fro becomes heavier from day to day. During my first year in England I heard people talking about the gradually sinking process of the famous Venice. Twenty-six years after I saw Venice still standing there as unchangingly beautiful as ever.

Dr. Lin Tung-yen told me that Frank Lloyd Wright was one of the many architects who submitted designs for the Bay Bridge. His design had an unusual butterfly shape in the middle span, but it was not adopted. A year before his death Frank Lloyd Wright was in San Francisco and the City TV Corporation arranged a panel discussion with him. Dr. Lin was asked to take part. The moderator was afraid my friend might want to decline the invitation, but Lin replied: "We professors and engineers deal with all kinds of people. Why should we be afraid of Frank Lloyd Wright?" Of course one only need look at any of the buildings Wright has designed to see whether he was the sort of person to comply easily with anyone else's opinion. But my friend had a good word and much respect for his opponent. He said that during their discussion Wright was very sharp and would easily corner his opponent but that he used beautiful expressions and was full of wit: he was a very good talker with wonderful ideas. "Usually," Lin continued, "architects only talk about architecture, but Frank Lloyd Wright talked about architecture with philosophy, art and literature. He was an architect-philosopher, not a philosophical architect." No doubt Lin was right, but he did not realize that these words apply to himself too. Dr. Lin is Professor of Civil Engineering at Berkeley; he is one of the world's leading authorities on pre-stressed concrete, was Chairman of the 1957 World Conference on pre-stressed Concrete, is head of the Los Angeles firm of T.Y. Lin and Associates, special consultant to the Government of Venezuela, the Government of Kuwait, the United States Navy, and the State of California Division of Architecture, as well as author of the Standard book *Design of Pre-stressed Structures* and numerous articles on the subject. He took the time to drive me round the World's Finest Parking Garage, which he built in pre-stressed concrete, in downtown San Francisco. Then he told me about his work for the New Hippodromo Nacional in Caracas, Venezuela, and also about his design for a Bering Strait Bridge between Alaska and Siberia in pre-stressed concrete. I gasped, not being able to

follow what he meant. He realized my predicament and explained that "Pre-stressing concrete simply means the squeezing or compressing of it. Prestressing makes concrete stronger by squeezing. Because of its strength, you can build bigger and stronger things, cheaper and faster . . ." "Oh, oh," I remarked, "many people in Europe think the Americans are a fantastic people, always trying to build things bigger and stronger, cheaper and faster than anywhere else. I did not realize that it is you, my fellow countryman, who are trying to do this!" I was wrong in regarding Lin's only interest as engineering, for he loves swimming, dancing, looking at pictures and places of historical interest of all sorts. When we first met in London in 1953, we, including Mrs. Lin and their son and daughter, dashed to all the well-known places of interest in a single afternoon and when we reached the Tower of London one minute after its closing time, young Paul Lin was very disappointed. When I came to see the Bay Region Lin sent me a note saying: "San Francisco has everything." He knew that I had taken a fancy to eating frog's-legs in Paris, so he drove me to a restaurant famous for the best frog's-legs on the west coast. I ordered the dish but the legs were the size of small chicken-legs, not so tender as the French ones, and certainly not cheaper. Lin laughed heartily. In 1960 I met the Lins in Honolulu, where Lin was giving a special summer course on pre-stressed concrete for the American Society of Engineers. We spent a week-end on the garden island, Kauai, and explored all the known beauty spots. Dr. Lin's interest is wide; he has sharp eyes and a quick wit and is a good talker. He sees his pre-stressed concrete as a ceramic artist sees a piece of clay.

Lin was born in Foochow, took his B. Sc. degree in Tangshan College in Tientsin, China, and then came to Berkeley for two years to study for his Master of Science degree in Civil Engineering, which he took in 1933. After that, he went back to serve as engineer and chief design-engineer for various Chinese government railways, and he travelled throughout the country under most difficult conditions from the Japanese invasion in 1937 to the end of the Second World War in 1945. He was then invited to come to teach in his old alma mater in 1946 and has been there ever since.

Trying to learn unacademically, I could not grasp much about the pre-stressed concrete beyond the term. But through Dr. Lin I learnt something about modern man in the world of men. A modern man enjoys a background of mixed cultures and makes use of the best conditions available to him to develop the greatness that is in him. He not only excels in his special field, but extends his interest to something beyond. Formerly scientists tended to become narrower and narrower in their thinking, interested in nothing beyond figures and formulae. They are different nowadays. Dr. Lin enjoys his life to the full with his happy family and goes with them everywhere he can. From Mrs. Lin I learned something about Chinese life during the war years. No one could imagine what she had passed through when meeting her now, a very slim lady, five feet three inches tall, with a less than twenty-inch waist, who is always quiet and walks as gently as if she dreaded to tread on an ant. When the invading Japanese army had moved inland so rapidly, the Chinese resistance force could not check them and there was the greatest confusion and havoc. A mass emigration to the southwest was started immediately by the people themselves without any plan or order. While her husband was cut off on some government service, Mrs. Lin carried her baby son on her back and held her younger sister by the hand, and they moved on and on with the throng. There was no means of transport for the masses. They just pushed on a few miles each day, the sisters keeping each other's spirits up as they had no relatives, nor friends, in the group. After many weeks they were not far from a safer area, but Mrs. Lin's steps had slowed down and she was left behind with her sister, like many others who had already dropped behind. The sisters moved on by themselves, much slower than before. Just before dusk they spotted a few houses, a small village. On reaching it they saw no villagers but only soldiers, or rather men in ragged uniforms. The sisters could not tell whether they belonged to the government forces or to a self-styled army, opportunists ready to fight for either side. An old village woman came out and offered them a wobbly long stool to rest on. The village was so remote it had hardly changed its way of life in the past few hundred years. No modern mechanical gadgets were known there. Exhaustion kept Mrs. Lin awake the whole night and she started to move on again as soon as dawn gave light to the path. They reached a town the next nightfall and joined another group to move on again until they eventually arrived at a place where a temporarily set-up university was to receive refugee students. Mrs. Lin stayed on till graduation before rejoining Dr. Lin in Berkeley. I have known the Lins for a few years but did not hear all this until we were watching a torch-dance in the back garden of the Coconut Palm Hotel on Kauai Island. Mrs. Lin is always gay in her own quiet way and likes to play a mah-jong game with me, for she knows that I can play no better than she. She loves dancing, including "twisting," and drives a car more efficiently than most Chinese ladies in the Bay area. I once asked her if she ever wished she could have had a car to take her and her sister and baby away from the ragged soldiers in that remote village in China. She just brushed the question aside, saying "that is different. Besides, there was no room for a car on that village footpath." Indeed, no one should underestimate the strength of a woman.

Berkeley houses another prominent China-born scientist. He is Dr. Chuh Hao Li, Director of the Hormone Research Laboratory, University of California. He is an internationally-known authority on hormones and has devoted the past twenty years to discovering the functions of a small part of a tiny, lima-bean-sized gland, lodged at the base of the human brain. His success won him many awards, including the Albert Lasker Basic Research Award. He once expressed his conviction that the hormone does double duties, controlling not only human growth but almost certainly lactation as well. It was Dr. Chuh Hao Li who informed me that the sea-lions of Seal Rocks beyond Cliff House are a separate species and who uses sea-lions for hormone experiments. He sent me a number of his publications but I could not make much out of them, for they cannot be studied unacademically; perhaps because I have an archaic mind and would prefer to believe that the sea-lions of the Seal Rocks were formerly humans whom the twin daughters of the local Indian Chief turned into sea-lions by use of a magic flower, as the legend says. In that case the sea-lions would have no different hormones from man. However, Dr. Li never talks shop to me when we meet, yet he likes to see me, for he always wants to display his newly-purchased art objects. His interest in pictorial art, Western and Chinese, is quite unusual. His house at Arlington was specially built to Mrs. Li's architectural design; Mrs. Li is a sculptor and wood-carver, as well, and takes a great interest in gardening and cooking. This explains why I never missed a chance to go there when I was asked. There is another thing I always remember about the Lis. At the back of their house is an unusual-shaped rock, called the Indian Rock, which has stood there erect since time immemorial. From the sculptural point of view and also from the love of natural rocks which belongs to the Chinese art of gardening, Mrs. Li is glad to have this Indian Rock close by her house. When I visited them for the first time in 1953, after a most sumptuous dinner Mrs. Li told her daughters, Ann-si and Yi-fan to show me the Indian Rock. The elder, Ann-si, related that the Indian Rock was known to have been a watch tower as well as a throne for the Indian Chiefs in days gone by. While climbing up the rock inch by inch after Ann-si and Yi-fan, I wished we had all put on Indian clothes and feathers, for Ann-si walked sedately just like an Indian Chief followed by two attendants ascending the rock for a Camp-fire Dance Festival. When we reached the top, Ann-si began to shade her eyes with her right hand, and to turn from left to right demonstrating how the Indian Chief would scan or watch the surrounding country. Yi-fan made the same movements. My hand seemed to imitate theirs involuntarily. For a good while Ann-si related what she knew about the rock in perfect sincerity, not for a moment ironically. She actually imagined herself in the part. Now she is studying at college and Yi-fan will not be long finishing her high-school education. Each time I was at the Lis' I have reminded them of my visit to the Indian Rock. I wonder whether Ann-si and Yi-fan will say my description of the visit is correct? And will their children show their guests to the Indian Rock in a similar manner? Perhaps their guests will not have an infantile brain like mine.

There is another Indian Watching Rock near the end of Cragmont Avenue in Berkeley. It is not like a watch-tower in shape, for it has an arbor-like structure built over it, from inside which I twice observed a beautiful sunset over San Francisco across the Bay. Not far away from it lives another prominent China-born scholar. He is Dr. Yuen-Ren Chao, Agassiz Professor of Oriental Language and literature, Emeritus, a much more senior member of Berkeley's faculty than either Dr. Lin or Dr. Li. Though educated in Cornell University, more than forty years ago, Dr. Chao went back to teach in Peking University for years. While in China, he travelled extensively and made a systematic study of various Chinese dialects in different parts of the country. Apart from

Cragmont Rock in Berkeley

students of the Chinese language, people in the West as a whole do not realize that China has a number of dialects, but only *one* written language. Although two Chinese, one from the north and the other from south China, may be unable to converse easily with each other, yet they can make themselves understood by writing. The written form of the Chinese language is the same for all native Chinese as well as for overseas-born-Chinese and has not undergone any significant change since at least the first century before Christ, though a somewhat simplified form for a few words has arisen from time to time. No English child of five or six can read Chaucer's writings, but a five-year-old Chinese child may be fluent in reciting Confucius' analects. The natural growth of different dialects in China is understandable. China should be regarded as a continent, not merely as a single country, for she covers a vast area, almost as big as Europe. If one thinks of the many different languages existing in Europe, there should be great cause for wonder that so big a country as China has only one written language. Dialects even exist within the area of London.

In the ancient days people anywhere who managed to find a piece of habitable land with favorable conditions first built a shelter to protect themselves from wind, rain and wild beasts, then cultivated the earth around it to grow food and in time busied themselves with all kinds of living problems. They seldom thought of going away from the land they had developed for themselves. However Chinese history tells us that many of our forefathers were forced to migrate south-eastwards and south-westwards from time to time because of famine, drought, floods and wars. Those who made a new homestead after their wanderings centuries ago did not want to move again. When I was working in China as a civil servant, I met many old peasants who had never even walked a few miles beyond the handful of houses which formed their little village, and who said that their fathers and grandfathers never had either. They kept to themselves and knew very little outside their village. By and by their language became somewhat different from that spoken in other parts of the country. Through the years and centuries the difference increased and so a dialect grew, almost unintelligible to outsiders. Of course there are other reasons for the existence of different dialects. For instance, the Wu dialect round the Shanghai area and along the south-eastern coastal line and the southern dialect round the area of Kuangtung and Fukien along the south-western coastal line must have had their origin in the very distant past. In the course of history these lands were brought under Chinese sovereignty by Imperial armies from the north, and so the people were forced to adopt the Chinese written language for convenience in administration. That is probably why the Wu and Southern dialects show such a wide deviation from the Northern (known as Mandarin) dialect at the present day, yet all have to use the same written language for any communication throughout the country. Any Chinese born in the Wu and Southern areas must learn to speak the northern dialect if he intends to enter government service or to do business on a larger scale. The old means of transport such as riding a donkey, horse or camel, or by a single-wheel barrow or sedan chair, made travelling very limited. Forty years ago no road in China followed a straight course for even a few miles. If China can build as many good, wide roads and highways as America has, and if most Chinese acquire a car and become as mobile as the Americans, they will all have to learn the northern (Mandarin) dialect and China will then be able to say that she has no dialects but only a slight difference in accent from one district to another. Then, only then, China will manage to eliminate some of her age-old ills. In recent years China has already undergone great changes; people have begun to move about and hundreds and thousands of the younger generation can speak the northern dialect in addition to what their parents speak at home. This is a good sign for the future progress of Chinese culture. Modern television and radio services will help too.

China cannot yet claim to have no difficult dialects, and in the meantime Dr. Yuen-Ren Chao's systematic study of Chinese dialects, in Chinese called *Fang Yen,* ranks high among works on the Chinese language. Other scholars have made brilliant studies of the subject, but none covers so wide a field so thoroughly as Dr. Chao. In fact Dr. Chao has become a world authority on the Chinese language and has been the leading speaker on the subject. He conducted some intensive courses on Chinese studies for army and navy personnel at the Harvard Yenching Institute during the Second World War and then came to teach at Berkeley. As he is our senior and most kind to all friends, old and young, we all want to pay him our respects. Each time I have called on the Chaos at Cragmont Avenue, their living room has been full of guests. Not once did I manage to secure a seat for long, for ladies have the first preference. We just lingered there for hours; no one wanted to make a move. The chief attraction is of course to be with Dr. Chao and to hear his inimitable storytelling, for he has a great sense of humor. He has translated *Alice in Wonderland* into Chinese, a feat which I never imagined would be possible. Another attraction usually proceeded from the back regions of the Chao's house; a savoury smell seemed to assail our nostrils and prevent our tongue uttering words of farewell. Mrs. Yuen Ren Chao was always cooking. Mrs. Chao is author of *Autobiography of A Chinese Woman* and also *How to Cook and Eat in Chinese*. The Nobel-Prize-winner Pearl Buck has the following words to say about Mrs. Chao's cook-book, which has been selling for years and is still going strong:

> It is as an American woman that I should like to say that it seems to me this is a perfect cook-book. There is not a dish in its pages which an American housewife cannot produce, without any qualms over its difficulty . . . I consider this cook-book a contribution to international understanding.

Indeed, Mrs. Chao's cooking is something to be experienced in Berkeley.

Recently I had a talk with my colleague at Columbia, Professor Hans Belinstein, an illustrious pupil of the illustrious Swedish Orientalist, Professor Bernhard Karlgren, author of *Sound and Symbol in Chinese,* and many other important works. Hans' eyes twinkled when I mentioned Mrs. Chao's cooking, for he had often tasted it during the year he spent at Berkeley doing research work before he took up a professorship in the University of Canberra, Australia. Now he has come back to teach at Columbia. One interesting anecdote of Hans' is that he moved six times during his year in Berkeley and each time the house he left was pulled down to become a garage. More and more people own cars in Berkeley and many families own more than one car. Hans also told me that he loved to ride on horseback outside the city and was very fond of the Yosemite landscape. These interests we both share.

Berkeley reveals to me its early inclination to be Hellenic in style of architecture, for this was the condition laid down in the international competition for a comprehensive university building plan financed by Mrs. Phoebe Apperson Hearst in 1896. As the University has almost outgrown its five-hundred-and-thirty-acre campus, the original plan has become lost in the multitude of buildings. The Ionic colonnades of white granite of the massive Wheeler Hall must have enjoyed an impressive glory in the early years of this century. Somehow I feel that they are being gradually dwarfed or obscured by the luxuriant growth of the many giant eucalyptus and other tall trees in full foliage. This is one respect in which Berkeley differs from Athens and other Greek cities. The Greek temples with their Ionic Colonnades always stand aloof on high ground commanding the surroundings. No big trees obstruct the view. There is a magic purity in the Greek air which cannot be described in words, but which I experienced there one summer. In comparison the air at Berkeley is either hazy under the brilliant sunlight or clammy with the Bay fog.

I spent a good half-hour in Berkeley's Hearst Greek Theater. It is built of concrete with a semicircular auditorium to seat over seven thousand. It looks big enough for the University musical and dramatic activities, yet I found it rather small when I recalled the ancient Greek amphitheater at Epidarros, traditional birthplace of Asklepios. It stands in a valley backed by rocky cliffs with no other buildings in sight nor any auto sound to enter the ears. The semicircular auditorium seemed to have been so well-calculated by the ancient mathematician and scientist that every single note or word from the players on the stage could be clearly heard and appreciated as it came through the pure air without obstruction.

I knew nothing about Berkeley's Greek theater when I first strolled on to the upper campus. I went there in order to enjoy a beautiful night-scene that I glimpsed through the hanging leaves of two tall eucalyptus trees: the slender campanile faintly lit up by the faraway moon against a deep blue sky. Though many cars were moving noisily behind me, they did not disturb me, for I was completely absorbed in the unbelievably tranquil scene. The size of the moon made it look like an ancient Chinese bronze mirror resting on a blue-satin wall; it gazed down on the ethereal edges of the Campanile and the motionless leaves of the eucalyptus trees. A very beautiful sight.

Certainly the Campanile is the symbol for Berkeley, gown and town. Its design is said to have been based on the lofty Campanile in San Marco Square in Venice. It amuses me to think of the early existence of both the Ferry Building and the Berkeley campanile, as if they were two tall towers for an imaginary suspension bridge long before the actual Bay Bridge was built.

I think the use of gray granite for constructing the Berkeley Campanile instead of the red-brick used for the ancient one in San Marco Square was a good choice. The beauty of the Venetian Tower is in its ornate frescoes in gold and brilliant pigments, as well as the many elaborate buildings in Italian Renaissance style adjoining it; it fits in with the flowing throngs of visitors and pilgrims day and night. I have been on the top of both campaniles. Standing so high above the earth I felt aloof, yet at the same time infinitesimal and a mere flash of existence. San Marco's campanile still breathes an antique air and commands a view that is international as well as local. Berkeley campanile is in its prime of life, though with a view rather local than international.

Professor Shih-hsiang Chen managed one morning to take me up to the roof of the newly-built University Hall. From there I got a better view of the campus as a whole, though most of it was hidden by the massive growth of the eucalyptus grove in the center. The grove helped me to compose an interesting picture. Inside the eucalyptus grove a number of seats cut out of huge tree-trunks are set. I once strolled there and encountered a group of people sitting and standing in some hot discussion. A very interesting location for a meeting, I thought.

In Berkeley there is much to learn unacademically. I, for one, gained a new piece of knowledge there; I learnt of "Ph.D. policemen." This will surely tickle the men of London's Scotland Yard, so highly praised for their efficiency. In my long stay in England, my ears constantly heard about the English weather and the English policemen. The English policeman stands out in any crowd by his tall stature, high helmet and peculiar, gentle gait. He is an English symbol and England is proud of him. Then in Paris I met a poet-policeman as I described in *The Silent Traveller in Paris*; he was naive and bohemian except for his uniform. The Ph.D. policeman of Berkeley is still only a name to me; I have not met one so far, for they are seldom seen on the beat. There is a Chair of Police Administration in Berkeley's Department of Political Science, the only one I know of in any University.

One morning Nancy Chao, third daughter of the prominent Chaos of Cragmont, dropped me at the entrance to the Botanical Gardens in Strawberry Canyon before she went on her way to business. I made a point of going there because of its two special collections: its five thousand rare rhododendrons and its two thousand cacti and succulents. Being no student of botany I am always a little confused about cactus and succulent. I have read that "succulents" are a class of plants which have bodies for their leaves or stems so that they can keep water for their nourishment for days in a dry sandy region or desert and which include cactus, aloe, mesembryanthemum, echinocactus, cereus, sempervivum and various others. However, from the layman's point of view, in spite of cactus being in the family of "succulents," the ordinary type of succulent is a plant with proper woody-like branches and stem as well as leaves which, unlike the usual thin tree-leaves, are somewhat thick, round and shiny like a green-jade carved by some skillful Chinese jade-carver. They grow in a well-set pattern, so evenly arranged in space and so uniformly designed in shape and form as to seem entirely made by human hands. Some are actually called "jade trees." In one of the greenhouses here I saw a plant with unusually-shaped leaves and a flower shaped like the head of a rattlesnake with a snakeskin pattern in pinkish-purple. There were several specimens of the common type of succulent that I saw outside many San Franciscan houses, the so-called "hen and chickens"; these were interestingly placed around other tall cacti. They have a beautiful pattern in their leaf-group arrangement which caught my gaze, crowded rosulate leaves looking healthy and neat. Many textile designers must have been inspired by them.

I think of cacti as a class of succulent plant usually in ball-like, rod-like or fan-like formation with spiky pins, long or short, shooting out to protect themselves. They are in a group on their own and do not seem to mix well with the rest of the botanic world. Every one of the cacti has an intriguing pattern with its numerous spikes. I must have come to the botanic garden at a good time, for there were quite a number of cacti in bloom. All their flowers are tubular with waxy-looking petals of yellow or red in different shades. My interest in cacti might have been less had I not also become interested in humming-birds some ten years ago when I managed to collect a set of *A Monograph of the Trochildae* by John Gould, with full hand-colored plates, published in the eighteen-sixties. As I grew up in China, I was trained by my father to paint on silk in rich colors, and I tried to see many original works by our ancient masters as well as reproductions. My father specialized in painting flowers and birds, and often told me that most types of birds under Heaven including the fabulous phoenix had been portrayed by our masters from earliest times. I only wish I could now tell my father that there are other birds, such as the hummers, that we Chinese did not know. I may have been the first Chinese to paint the ruby-throated humming-bird in our traditional style on silk. The painting is reproduced as one of the illustrations for my book *The Silent Traveller in New York*. There are many species of humming-birds, some of them only slightly bigger than a bumblebee. The humming-bird hums like a bee while it flies. Not only does it fly and hum, but it can direct its flight backwards as well as forwards; I know of no other bird that can do this. To watch birds in flight is one of my special delights, but only the birds with larger wings which flap slowly or glide in the air can be watched. Small birds like the orioles, finches, tits, robins, chickadees, etc., are gone in a flash. To see a humming-bird flying in all directions at will adds new satisfaction to my delight. I have come across the ruby-throated humming-bird in flight high up Mount Tamalpais, but such a tiny bird cannot easily be spotted or watched among the luxuriant growth of manzanitas and other shrubs on the mountain. Now in the botanic garden the ruby-throat, though minute, became conspicuous when its glossy plumage, particularly around the throat, was caught by the sun's rays. I saw two ruby-throats flying around different cacti in bloom, one directly against the sun and the other in the shade. Their hovering wings beat so fast as to be indistinguishable as wings and I was fascinated by their acrobatics. One soon was lost to sight; the other hovered in front of a flower, stretching its long beak into the flower-cup while its wings continued to beat at a fantastic speed. Later I met another hummer darting up and down, to and fro, by a yellow cactus flower. It was even smaller than the ruby-throat and when it flew across the path of the sun I saw a flash of emerald green throat surrounded by black feathers. I could not have imagined such a brilliant emerald. It may have been the broad-billed hummer but I cannot be sure, for I do not know which species of hummers are to be found in the Bay region. The flowers of the cacti are said to be the hummers' favorite, and the cacti with their ball-like or rod-like or fan-like body and waxy flowers and the humming-birds together formed for me an interesting but unusual composition for a picture. The Berkeley botanic garden gave me much to chew on mentally.

The next mental food I absorbed was its five thousand species of rhododendrons. I am fond of rhododendrons, including azaleas (which are actually rhododendrons with a different arrangement of stamens) , just because many of them originally came from my native land. The hardy species of the rhododendrons are confined to the northern hemisphere, and the greatest aggregation of them is found in the Chinese-Tibetan-Himalayan region. I have seen many, many small mountain rhododendrons in Kew Gardens in London, that have all come from Yunnan Province of China. Many botanists such as Fortune, Forrest, Farrar, Kingdon Ward, Wilson, and others were sent to China to collect rare plants in the nineteenth century and each brought back some rhododendrons. Wilson of Harvard's Arnold Arboretum brought back at least fourteen rare specimens. He wrote in his famous book, *China: Mother of Gardens*:

> My attention and interest, however, were chiefly taken up with the rhododendrons. The gorgeous beauty of their flowers defies description. They were there in thousands and hundreds of thousands. Bushes of all sizes, many fully thirty feet tall and more in diameter, all clad with a wealth of blossoms that almost hid the foliage. Some flowers were crimson, some bright red, some flesh-colored, some silvery pink, some yellow, and others pure white. . . . How the rhododendrons find root-hold on these wild crags and cliffs is a marvel. . . .

There is a very narrow valley in Mount Lu in my native province called "Ching-hsiu-ku" or "Brocade Ravine," where masses of azaleas and rhododendrons bloom together profusely. I have seen them there many a time.

At first I was a little puzzled at the planting of so many species of hardy rhododendrons in the sunny grounds of Berkeley, until I realized that they were not planted in the open ground but behind the cacti in shaded areas and down the ravines. On this occasion they had passed their season for blooming except for two bushes which were in full bloom. They made a great contrast to the flowers of the cacti, but they did not vie with one another, each enjoyed its own glory. My special liking for Berkeley botanic garden is because it specializes in these two collections instead of having everything possible like other botanic gardens. The garden and Arboretum in Golden Gate Park are there to supply many other species for study.

Before finishing my unacademic learning in Berkeley, I was fortunate enough to be taken to its only long fishing pier, which used to stretch far out into the Bay water. Now it is abolished. Four years ago when Professor Hans Frankel of Yale University was still with the University of California, I asked him to drive me to this long pier on his way to his office. It was a long walk to the end of the rather dilapidated pier, of which many planks had been missing for some time. Many people were already there with their rods and other fishing tackle; youngsters were excitedly shouting or quarrelling about their catch; everyone was in a completely relaxed mood and no one was in a hurry. I looked at them and then at the highway where I had just been dropped from my friend's car. The contrast was amazing, with autos passing in a continuous chain from the Bay Bridge. A shout heralding a catch rose often. I moved nearer the fishermen and saw fish-like creatures but not quite the usual type of fish. Someone told me they were sand-sharks. Harmless and inedible, there are plenty of sand-sharks in the Bay water. I also saw a few young boys who were busy dropping their home-made baskets into the water: in no time they drew them up again covered with little crabs. All ended in laughter. It is a pity that the pier had to be abolished; where can the people of Berkeley, old and young, take themselves off now for a few hours' amusement in the open air?

XIX

Murmuring Secretively

After I had lived many years in the mountains, I spent my first winter in San Francisco, writing up notes. I used to run out on short excursions to Mount Tamalpais, or the hills across the Bay, for rest and exercise, and I always brought back a lot of flowers— as many as I could carry—and it was most touching to see the quick, natural enthusiasm in the hearts of the ragged, neglected, defrauded, dirty little wretches of the Tar Flat water front of the city I used to pass through on my way home. As soon as they caught sight of my wild bouquet, they quit their pitiful attempts at amusement in the miserable dirty streets and ran after me begging a flower. "Please, Mister, give me a flower—give me a flower, Mister," in a humble begging tone as if expecting to be refused. And when I stopped and distributed the treasures, giving each a lily or daisy or calachortus, anemone, gilia, flowering dogwood, spray of ceanothus, manzanita, or a branch of redwood, the dirty faces fairly glowed with enthusiasm while they gazed at them and fondled them reverently as if looking into the face of angels from heaven.

THE ABOVE PASSAGE written by John Muir, a Scotsman, in the eighteen-eighties tells a great deal about the San Francisco of that time. He could not have written like that if he were alive now. With the passing of time, many things once common are now rare or even non-existent. I have hardly once seen a single "ragged, neglected, defrauded, dirty little wretch of the Tar Flat" or any other water-front of San Francisco in all the times I stayed there. Some people tend to hanker after the past, but in doing so they quite forget the relief they must now feel at the disappearance of those "little wretches." Are we not living in a better time after all? I cannot deny that I often wished I could have been born in the golden days of China, but I still maintain that I am glad to be living in this saner world of ours. Before long this passage of John Muir's will appear senseless and almost incomprehensible to San Franciscans. Provided with every possible comfort for life, they would not be able to imagine how children could be neglected, ragged, defrauded, and dirty. This reminds me of Charles Dickens' stories, such as "Oliver Twist" or "David Copperfield." Before I went to England I read translations of Dickens' work in Chinese and many passages describing the way of life in those times seemed utterly obscure to me. After a few years' stay in England before the Second World War, I enjoyed reading these novels again, in their original versions, for I had the background before my eyes. This reminded me of many an "Oliver Twist" in China but we have no Dickens to write about them. However, there is no "Oliver Twist" in the London scene or anywhere else in England now, and such characters are unlikely to appear in novels again. With the abolition of the slums everywhere in the United States and in Europe the nature of western literature will no doubt undergo some change and it has, in fact, already been changing fast. Nevertheless, Dickens' "Oliver" and John Muir's "dirty little wretches" still exist in large numbers in other parts of the world. In former days their existence was unnoticed or completely ignored by Europeans and North Americans, but time and change have brought them to the notice and conscience of all. They could not be ignored any longer. This is an aspect of this new era of ours that makes me glad to have been born when I was.

In some ways, this era is one of the great turning points in the history of mankind—I mean "mankind" in its fullest possible sense. The history of mankind before our time was exceedingly fragmentary —that is, in each nation a good proportion of the people were completely ignored and suppressed as if they were unmentionable. The greater part of the world's population was unrecorded in any history book. In the past men were arbitrarily divided into "superior race," "other races," and "backward races," there were "super-men" and "subhuman men" and so on. This kind of concept has been in existence for thousands of years. Now there is a real change, a change that has been going on for a century and now emerges. This is what I mean by the beginning of a new history of mankind in its fullest sense. It is the era of the evolution of mankind as a whole. Until every single member of mankind throughout the world reaches a similar standard of living in his or her own right and ability, such evolution will not be complete or the history of mankind as a whole described as finished. No matter how many theories, ideologies and arguments the so-called great philosophers, historians, economists and scientists may put forward, they are valueless unless they take the right and ability of every single human being into consideration. I feel happy to have realized this and am therefore unable to share others' dim and miserable views for the future of the human race. I do not mean that I have not suffered enough in being born into this much-divided world of the twentieth century; yet I feel it worth while to have endured personal sufferings for the sake of being a witness to the greatest evolution of mankind. This explains my enjoyment in seeing new and interesting things on my travels instead of brooding and lamenting for the past. I am happy to see the disappearance of those "ragged, neglected, defrauded, dirty" little wretches of John Muir's days in San Francisco. It is my great hope that the future will see the disappearance of many, many more of those dirty little wretches from China, India, South-east Asia, the Middle East, South America and everywhere else on the globe, though it may not happen in my lifetime.

No doubt John Muir, if he were still alive, could not have understood what I have just said. But he would be amused to know that I envy him very much that he "used to run out on short excursions to Mount Tamalpais, or the hills across the Bay, for rest and exercise. . . ." How could he manage that so effortlessly? I myself failed in every attempt. It would take me at least half an hour from where I was staying to reach the Ferry Building for a train or bus to cross the Bay. After reaching the Berkeley side I already felt it a hopeless task to take myself on foot to Richmond and then on to San Rafael by ferryboat. Had I been in San Rafael I would have had no idea how to climb up Mount Tamalpais, etc. Now the ferry between Richmond and San Rafael has long disappeared: it is simply impossible for me to walk over the Golden Gate Bridge even to Sausalito. How did John Muir run out on short excursions then? He must have been a Chinese immortal if not a Scottish Genie!

Fortunately my good friends have motored me up to Tamalpais and to Muir Woods on many an occasion. Muir Woods is a grove of redwoods set inside a hill slope on the way up Mount Tamalpais, found by John Muir and named after him. I said in my New York book that "man is a greedy creature, greedy for wealth, food, clothes or fame, but I am more often greedy for things that delight the eye or the mind." It was my greediness for this sort of delight that made me ask a friend on one occasion to drop me down at Muir Woods when he drove to Mill Valley for a business appointment.

This time on entering the Woods, I could not help admiring John Muir as a man who made full use of his legs as described in *A Thousand-Mile Walk to the Gulf,* the title of one of his books. Many places and things have been named after John Muir, such as Muir Glacier in Alaska, Muir Lake and Muir Knoll in Wisconsin, Camp Muir in Washington, Muir Peak in Los Angeles, Muir Gorge in Yosemite, Muir Pass in Kings Canyon, Muir Crest and Muir Grove in the Sequoia National Park, and also John Muir Trail, winding high up the high peaks of the Sierras. I would not have known of all these had I not been to Muir Woods and begun to wonder why it was so named.

After I had read something about John Muir my interest in him grew, for he was a Scotsman born in Dunbar, which I had passed through many a time during my year's stay in Scotland, when I was writing *The Silent Traveller in Edinburgh*. The Chinese and the Scots both enjoy walking. Whenever I went walking in the Scottish countryside I always met other walkers too. Once I walked almost the whole way from Fort William through Glen Coe to Inverness. I expected to be a lonely trotter, but now and then someone would come along and exchange greetings with me. That was more than fifteen years ago. Since I came to wander in the United States I had never given a thought to whether people walk or had walked here until I read of John Muir. He was a much better walker than I, for he never questioned whether the distance would be too far, but just set off, sleeping wherever he was tired and sometimes even going without food. He was a great Scotsman. Both he and John McLaren, who created Golden Gate Park, did much for San Franciscans and for those who come to enjoy the Bay Area.

Once I was taken to Mill Valley. This was on a Wednesday morning, rather cool, and the hill road we followed was so deserted that it might have been a drive leading to an aristocratic château

An Oriental in Union Square.

or castle in France or England. No other car followed ours. I caught
sight of a rather unfinished-looking wooden structure by the side
of an almost dried-up creek. My friend told me it was the remains
of a sawmill, built here near an entrance to Cascade Canyon in
1843 by an Irish sailor, John Reed, who had helped to establish
a regular boat service between Sausalito and Yerba Buena—the
former name of San Francisco—and was awarded by the Mexican
Governor, José Figueroa, one square league of land in what is now
called Marin County. John Reed had then four thousand four hundred
and nine acres of ground. The Cascade Canyon has long ceased to
exist. Eventually the sawmill community earned a name for the valley.
I wonder what happened to John Reed's descendants and whether any
are still alive today. Before I came to the West Coast I heard much
about the pioneers, chiefly New Englanders, who had crossed the
country in covered wagons. It seems to me that the Scots and the Irish
were the real pioneers such as John Muir and John Reed.

Unlike on my previous visits, this time I was the only one to look
around the little gift-shop at the many interesting species of plants and
birds to be found in Muir Woods. I was specially interested in one type
of gift made of the variously shaped odd growths known as *burls*.
These objects made out of burls vary in size and are all highly polished
inside with the original shape of the odd growth still intact. There is
ingenuity in the making and a specialty here. On stepping out on to
the main footpath I was again alone facing the tall redwoods all around
me. Lifting up my head I could not find their tops, nor see a streak of
sky. I thought I owned the entire grove, yet I realized how infinitesimal
I must have looked by comparison. Actually I lost the sense of my own
reality and became a nothingness. How long was it since I began to feel
the illusion of my infinitesimal existence? Does the redwood bother
about my presence or existence? Do I have to bother about my own
reality? All these are questions without answer: I only know that while
the illusion lasts I have a brief existence. It is this flash of reality or
existence that gives a sense of the joy of living, however infinitesimal
I may be in the Universe. So I strolled on. I soon reached the point
where a huge cross-section, cut from a large redwood which was said to
have lived at least two thousand years, was displayed, so that people
could read its age from the rings. Confucius, who was born in 551 B.C.,

Trying to see Australia over Seal Rocks.

could have admired that tree in its younger days!

On and on I walked slowly and gazed around without a care. At places the sunshine probed through from above and illuminated parts of the green leaves on the hanging branches, transforming them into fresh, sparkling emerald-jade, against the background of the brown-red trunks of enormous size. To my surprise and amusement I saw a shaft of sunlight shining on a huge burl by the side of a tree-trunk. It looked like a hairy face with a large pair of eyes fixed on me, peering from behind an exuberant growth of ferns and shrubs. It reminded me of something very familiar and I cried out to myself that it was a satyr! How did the shape of a satyr come into my Chinese head? It must mean that I have been out of China far too long, and that I have frequently seen satyrs portrayed in drawings, oils and sculpture in Western art, and described in Western literature. My mind must have long been remoulded by my new environment. "Huan ching yi jen" or "Environment shifts man about," says a Chinese proverb. Actually three years ago I spent a month in Greece and saw a good many sculptured satyrs in stone and bronze in various museums. A young lady lecturer of the National Museum in Athens explained to a party of us that satyrs did not care for bad weather and were always frowning at the downpour or scorching sun when they perched on a rock in one of the Greek islands. She also said that some people believe that satyrs still exist. Indeed, a satyr had crossed the Atlantic, as he used to jump from one island to another in Greece, and had just appeared to me by the side of a huge redwood in Muir Woods!

The main species of tree growing in Muir Woods, the *Sequoia Sempervirens* or redwood, can reach the extreme height of three hundred and sixty-four feet; it can have a diameter of about twenty feet, and its maximum age is probably about two thousand years. The tallest redwood I myself noticed in Muir Woods was more than two hundred and forty-six feet high with a diameter of seventeen feet, and its bark was about a foot in thickness. How long had it been living there, I wonder. There must have been redwoods growing in that part of Mount Tamalpais long before—say, three or four or five thousand years ago. Why might not one of the Greek satyrs have actually come to roam round here long, long before it was named Muir Woods?

Perhaps the burl which looked to me like a satyr was a real one eventually petrified!

My good friend Carrington Goodrich once told me that he had read about the discovery of the Dawn Redwood or *Metasequoia,* a close relative of the *Sequoia Sempervirens* of Muir Woods, in Szechuan Province of China by Mr. Tsang Wang. An interesting point for me was that Mr. Wang had taken branches with leaves and cones to my old college teacher, Dr. Hsien-su Hu of the Fan Memorial Institute of Biology, for identification. He found them similar to certain fossil redwoods in Japan. Thus, in a sense, a fossil had come to life—a tree thought to have been extinct for some sixty million years was actually surviving in the hidden valleys of Central China. This discovery excited much interest, and expeditions were organized by Professor Wan-chun Cheng of the National Central University at Nanking under the leadership of Mr. Hsueh with the financial help of the Arnold Arboretum of Harvard University. Six hundred packets of seeds were collected and distributed all over the world. I have seen many young Dawn redwoods grown in my friends' gardens in several places in the United States, and they look very healthy and keep growing. Another interesting point for me in connection with this discovery was an article I read in *Natural History* by Dr. R. W. Chaney, of the Department of Palaeontology, University of California, who made an expedition to Szechuan together with Dr. Milton Silverman, Science Writer for the *San Francisco Chronicle.* Dr. Chaney has the following to say:

> Summarizing the evidence of *Metasequoia* distribution, we find that it appeared at high latitudes in the Cretaceous period, was widely distributed there in the Eocene, had moved south and was abundant in the United States and Northern China in the Oligocene, was more scattered in distribution during the Miocene, and disappeared from the fossil record on both sides of the Pacific before or during the Pliocene period. Why has it survived only in Central China after living so widely around the world in earlier ages? . . . So it is important to learn as much as we can about environmental conditions in these valleys of Central China. It will tell us what Manchuria and Oregon looked like forty million years ago. . . . Observations on the existing climate in the area now occupied by Dawn Redwoods will enable us to make some long

range weather predictions in reverse regarding the rains and winds of Manchuria and Oregon in the days when *Metasequoia* lived there and left behind its leaves and cones to be preserved as fossils.

Being no student of biology myself, I just ponder from the above quotation who can really say which country is actually older than the other?

Presently I was standing by an enormous redwood. The lower part of the trunk was hollow inside, big enough to hold a divan bed for sleeping. A split at the bottom could be the door and two or three large holes would make good windows; there must be big burls to be taken off. I wonder if the design for the early American-Indian tents or hogans was derived from such a hollow redwood. I once saw a guide leading a group of tourists through this trunk; walking through, the guide said, would bring luck. The guide seemed to have a great deal to tell about ghosts and Red Indians. The most vivid memory I have about this trunk is of when I joined a party including the Jessett family with their two young girls, Patience, aged nine, and Regan, only three. They soon engaged me in a game of hide-and-seek behind the tree trunks and inside the hollows. Little Regan often hid herself behind some outgrown burls in the midst of tall ferns. Some holes in the thick bark were big enough and not too high for Regan to slip through without my noticing her. Then her happy giggles gave her away. Patience ran faster than Regan; the faster she ran, the happier her soft giggle sounded. It was natural that Regan could not run so fast, but I somehow felt that she made an effort not to run away from me. So young at only three, yet so much she had to say to me. "Oh, isn't this fun?" she exclaimed, pausing for a moment with a satisfied expression. I became speechless. That laughter of the youngsters was simply magic to me and the scene came back to me so vividly now. Life is a strange and mysterious thing which nobody can define in a few words. Many find much bitterness in it. But one flash of a moment of sweetness is enough to make my brief existence worth while.

After this moment I felt my body lighter and strolled along buoyantly. I did not gaze at much, nor think much, for that sweet memory was still with me for a while. Involuntarily I heard some strange sounds,

In Muir Woods

yet no trace of the source could be discovered. Little sky was to be seen overhead, yet the deep-set valley of the redwood grove was full of light. No wind, not even a breath of breeze, was about, yet many leaves on the upper parts of the trees were rustling against one another. Was there a squirrel running along the hanging branch, or a bird hopping from one twig to another, or a chipmunk cracking a hard nut which unfortunately fell from its hold? I could not say. Faintly and at intervals, the murmuring sounds floated on, stirring in me a blissful and innocent sensation. Up and a little farther up still I stepped along the winding trail amidst the surrounding higher lands that enclose Muir Woods. I regained my repose of mind and calmness of heart, and let the everchanging forms of Nature pass before my eyes as I moved by. I was now higher than before and could see more of the upper sections of the redwoods, though not their tops still. Strangely each redwood seemed to me to have the architectural shape of a Chinese pagoda, or a

Chinese pavilion with curved roofs, some with more stories than others. It is not impossible that Chinese architecture had its origin in the appearance of a prehistoric *Sequoia*. Quite a few birds, undistinguishable as to species, flew from one branch to another or from one redwood to another. They flew high, active and lively; perhaps they could not have as much freedom for their wings down below, for I saw none of them before. Some looked so tiny, far more infinitesimal than I in comparison with the huge redwoods, yet they could make the redwood's twigs vibrate. Nothing is too small to enjoy its flash of existence, if it is left to live in peace. Occasionally now I felt a breath of wind making many long branches sway at once. Each thick cluster of leaves along the branches up to the tips fluttered gaily in the breeze; some caught the sun-rays to look even brighter than others, splendidly elegant, delicately unfamiliar, and mysteriously tangible. Gradually the footpath descended and I detected a dewy feeling in the air. I had come to a very shady quarter, surrounded by a most picturesque confusion of ferns, long grass, and stretching, intersected branches of Bay trees. The farther I stepped, the more entangled I found the luxuriant growth of plants. There was a lazy stream moving invisibly underneath them all.

For the moment I was interested in the Bay tree, which I was told was the typical California laurel. In this connection, I remember reading about the California poetess, Ina Coolbrith, who lived in San Francisco years ago. She was a friend of many eminent people including Alfred, Lord Tennyson, George Meredith, Dante Gabriel Rossetti, John Greenleaf Whittier, Marie, Queen of Rumania, and Henry Wadsworth Longfellow. After the earthquake and fire of 1906, she lost her home high on Russian Hill and became Librarian of the Oakland Public Library and later of San Francisco's Bohemian Club. It was she who induced Jack London to read and to write. Her favorite poet was Lord Byron and she poured contempt on the Victorians in London for treating the poet so disgracefully, though she herself was regarded as the last of the Victorians in her San Francisco days. Later she started a campaign to restore Byron's reputation, by writing letters to influential Londoners. She went tramping through Muir Woods in search of something worth while to make a memorial wreath—eventually she chose the typical Calfoirnia laurel, a Bay tree. To the wreath she made, she attached a poem of her own and entrusted both to her emissary, Joaquin Miller. When the remains of Lord Byron were removed from Italy and re-buried ceremoniously in Westminster Abbey the California laurel wreath that Ina Coolbrith made was placed on Byron's bier. She had an indomitable spirit of persistence,

House on Russian Hill

but her act means very little to anybody nowadays. Nevertheless, Byron's work will always be read even if he had not been re-buried in the citadel of all great Britishers. How many know Ina Coolbrith in San Francisco now? There is a small but neat Ina Coolbrith park not far from Russian Hill and I was taken there once by a friend.

My thoughts on Ina Coolbrith were driven away by the murmuring notes that I had heard before and which now became clearer and fresher. By and by some stray sunbeams glanced over the negligible, nameless brook which reflected them back in flashing sparkles now and then. On and on I strolled until I reached a quarter where the twinklings were no longer fully covered by the thickets. The water was shallow but pure, exposing every little pebble at the bottom. Actually it could hardly be termed a brook, for there is so little water there; nor was it visibly moving, either. On the other hand, it revealed its liveliness, sparkling and fascinating. It had excited and fed my curiosity; it is motion and life. At first, on my entering Muir Woods, I was solely impressed by the gigantic, enormous, tallest trees. I felt as if shrunk to nothing there. Gradually, though my eyes were stunned by the redwoods so close at hand, yet the insignificant murmurs did manage to enter my ears. This reminds me of the much-talked and much-written about *Space Age* of ours: everything assumes stupendous, colossal dimensions—no one seems to realise that a tiny, unnoticeable effort is also to be taken into account. It is that tiny, insignificant trickle of water which must have kept all the plants and giant redwoods growing and alive. The occasional murmurs that I heard in Muir Woods are symbols for those fleeting pleasures that linger on and on during my flash of existence.

Satisfied and gratified I felt when my friend came to fetch me down to the city. He wondered why I became more silent than ever in his car, but he did not know that I was composing a poem. I translated it roughly as follows:

古木共擎天 似恐天下墜
天無下墜理 排雲聳立幾何年
不知千千萬萬世
應有天女天神巢雲顛
我今呕行自東土 未遇神仙不見天
候忽陽光穿樹出 鵝黃嫩綠各分妍
樹大始知我渺小 山深曲處有流泉
泉聲斷續遶幽靜 飛蘿挂壁搖青煙
青煙紆迴遶樹杪 隱隱中藏數飛鳥
鳥語聽到聽不到 一時喃喃一時香
暫了人間塵俗心 且識潺潺萬古音
我生豈能有二次 流連樂此漫間吟

The ancient trees stand to support
   Heaven
Lest Heaven should fall.
No such fall is possible,
Yet they have stood there, upholding the clouds—
   how many years?
In the thousands of centuries before my knowledge
Fairies and spirits lived above the clouds.
I come now from the Eastern land to travel silently;
I neither met immortals nor was able to see the sky.
Suddenly a shaft of sunshine shoots through the trees,
Bright yellow and young green divide the beauty.
These giants of trees reveal my insignificance.
From some hidden corner, deep in the hills
   a brook flows on—
Its intermittent murmurs make the peace profounder.
Swaying creepers, hanging from the cliff,
   disturb the clear mist.
The clear mist spirals up to circle the tree tops;
Invisibly a few birds perch in the foliage:
Their birds' talk is audible then inaudible,
At one time they chatter, at another not.
For the moment I close my mind to dusty,
   earthly affairs,
And receive the murmurs that come down from
   ages long past.
How can I hope for a second living span?
Lingering on I hum leisurely for my enjoyment.

XX

Seeking Objectively

I WAS TAKEN TO San Quentin one day. But not in a police car. I had casually asked Shih-hsiang Chen if anyone was allowed to pay Alcatraz Island a visit. The answer was "never heard of it happening."

However, Shih-hsiang started telephoning. After four or five calls, he told me smilingly that we might go to San Quentin next morning. Shih-hsiang has acquired much of the typical way of life of university professors and does not care to be troubled by what he considers unnecessary questions. He was living alone *then* (1953), and I was a traveller drifting about. We seldom started on an outing exactly as scheduled, nor did we ever reach our destination on time. It never bothered us. We were always forgiven by friends on the score that we had been born in China, where time does not matter.

The next morning proved an exception. An appointment with the inmates of San Quentin was different from one with friends, Shih-hsiang said. We had our breakfast and left the house punctually at ten o'clock, arriving ahead of all other cars at the landing stage for the ferryboat to take us to San Rafael. We were the first on the upper deck. The fresh sea air dispersed my queries and anticipations for the moment; the wide expanse made me draw a deep breath. Beyond the farther shore, some rounded hills looked quite hot and brown, with dark green patches here and there. The morning sun was already strong enough to evaporate the dew on the grass and trees. The San Francisco fog-horn could be heard at long intervals, yet no sea fog was to be seen as far as my eye could reach. We were behind Raccoon Strait and far away from the Golden Gate. Tranquillity reigned in the air and over all on the ferry except for the sound of the engine and the occasional dash of a few children across the deck and up and down the stairs.

Someone remarked that the ferryboat would not be running much longer. A new bridge was to be built between Richmond and San Rafael. I could not help asking myself why another bridge was needed, with two good long bridges like Bay Bridge and San Mateo Bridge; the word "enough" has a different significance in the eyes of Californians, it appears.

I, for one, feel sorry to think of the ferryboat disappearing. Before the construction of Bay Bridge there used to be a ferry running between the Custom House and Berkeley, I was told, but I came to San Francisco too late to enjoy it. The ferry between the Ferry Building along the Embarcadero and Oakland was running when I was there; I crossed the Bay on it three times, just for pleasure. It was from the ferryboat that I admired the setting of San Francisco, its natural beauty and its man-made panorama of buildings. To stand on the upper deck of a ferryboat lifts one's spirit, halts one's endless hurrying, relaxes one's body and causes one to feel aloof from the bustling throng. It is there that one realizes in what beautiful surroundings one is living and working; there that one can undergo healthy, fresh-air treatment without the formality of an appointment with a doctor or hospital. Why, in this modern age of ours, is so much designed for efficiency and money-making but not for health?

If the last ferryboat in San Francisco Bay has to go, it is not for me to try to stop it. Our ancient thinkers never took the circumstances of life to be unchangeable; I take change as it comes and seldom lament it. All the same I cannot help feeling a little sentimental about the disappearance of the ferryboat, and inevitably enjoyed my trip on the ferry to San Rafael when I learned that it would soon run no more. I moved from one side to the other in order to see more of the Bay scene. I watched Angel Island, shaped like a huge boat anchored not far from the tip of Belvedere. I also observed a large flock of hell-divers, flying close to the water surface. The part of the Bay over which we were moving was very calm and spacious with hardly a ripple.

Shih-hsiang was on the deck busy making notes, for he was going to give a lecture to a number of old-timers in San Quentin. He had been asked to lecture there a year previously but had declined. Simply trying to accommodate my wish, he had managed to make arrangements for this trip of ours, thereby letting himself in for a lecture. His friendship for me is immeasurable. "Te-yi-chih-chi, szu-er-wu-han," or "Having one good friend in life means no regret when dying," is a common saying in China. This kind of feeling for friendship has, however, been changing among us modern Chinese, considerably. I appreciated Shih-hsiang's feeling towards me all the more.

Not one of the other cars followed us to San Quentin; the much winding road belonged to us alone. After a while came a larger car with two men in uniform. They passed us without a look. Eventually we drew up in front of a locked gate, through which I spotted a guard walking to and fro on a high tower. Our approach must have been watched. First we were asked to hand the gate guard the cameras. We had none. Then the car was conducted into the open yard and we were led into a modern canteen restaurant and given seats near the counter. Mr. Short, Shih-hsiang's friend, soon came to greet us. He explained that this canteen was for the staff only; the mess canteen was elsewhere. A good lunch was neatly served. Afterwards Mr. Short expressed his difficulties in attempting to show us the buildings, for they had been re-modelled and the movements of the inmates were freer than before. Presently we approached a hall. While the guard was unlocking the gate into it, I noticed two stout unshaven fellows being led behind bars. "Those have not been here long," remarked Mr. Short; "the group we are going to meet are old-timers. They have proved their good behavior."

We were then led to a row of chairs on a raised platform, while a considerable crowd streamed in and sat down below. Then as chief organizer Mr. Short gave the word for the meeting to start. A young man in blue jeans came up to take the position of chairman. Another, the secretary, read the minutes of a former meeting. Discussion of each item followed and argument soon arose. It became heated over a demand for the withdrawal of membership from someone whose conduct was condemned. The member in question refused to withdraw and instead put forward many suggestions for the reform of the regulations. The chairman became impatient and began to stamp his feet on the floor. The situation seemed to be getting out of hand. Then a young man, neatly dressed, stood up and addressed the meeting with control and courtesy. First he read a number of the regulations of the organization, expounding them one by one in defense of the member who had been criticized. His speech was rather long but it impressed me more than many harangues by well-known politicians which I had heard. Perhaps I was biased, for I did not expect to hear such a speech in San Quentin. There was a marked silence after his remarks; the others may have felt they were no match for him. The chairman, however, was still impatient and unconvinced, and the problem seemed no nearer a solution.

Eventually Mr. Short stood up to say the procedure of the meeting had been well carried out and that it was time for him to introduce the speaker. Shih-hsiang rose to give a talk on "An outline of China's history." Everyone seemed to be greatly interested in the subject and listened attentively. One of the audience declared that he read every book on China he could lay hands on. He even offered to go up on the platform and draw a map of China for the speaker when the need arose. To my surprise, the rough map gave the shape of China and the positions of a number of big cities with very reasonable accuracy. The talk lasted a good while, for it is a huge subject. After a thunder of applause a stream of questions came up one after another. The enthusiasm was great, and it was a wonder to me how those living in San Quentin, under rigid discipline, could have so much interest in another country which they had never seen. Again Mr. Short rose to end the confusion, but a stone was dropped on my head when he said that he was sure the audience would like Professor Chen's friend to say something. We had never met before and he did not know whether I was really a silent man.

However, I had to pluck up my courage and meet the request. I thought they had all had an interesting but rather strenuous hour: I ought not to keep them sitting much longer. So I just told them a well-known Chinese joke. I began by saying that people in the West had all heard of the Chinese family system originated by Confucius, and also believed that Chinese women were looked down on by the men. Yet few realized that the real head of a Chinese family is always the woman and how powerful she has always been. The Chinese family system has produced many tyrannical women and henpecked husbands. Once ten henpecked husbands in a well-known city gathered together and organized a society sworn to resist the deadly oppression of their wives. They planned their first meeting with due ceremony in order to elect a president. At first they all drank wine, exchanged verses they had written recently, and discussed art and literature happily. They did not realize that their wives had got wind of the project until the women suddenly appeared on the scene. The stampede caused was terrific; the husbands ran for their lives like mice at the first mew of a cat. Cups and saucers went flying and chairs tipped upside down. However, one of the husbands remained unmoved by the commotion and continued to sit there calmly to face the music. The wives merely enjoyed the raid and laughed at the scene contemptuously. None of them took any notice of him and presently they left the garden. Afterwards, the nine mice-like creatures crept back again and agreed that the tenth member who had not run away should be elected their president for having shown real courage. When they came up to offer him the post, they discovered that he had died of fright!

All had a good laugh before I sat down. Mr. Short asked the audience to show their thanks by applauding. In addition, they were asked whether Shih-hsiang and I should be elected as two honorary members of their club—the Seekers' Club. Since that day I have a new title after my name! Though the meeting was over, we did not get away easily. There was a group of Seekers round Shih-hsiang and I had a few too. A young, tall, dark-skinned fellow, with a merry, happy-go-lucky look, dubbed me "Confucius" and Shih-hsiang a great scholar of China. A rather sunken-faced Seeker, middle-aged and short, began to follow me about. Eventually he stepped forward and remarked: "I think those ten husbands were all cowards." "Why?" I asked. "They should not have let their wives boss them about; I killed mine!" Now I realized that at least one person in the audience had not laughed at my joke.

On our way out of San Quentin to go to Mr. Short's home at Sausalito we learned the history of some of the inmates. Though all the men attending the meeting had looked friendly and normal in their behavior, many had taken others' lives, directly or indirectly. Years of confinement within a restricted area ensured their good conduct. They now worked to order, and rested to order, and they made good use of the library, whenever they wanted to. The young speaker who had intervened at the meeting was noted as one of the regular readers in the library. He was known to have been a bright student at High School with a great ambition to become a Congressman or Senator. He was always an outstanding figure at the meetings, for he always brushed his hair till it shone, dressed neatly, and spoke as if used to addressing a public gathering. He came to San Quentin after setting fire to a house and causing several deaths. He claimed to have been a close friend of the film star, Sabu, of *The Elephant Boy*, and that he had acted as a knight-errant by setting fire to the house when he found that his friend had been wronged by its owner. At the time of the meeting he still believed that he had done a good deed. In fact, we were informed, many stuck throughout to what they had said on their first day in San Quentin.

On reaching Sausalito Mr. Short wished to take us to see his Greek artist-friend Verda, a noted figure in San Francisco, who lived nearby. Leaving the car on the shore we began to walk up a sort of gangway over the water. It was explained to us that the artist did not care much for visitors, particularly women, intruding on his living quarters and that he purposely disconnected the landing-stage from the boat in which he lived. Our host called to his friend, but there was no answer. Then we took hold of a strong rope and swung ourselves across the gap, landing on board the artist's antique-looking barge. No one appeared. Mr. Short knew this friend of his so well that he just told us to have a good look round at the paintings on the walls of the barge. They were colorful and many were paper-cut symbolic figures pasted on to colored-paper backgrounds.

The house in which our host lived was a modern houseboat with all modern comforts. Mrs. Short had cold drinks ready for us and we were taken to sit on the upper deck above the stern to gaze at Angel Island and Belvedere in turn. But my eyes could not discern the real form of either, for the thick San Francisco sea-fog was rolling along. I could not help admiring the Shorts' way of life. I also felt thankful that I was merely an honorary member of "the Seekers," not a regular one.

After supper that evening, being alone, I began to read the Seekers'

Constitution and by-laws, which had been given to me. It is not a bulky publication but contains a good few pages. I read:

> The purpose of the organization is to exemplify the Golden Rule; to help one another and ourselves; seek correct answers to problems of good social living habits inside the prison and outside.
>
> 1. To help each individual member discover himself, realize that he is now a part of a minority group, and develop the fortitude to make the best of his situation.
> 2. To cultivate a deeper appreciation for law, for democratic ideas, and for social institutions.
> 3. To afford practice in:
>   (a) Participating in group activities.
>   (b) Making and enforcing laws.
>   (c) Conforming to laws.
>   (d) Conducting on one's feet and using democratic discussion to formulate opinions and discard unreasonable prejudice.
> 4. To provide a medium through which free people may have some contact with inmates, learning about their problems, outlook, ambitions, purposes; in the hope that the gulf between inmates and free people may be narrowed.
> 5. To constitute this organization in prison as a growing institution for the benefit of future inmates who may become prisoners through failure to make the right social adjustments.
> 6. To advocate and practice racial equality, helping in some small way to lessen antipathy and prejudice and so aid in advancement of world peace.

These purposes are as sound as those of any useful organization. But I wonder if the "golden rule" which is to be exemplified is similar to that which is so important in Chinese Confucianism. Confucianism has been much attacked in the past few decades, but that is because later rulers and ruling classes in China abused it by insisting on less fortunate people following it but failing to practice it themselves. I myself still give Confucius my highest reverence, for he who lived so many hundred of years ago had the foresight and vision to define the perennial causes of trouble among men. His golden rule rests on measuring man by man's own self. He demands:

(1) hsiao —that one be filial to one's parents
(2) ti —that one show brotherly love to one's fellows
(3) chung—that one be loyal to one's work
(4) hsin —that one be sincere in friendship.

We must conduct our life according to *li,* good manners, *vi,* righteousness, *lien,* incorruptibility and, *chih,* having a sense of shame. In this way a man would be "good" in the full sense of the word. I am not suggesting measuring the inmates of San Quentin by these eight points. But I wonder whether we modern men still have the sense of righteousness and the sense of shame. It seems to me that modern life and modern standards of morals have done away with these two senses. It is the lack of a sense of righteousness which probably makes the inmates of San Quentin stick to their belief in their own innocence, which they held on the first day they entered. With no sense of shame they may not be able to prevent themselves acting shamelessly. In the face of the ever more populous and more complex world it is difficult to infuse man with the sense of righteousness and that of shame. Yet to lessen antipathy and prejudice it is necessary to create just these senses. But how? I seek objectively.

XXI

Drinking Inordinately

THROUGH an introduction from our mutual poet-friend, David McCord, I was entertained in 1953 by Joseph Henry Jackson of the *San Francisco Chronicle* with a few anecdotes of the City he had known and loved almost his whole life. We had a drink together. He knew that I was a brand newcomer and that he could tell me what best to see. Modestly he did not mention the title of a single one of his many books on San Francisco and California. Alas! Henry is no longer with David and me in this world.

Handing me a bowl of nuts and another of corn-chips, as we drank that evening, Jackson remarked that years ago in almost every drinking house in San Francisco the bowls would be filled, not with nuts or corn-chips but with freshly-cooked shrimps. The bowls were all Cantonware in pleasing colors and looked quite attractive, lying on the long counters of the drinking-houses. Customers were free to eat the shrimps with their drinks and could add a little salt, pepper, even ginger or soya-sauce if they liked. But Jackson preferred to eat them plain, for he enjoyed their fresh-sweet taste. "The Chinese," he remarked "were resourceful and found ways to introduce many new things into the life of San Francisco." They used to fish for small shrimps in the Bay under the Presidio every morning. Nobody had thought of doing so before. They cooked them and went from house to house selling them. Who first introduced them to the drinking places Henry did not know, but they soon became a vogue and a much liked delicacy. The place where the Chinese fished soon became known as China Beach and their fishing area extended to include San Rafael Bay too. In the early mornings, particularly on a Saturday, many San Franciscans would take their youngsters to watch the Chinese fishing for shrimps at China Beach. All of a sudden, with the beginning of the Second World War no more bowls of fresh shrimps appeared in Bars. "Changes always come quickly in San Francisco," said Jackson with a smile.

"It is the incredibly rapid changes which have built up this city as it is now. Even while you are here, you will notice changes going on yourself. San Francisco will *never* rest contented or it wouldn't be San Francisco. Nevertheless there is something in its character which stays firm always. Other cities become totally different in the process of developing, but not San Francisco. That is why I love this city so much." I hazarded that the natural setting of San Francisco must be the element which has kept the city so true to its original character. Jackson gave me a smile but made no comment. I was very interested in his talk about changes and told him that people in the West, deluded by Chinese culture being so persistent in its age-old traditions, have the notion that China itself has not changed at all for four thousand years. When they saw China suddenly changing they could not believe it was possible. Actually China has been changing all the time, unobserved perhaps, by other nations. It is interesting to note that China has produced a Classic work called *Yi-Ching* or "Canon of Changes," thought to have been written in about the eleventh or twelfth century B.C. and dealing solely with the *changes* in the universe and man. But it is a book very few Chinese can understand. Even Confucius, who lived in the sixth century B.C., once said that should Heaven grant him a few more years of life he might be able to study and understand the Book of Changes.

A few days after this meeting I had a message from Henry Jackson's secretary, asking me to go to 1335 Sutter Street. I found the number and was well received by the Grabhorn brothers, Ernie and Bob, of the Grabhorn Press. The Grabhorn Press is the oldest printing establishment in San Francisco and its fine printing is known not only in this city but in the whole United States. My friend, Dr. Walter M. Whitehill, Director of Boston Athenaeum, knows it well and once in his Library showed me a few first editions printed by this Press. Another friend of mine, Mr. Harold Hugo, Managing Director of the Meriden Gravure Company, never failed to mention his association and friendship with the Grabhorn brothers whenever we met. I had also heard of the Grabhorn Press from the late Strickland Gibson, keeper of the Bodleian Library at Oxford, and from the late George Fishendon, an authority on printing in London. So I was grateful for the chance to visit this famous Press and silently sent my thanks to Jackson.

Fishing by the old fort

Bob Grabhorn was busy at the machine while his wife, Jane, worked hard at composing. The elder brother, Ernie, told me that the three of them ran the Press entirely alone and that no other person had ever been employed. It was Ernie who started the Press in Indianapolis some fifty years ago, training his brother, Bob, in the trade; Bob in turn interested Jane in it. After having made a good start in Indianapolis, Ernie decided to move the Press to San Francisco in the early nineteen-twenties, almost single-handed. Ernie has always specialized in fine printing and never accepted any work which he did not like and which he regarded as not worthy of his skill. Bob and Jane have maintained the same attitude. From the very beginning, each of their books has turned out to be a collector's piece. Ernie's collection of early Japanese

woodcuts which he showed me was ample evidence of his good taste.
He had plenty of anecdotes to tell me too about how he acquired the
prints in Japan and other countries and also how he sometimes had to
refuse very harshly to take on a piece of work. I enjoyed his comments
on human nature, which he seemed to understand very well. I suppose
a single-minded person has to be firm and even rude in his dealings, if
he wants to achieve his aim. Nevertheless, I still believe that if we
human beings could only understand each other's problems better, a
firm attitude need not become a rude one. Some improvement in
human contacts is a goal to aim at all the time. Before I said "Good-
bye" to the Grabhorns, Ernie told me with a broad smile that they had
managed to get a good stock of best quality paper just before the out-
break of the Second World War and had plenty of work to keep them
busy for a number of years. "That sounds like a definite refusal if I
asked you to print something for me," I grinned back at him.

I was filled with admiration for the Grabhorn brothers' independent
way of working and their persistence in carrying out their beliefs. I
remember reading somewhere that Bret Harte once shouted at his wife
that he would never write another word and that no one appreciated
art, when he arrived back in his small apartment in San Francisco with
the rejected manuscript of *The Luck of Roaring Camp* under his arm.
"Very well, Frank," rebuked his life-partner, "never write another
word. But remember, I've got to eat even if you don't." In Bret Harte's
days literature and art ranked far behind gold in San Francisco. Yet
Bret Harte's name lives to this day and Mark Twain's too, and those of
many other noted writers of the West. No important literary work
appeared in this West Coast of America in the late nineteenth and
early twentieth centuries; yet now the Grabhorn Press had earned
distinction for San Francisco as a city possessing one of the finest presses
in the whole United States. Ernie Grabhorn must have had the pioneer
spirit in him. I feel glad to know that "in an age of man's technological
progress toward total automation when any type of work is undertaken
for material advantages by the use of implements according to specifi-
able rules," as my friend, Sir Herbert Read wrote, there are people
like the Grabhorn brothers who have resisted the "total automation"
dictated by material advantages and also that there are some who still
admire work done by individual artistry and skill.

A few days after this visit came a letter from Mr. Kenneth O. Dills asking me to pay the Charles Krug vinery at Napa Valley a visit. This invitation I also owed to Joseph Henry Jackson's recommendation. Of course I was delighted at the opportunity, but a little worried as to how I could get there, as I do not drive a car. Besides, I am no expert on the subject of wine. However, I went to discuss the matter with my "screwy brother" Professor Shih-hsiang Chen of the University of California, who shares delight in the wine-cups with our famous poet, Li Po of the T'ang Dynasty. He was quite excited about the visit, and suggested asking Professor Otto and Annya Menchen to go with us. On the appointed morning I went over to Berkeley and thought at first I must have gone to the wrong address when I saw a brand-new car sitting outside my screwy brother's shack instead of the familiar friend, the ten-year-old jalopy. He explained that he did not think his jalopy could take us such a long distance and that its unusual appearance might cause some difficulty in gaining admission to the vineyard. He wanted to give a good impression for my sake. But he said with a laugh that he had been rebuked by the University-gate police when he drove the new car inside the campus. "Oh, no, no, that car does not suit you. You look more impressive in your friendly jalopy"!

Later Shih-hsiang showed me the following poem which he had written "Fare Thee Well, My Dear Jalopy":

為僭吥子御風行
肯捨跎駘買玉驄
共畔九洲晚千罘
浮雲澈慮志猶同

Riding the wind to go about in the
company of The Silent Traveller,
I give up my lamed horse for a jade-like steed.
Together we glance over the numerous lands
and myriad scenes of life;
Wealth and fame have no meaning for either of us.

I do not usually lament the past, but when I think of the jalopy in which I rode with my friend many a time and for hundreds of miles, I cannot help feeling sad that I shall not see it any more.

We exchanged greetings with the Menchens and were soon on our way to Napa Valley. Both Otto and Annya Menchen came from Vienna. Otto has been teaching Far Eastern archaeology and art at the University of California for many years, while Annya, a pupil of the famous Dr. Freud, is a noted psychiatrist in the Bay Area. They are great story-tellers and the best companions one could have for a long journey. While Shih-hsiang displayed his unconcealed pride in driving his new car, we were entertained by anecdotes from Otto and Annya in turn. One of Annya's stories impressed me greatly. It was about a Polish professor formerly in the University of California, who remained obstinately Polish till his last days. Nothing was as good as what he had known in Poland. Once as he was watching the sunset over San Francisco, he remarked to his friends that it made him think of Poland. His friends, who were exclaiming enthusiastically over the beautiful scene were surprised and asked him why. "Simply because it it so different from a Polish sunset," was his reply! He was a good talker and could beat almost everyone at Berkeley if an argument started. For the four of us in the car, none of whom had been born in America, Annya mimicked the stubborn attitude of the Polish professor being so proud of his Polish birth, and caused much laughter. But who is not like him? I asked myself. I have travelled in many countries during the past twenty-odd years and a typical attitude which I have encountered everywhere is the pride in the beautiful scenery and lovely attributes of the place where one was born and bred. The English and Scots are known to the world as always being English and Scots. So are the French, the Irish, the Indians, the Japanese, the Austrians, the Chinese.

... This seems to me a deep-rooted human instinct. But will it remain so in the restless, mobile sort of life we live nowadays? Again, in view of the mingling of so many different races in the big cities of the world today, can there continue to be many people like the Polish professor, so strictly national in outlook? I hope there will still be some, or life would be much less interesting.

Presently we reached the town of Sonoma. The hot, bright sun lit up the red-tiled roofs of the Spanish-styled houses, and made them positively glow. Not a leaf of the many tall palm trees, which bore clusters of coconuts high up, showed the slightest movement. They were all pointing upwards and each led my eyes to the sky far above and spotlessly blue. Between the sky and earth I felt baked. When I saw two ladies sitting on a long balcony fanning themselves incessantly I almost imagined that I had become a piece of cooked yam. Sonoma has a typical Spanish setting and it is this type of man-decorated landscape that contributes to make California so different from other States.

Sonoma Town Hall

Following the directions given to us we were soon on our way again, stopping only once at a little town near a lovely, rustic old creek, where we had a cold drink. I explored a little distance along the creek, which was much more European in aspect than American. There was an unusual feeling in the air of a peaceful countryside. On reaching the vineyard, we were met at the entrance by Kenneth O. Dills, Robert Mondavi and Paul Stern with welcoming smiles. At first we had a look round the vineyards and I exchanged a word or two with one of the gardeners, who seemed to be enjoying his work. All the vine plants were neatly trimmed, and I was told that the Californian climate and the fertile soil of the Napa Valley helped them to grow even more vigorously than vines in the south of France. Then we were led into one of the main buildings known as the Oak Room. Robert Mondavi explained that the Oak Room was the original carriage house and stable built by the founder of the Charles Krug winery in 1881. Charles Krug, a Prussian, came to San Francisco in 1865 at the age of thirty-three with the same idea as many others, the hope of making a great fortune in gold. However, he did not go digging but engaged in several enterprises, including gold-refining. Gradually his mind turned to the fertile soil. Perhaps he could strike gold in a vineyard? He did. In 1858 he used a small cider press which he made himself and which was shown to us, to produce the first wine in Napa Valley. The first winery Krug built in 1861 was destroyed by fire; then he built another in 1874 and again in 1881, together with the Oak Room, which is now one of the historical landmarks of California. Its exterior has been well preserved by Krug's successors, C. Mondavi and Sons, but it now serves as a shell for a vast reinforced concrete storage area protecting fine vintages aging in barrels and bottles. Our noses began to complain of being tantalized. Fortunately we were then led to a small room where there were numerous big bottles full of different kinds of wine for us to taste. Otto's eyes opened wide and Shih-hsiang's mouth fell open too. Otto displayed his European upbringing by pronouncing the names of various German and French wines; while Shih-hsiang felt relieved that Li Po was no longer alive. The name Li Po suddenly came into my head and so did his famous poem, which I translate roughly as follows:

處世若大夢
胡為勞其生
所以終日醉
頹然臥前楹
覺來眄庭前
一鳥花間鳴
借問此何時
春風語流鶯
感之欲歎息
對酒還自傾
浩歌待明月
曲盡已忘情

Life in this world is but a great dream;
Why should we spend it in toil?
So I shall stay tipsy all the day long,
Lying in a daze on the front porch.
When I wake and gaze at the courtyard before me,
In the midst of the flowers a bird is singing!
May I ask, what season is it now?

The Spring wind is chattering with the gliding oriole.
Touched by the scene I feel like sighing;
I turn to the wine and pour myself another cupful.
Singing lustily I wait for the bright moon:
By the end of the song I have quite forgotten my emotion.

Annya, unlike Otto and Shih-hsiang, has only a mild taste for wine. I told her that one of the best known wine-tasters in the United States, Mr. Charles Codman of Boston, said, "There is really nothing scientific to wine-tasting. It is all a matter of memory. The whole secret is being able to remember how a previous wine tasted. There are established tastes to certain wines, and if there is a difference, this change must be noted." Annya said with a smile that she has not a good memory, but I for one have never used my memory for wine. However, I have a great attachment for the vine plant and its grapes, as its creeping stems with their intriguing patterns suit my brush-work.

When we were about to get into the car for our return journey, three huge cases of wine were given to us to take home. Otto and Shih-hsiang wanted to show their great appreciation of Charles Krug's wine which they had just tasted, and ordered four more cases of various wines, each case bigger than the others. A problem arose as to how we four were going to sit in the car; finally I became the guardian of the wines in the back seat.

Each of us had been hearing from within a constant call for food. Shih-hsiang drove to a well-shaded spot under a huge tree. Annya carefully spread out the tablecloth and her well-prepared foods for the picnic. This was Annya's day; she is always busy with her work and very seldom has a chance to go out. Just as we began to eat, an elderly gentleman shouted at us from a little distance away. We could not make out his remarks but thought that perhaps he did not like us trespassing on his property. However, since there was no notice to be seen, we ignored his shouting and went on eating our lunch. Otto and Shih-hsiang clinked their glasses repeatedly: I was a little more abstemious. I have read that Padre Junipero Serra who established the Mission San Diego in 1760 and planted wine grapes there, discovered that Californian soil was specially good for wine-growing. The vines the Mission Fathers planted were descendants of the Spanish wine grapes. Later Jean Louis Vignes, a Frenchman from the wine-famed Bordeaux district of France, realized that he could produce finer wines with choicer grapes from Europe. He started to import French grapes into California. Then Agoston Harazthy, a Hungarian nobleman, brought some hundred thousand vines to California; he has since been called the father of California's viniculture.

One summer, Walter and Jane Whitehill and I spent a few days at our mutual friends', Betsy and Bill Tyler's château at Antigny, Côte d'Or, France. We had a drive through the countryside of Burgundy. On the way Bill remarked: "Near the end of the nineteenth century a vine disease called *Phylloxera* spread through France, and many vineyards gradually perished. It was discovered that the Californian vines, which had been brought from France, were immune against this particular disease, and so, gradually, the vineyards of France were replaced by the hardy stock from the new world. And the magic is that the soil and climate in France caused them to produce far better wine than they did in California! Like man, Nature's product comes from a host of circumstances, in origin, in particular condition, and in treatment. Thus the simple universality of life is as complicated as are the laws that determine the nature and the role of the atom." Bill Tyler is a scholar of medieval art and has been in the American diplomatic service in Europe for years. I particularly enjoy his philosophical outlook on life.

The tree with its wide-stretching branches and masses of leaves that shaded us well now looked a little weary, for the sun had never left it for a moment. Its leaves seemed to cluster in big drops or hazy balls. I could not see very far beyond where Otto and Shih-hsiang sat back to back, more silent than I had ever known them. Well-fed and wined, none of us cared even if the Heavens should suddenly fall on us. It was Annya who started to collect the spoons, forks and the rest into baskets again and who thought we should make a move. By and by we gathered up our strength and climbed into the car. To Shih-hsiang's greatest surprise—and ours too—the car refused to move. Shih-hsiang tried again and again but it would not budge. "The car is drunk," declared Shih-hsiang. We all got out and thought something had to be done with the cases of wine. Then we all tried to give the car a push until we realised that it was deeply sunk in the heavy soil. We now understood why that elderly gentleman had shouted at us. We felt quite ashamed. Since the only house in the neighborhood was the one which he had entered, Otto and I plucked up courage and went to borrow a spade and some planks in order to raise the car out of the mud. He gave them to us with a smile but without a word. All our efforts still achieved nothing, and we had to telephone the A.A.A. for help. Almost an hour slipped by before the A.A.A. truck arrived to pull Shih-hsiang's pride out of the mud at last.

The car was now in good form again and we were all in the highest spirits. Otto remembered having seen an Italian-style Castle not far from where we were and suggested having a look at it. Unfortunately he did not remember its name nor the exact road, but he felt pretty sure of the direction, so he guided Shih-hsiang up a hill. After a while the car reached a point where no pathway of any description was visible: we had to find our way down somehow. The road turned out to be a newly paved one of red sand, not yet set hard. Though Shih-

"The car is drunk."

hsiang had all along displayed pride in driving his new car, he now
seemed a little scared, for the downward journey was a long succession
of irregular zigzag curves and rather slippery when the sand moved.
We knew he was an old hand at driving and were sure of our safety.
Then we tried another approach but this time were confronted by
some impassible rocks. Otto had great faith in his memory and just did
not like to give up. Although we had already spent some time in fruit-
less wanderings, we went on along narrow pathways through bushes
and behind trees. I asked Otto why an Italian Castle had been built in
this part of the earth and not a Spanish one. He supposed that in the
early days Italians immigrated here and made their fortunes, like many
other Europeans. At last, Shih-hsiang sighed and said that he was
beginning to feel quite dizzy from going up and down hills, and that
we should have to call off the search.

After the excitement of trying in vain to see a castle in California we
all sank into silence on our way back to Berkeley. But my mind
wandered off to Italy. I once read a description by Professor C. T. G.
Formilli of how he and a friend went to explore the oldest castle in
Val d'Aosta. Though they knew its exact location, it was in a very

inaccessible spot. Having struggled on for six hours of hard climbing, they eventually found themselves in a large square leading to a small but well defended doorway in the massive walls of the back of the castle. Professor Formilli and his friend had been more fortunate than us four.

He tells a good story about this ancient Italian castle. On a rainy night in 1450, came a great man of the time, Guido de Fessigny, President of the Senate of Chambéry, at the invitation of his relation, the Count of Montmayeur, the owner of the castle, for a great celebration with a sumptuous feast in order to make up their little quarrel during which the Senate of Chambéry had decided a law-suit against the Count. Guido de Fessigny, a huge, upright man, rode up to the door in pouring rain. There was no light in any window and the whole square was deserted and pitch-dark. He thought he had come on the wrong day and was about to ride home when suddenly the doors flung wide open, to reveal the smiling face of the Count himself. He apologized profoundly for the delay and explained that the other guests had declined the invitation owing to the bad weather. He expressed great joy at seeing the President defying Nature's challenge. The table was loaded with choicest food and wine. The host and his sole guest exchanged friendly and courteous conversation. After the first glass of rare wine and when the butler had left the room, the atmosphere suddenly became tense and the candles were blown out by the wind as a door swayed open. The host turned to his guest and asked in a flat and solemn voice if he was a good Christian. The answer was in the affirmative, but why should he be asked such a question? The Count then told him to look behind him, whereupon the guest saw with horror through the door of the adjoining room, a wooden block, draped in black cloth, and an enormous axe in the hand of a giant executioner surrounded by twelve old monks chanting the prayers for departing souls. The President thought it was a joke, but the Count said that he had had to pay for the loss of his law-suit the sum of one hundred thousand *lire*. He added that the guest's last moment had come. At the Count's signal the victim's head rolled on the floor, while the monks chanted their prayers and disappeared. The Count calmly wrapped the head in a leather bag and made it his pillow for the night.

Next morning he took the leather bag with him and rode to the City Council Chamber and, declaring that he had brought an important document concerning his law-suit, threw the leather bag down for them to examine. By the time the horrible contents of the bag had been disclosed, the Count was already far away, and had crossed the border into France before he could be apprehended. He was said to have lived there quietly until his brutal deed was forgotten. Years later, after death had taken each of the other councillors in the law-suit, the Count returned in great state to his old castle to end his days without disturbance.

This was a story from fifteenth-century Italy; I know many similar tales in the early history of China. Perhaps, after all, we were lucky not to have found the Italian Castle in Napa Valley. Certainly we were all glad to reach home. The cases of wine were removed from the car, and we four finished another bottle. By then I was actually drunk and did not remember the Count any more.

XXII

Darting Surprisingly

I HOPE Olive Cowell will not mind my using the word "darting" to describe our various trips to the outlying districts of San Francisco Bay. The trips were made in a *surprisingly* short time and could only have been accomplished by "darting."

I lived in China for the first thirty years of my life, but I spent such a sheltered childhood that it was only after I entered College in Nanking that I began to distinguish one type of person from another. I then only had a little more than ten years to study such differences among all the people of my own country. But what a variety and what a countless number of types, though we each have the same pair of lips, eyes, and ears. Not all my fellow countrymen are inscrutable and none of them really wears an emotionless face! Then since 1933 I have lived in Europe and America and have constantly encountered new types of people from all corners of the globe. None of them all has so quick and lively a mind as Olive.

In August, 1953, I met her and her husband, Harry Cowell, who was then ninety years of age, in their house not far from Mount Davidson. I was taken there by our mutual friend, Shih-hsiang Chen, who came to know them through Mr. Cowell's son Henry Cowell, who has been regarded a striking musical pioneer and *enfant terrible* for over fifty years and has incorporated many tunes from other countries such as India, Japan, Indonesia, and China into his work. On reaching the Cowell's house the door flew wide open and two long, slender arms spread like parting waves to embrace our friend in hearty welcome. Those arms were Olive's. She is tall and slim and looked even taller in a new, stiff purplish linen gown. She at once unfastened some pins and spread open part of the gown to show us that it was a long piece of freshly-bought Irish linen, which she had made into a sort of Indian

304

The Berkeley Campus at noontime.

sari specially for the occasion. There was much merriment in the big living room. It was also of Olive's making.

I was then taken over to sit by Mr. Harry Cowell for a quiet talk. He had been born in Dublin and knew that I had lived there for a while. He had come to San Francisco before the beginning of the present century and told me many anecdotes about the city before the earthquake and immediately after it. He said that he landed in California from Ireland as a young lad ready for anything that came his way. He walked everywhere and tried everything. He used to sing old Irish songs, which perhaps explains the musical gifts of his son. He even drove the cable-cars up and down Nob Hill when they first started. Smilingly he said that he had made a success of every undertaking. "Of all your successes," I suggested, "none can have been as great as securing Olive for a wife." He grinned appreciatively. We became good friends, and each time Olive took me on a trip, she said how sorry Harry was that he could not come along with us. Once she gave me a sheet of paper, on which were the following words:

To the Golden-Voiced Silent Traveller
        To Chiang Yee, charming host,
        Travelling from coast to coast,
        Who guests galore can boast.
        I, thinking, drink this toast:
        He who gives most
        Of his fine heart,
        Of his fine art,
        His central part,
        Lives best, lives most,
        Till he gives up his ghost;
        Then still he lives,
        Despite the chilling grave,
        The joy he, living, gave.
        With my small voice I sing
        The immortality,
        Albeit relative,
        Of painting, poetry,
        And their fair fadeless spring
        In beauty blossoming.
        They live millennia,

Moonlight scene from Telegraph Hill.

Outlive Methuselah,
Continue still they live,
To give joy, smiling, give.

(From Harry Cowell, The Silent Traveller's grateful guest.)

Olive told me that this was written a few days before Harry passed away on January 19th, 1954. I blush to expose these words about myself, for I do not deserve them. But I quote them here in order to pay my homage to Harry, my good Irish friend. I only regret that I was born a little too late to have wandered round with him all over the Bay area on foot. What fun it would have been!

Olive and I spent four afternoons together on rather long trips. She was then Professor of Political Science at the San Francisco State College and had to teach and work in the mornings. Before dusk she always darted back to Harry and the household cares. In view of all this and other social activities, it was most kind of her to spare the time to show me round. I was introduced to her after I had already explored San Francisco in my own way, wherever my legs could carry me, so she suggested trips outside the city.

The first arrangement was that she would meet me at the Mountain House half way up Mount Tamalpais at noon, after I had spent the night there in order to see the sunrise. She arrived punctually, and wasted no time in asking what I had been doing up the mountain the whole morning after the sun had risen. No sooner had I gobbled up a piece of sandwich than we were darting down the slope into Marin County. The panorama of the distant hills, some brown, some bright yellow and some of purple and blue hue, as they always are in the summer months, was most interesting to look at, but they flashed past my eyes, one section after another, as if I were watching a cinemascope. Our car sped on very fast; sometimes I felt that I was in a boat on the high seas, one moment on the top of a tall wave and next moment deep down in the trough. My friend intended me to meet a famous ceramic artist without losing any time. We passed a riverside where masses of people were vacationing with canoes and colored sunshades. I was informed that it was Russian River, where the Russians used to trap otters for their furs. Immediately afterwards we were driving steeply uphill again. This time the road wound spirally upwards and was only wide enough for two cars to pass with some difficulty. At each bend I thought our car would go over the edge, instead it made a quick turn and we continued climbing. My friend took pride in her dexterous steering and grinned at me when she pulled the car around. At long last we reached the house, but to our disappointment could not get in. Apparently the artist was away and there was no means of telling when she would be back. I peeped through the cracks of the gate and saw that the central garden was decorated with different ceramics of fine taste and modern design. There was nothing we could do but return to the city. All the way back my friend's words rolled on faster than our car. She had much to say about the Bay area and had strong opinions on how to see San Francisco at its best. But I was quite satisfied with my new experience and with our general survey outside the Bay. Who was not? Olive.

A second trip was arranged to make up for the imperfection of the first. I should see a most enchanting spot outside San Francisco Bay, said Olive. Off we went. Usually when I was driven through the Golden Gate Bridge I never failed to observe closely the rolling fog which either covered up the base of the towers or billowed against our car and slowed it down; but this time I did not and could not, for I did not even realize that we had passed it until we were on the Manzanita-Bolinas Road. At Stinson Beach we got out for a walk. The fine sand was piled up deep enough to bury my shoes and feet up to the ankles at every step and I enjoyed our slow progress pulling out each foot in turn, after the fast pace of the car. Only a handful of people were around and no one was in the water, for the ocean wind was quite strong. The liveliness and the amazing power of the wind can best be seen in its effects: I saw myriads of thick-foliaged willow branches swaying together towards the land. A willow-lined beach was a new sight for me. It was also the first time that I had seen willows covered with sand; they did not look as fresh and gentle as they usually do swaying beside a stream or river in the spring breeze. What a strange idea to have planted them beside a beach! My friend remarked that we must not linger too long, so we drove on again and in a couple of minutes we were standing on the rocky cliff of Bolinas facing a tranquil lagoon.

A moment ago we had been on an open beach facing the Pacific Ocean, over whose surface the invisible wind rushed and roared. Now the surface of the lagoon looked like a sheet of glass reflecting almost everything clearly, so that from high above, I saw the fine azure blue sky surrounded by short upside-down trees and cliffs. There is a long narrow strip of land that stretches from Stinson Beach, almost joining the rocky bottom of the cliff where I was standing. The ocean waves never manage to enter the lagoon. It looked like a lake and yet not quite. Only two small trees grew on that long narrow stretch of land. Perhaps they were big trees but they looked small from where I stood on the higher ground. They must have been battered heavily by the ocean wind at times, yet they looked healthy and quite striking between the two waters, one side so calm and the other side so turbulent. My eyes rested for a good while on an unusually bright, fresh patch of color—spring-like green or more yellowish than green—in the middle of the narrow land behind the trees. There must have been water there —perhaps, a marshy patch where grass could still grow freshly. During the summer months, particularly in August, I was informed, the grass on the hills all turns brown and orange. Among all the browns and oranges, and the dark-green patches of trees, this fresh young yellowish green was conspicuous and delightful. The village of Bolinas, though close to the ocean, does not face it openly like Stinson Beach. The prominent rock of Duxbury Point seems to break the ocean wind before it can reach Bolinas. Thus the few houses on Bolinas are sheltered and secure and have lovely cottage roses growing on their fences. It struck me as a likable spot for retirement.

When Olive came back from wandering among the houses, I said I wished I could have a walk on the strip of narrow land down below. "No time for that," she replied, "I have many other places to show you." Soon we were on the move again. "Last time we went down, down," said Olive with a wide grin, turning to me; "this time we are going up, up. I want you to see how beautiful it is all the way up Mount Tamalpais along the coastal line." I soon realized that I was on a swaying ship again. Nevertheless, I kept turning my head to look back where we had come from; there lay the coast and the uneven land with the group of trees scattered on an enormous carpet of camel's-hair.

Then I looked forward again and the shore line of San Francisco peninsula was clearly in sight, but the Golden Gate Bridge and Cliff House were hidden behind Mount Tamalpais. We were travelling on Mount Tamalpais Ridge Crest Road, which ran all along the crest of the hills to the State Park. A small group of tall trees clung together with their dark-green foliage, showing part of their whitish trunks against the background of blurred, camel's-hair-carpet-covered hills, as if they were cut out of paper. These paper-cut trees fascinated me and it was altogether a very different landscape from any I know in China, Europe and the New England States. This was California in summer. All of a sudden my head began to swing round violently as if my neck had turned into a copper-wire screw: Our car had made a quick turn to the left, and was diving steeply downhill again. "You don't want to see Mount Tamalpais State Park again," said Olive laughingly, "you have been there many times. I want to show you some beautiful mountain lakes—those enchanting waters high up the hillside." The noise of our wheels grating over pebbles on the not-so-well paved road, little used by motorists, filled my ears. Only my weight kept the car from bouncing right up in the air at times. Then, all of a sudden, we had drawn up by the side of Phoenix Lake. I moved round the edge and saw not a ripple, not even one tiny insect to cause a disturbance on the water surface. The whole lake is shaped like a capital "L." No big trees grow round it. It must be deep, and its waters could never be painted so evenly dark-blue by any mortal artist. It is surrounded by brownish yellow sandy earth and grass. "Why was it called Phoenix?" I asked. "Was it after a European phoenix symbolizing resurrection? Or a Chinese phoenix which only appears when there is great peace over the human world?" "Oh never mind about that!" remarked my friend.

The next time we got out of the car was at Lake Lagunitas, which is joined by a long narrow stream to Alpine Lake. I did not dare suggest walking round Alpine Lake, but I managed to go across the narrow cemented bridge, built over the stream near the end of Lake Lagunitas. A few oil-barrels standing by some machinery suggested that a dam was being made there. A workman in muddy blue jeans walked ahead of me. A number of strange-looking trees which I could not name, growing from a hillock on the other side, lent some green color to the scene, but the atmosphere was not as peaceful as at the "L" lake. All the same, Olive was beaming all the while. Off we went again and soon entered a shady avenue of royal palms with many beautiful houses and gardens full of flowers on both sides. This was the town of Fairfax, through which our car passed rather slowly, for my friend wanted me to have a bird's-eye view of the place before we darted through the towns of Ross, Kentfield, Corte Madera, Alto, Sausalito, and then back to Lake Street where I was staying. There was no time to express my gratitude as we quickly made arrangements for an outing another day. The memory of the town of Fairfax returned to my mind again and again; it is indeed a pleasant place to live. Who had told me the story of Charley "The Baron" Fairfax, which I recorded somewhere before? Not Olive!

The date for the third trip arrived. I was whisked through Golden Gate Bridge, Sausalito, and then San Geronimo, the name of which I read on a signpost after a fast smooth run over the Sir Francis Drake Highway. We got out in the shade of a large group of trees, mostly eucalyptus, in Samuel P. Taylor State Park, for my friend saw a number of people in blue jeans digging hard in the creek. A new find of gold? No, it was the driest summer California had ever experienced, one of the workers told Olive. There used to be some water, though not much, in the creek, but this summer they had to dig for it. We could not stay long, for there was something my friend wanted me to see, something extraordinary, something she thought I had never seen before. So on we went along the inland part of Sir Francis Drake Highway. After Point Reyes I saw a lovely stretch of water, so tranquil-looking in between hill-ridges, with a good many sailing-boats and yachts anchored here and there. Both banks were quite green, unlike the brownish yellow landscape we had just passed. "That is Inverness," was the information I got, still inside the car. After we had driven for another ten minutes or so we got out to walk in fields full of long grass with tall trees on the higher ground. I followed my friend down and down to the edge of the hillside from which I could see water far below. "Look, here is the beautiful Spanish moss tree," called Olive, pointing to my right, "How beautiful it looks; I don't think you have seen any tree as beautiful as this. China must have that kind of tree; I have seen

Chinese pictures with trees rather like it." "Well, how do you know that I haven't seen this kind of tree then?" I teased her. "Indeed, it is beautiful. What did you say it was called?" My friend did not hear what I said, for she had strolled away leaving me alone to admire the Spanish moss tree. The tree was very big and rugged with wide spreading branches, looking as if it had been standing there for hundreds of years like an old English oak, but the shape of the leaves was new to me. The moss hung softly, very softly like a mass of long silk threads clustered together all along the branches, as if taking the place of the actual leaves of the tree. The ocean wind at this rather sheltered corner was no more than a breeze which swayed the tassels of moss hither and thither like young branches of weeping willow. Perhaps it was this which made the Spanish moss tree resemble the willows in Chinese paintings. It was true I had never seen a tree with Spanish moss attached to it before. It occured to me that this Spanish moss was a proof of the great Chinese philosopher, Lao Tzu's saying: "Existence grows out of non-existence." The sea-fog is purely vapour of minute water-particles loosely held together, having no real substance after dispersal or evaporation. Yet when it came into contact with this huge tree, it seemed to have materialized and left something behind, which continued to grow and grow into moss, short and long at random. All the moss that hung along the tree branches looked soft and young in its yellow-green color with a slightly whitish powdery surface, as if it would fly away at a touch. But it grew on such a strong, rugged, old tree. In other words, the young, the old, the weak and the strong, co-existed most happily. The sight gave me deep pleasure.

Presently we began to walk through a field of long grass. All along here the land was green, with trees and grass, and with rocks projecting here and there, not unlike the Scottish highland country round Inverness, where I once walked from Fort William through Glencoe. An Inverness Scot, James Black, had settled here in 1832, hence the name of the nearby town, founded in 1908. We did not follow Sir Francis Drake's Highway to the land's end; we had been trying to get a glimpse of the head waters of Drake's Estero—the water flows inland there to become a big lake in a similar manner to Bolinas Lagoon—and cannot be seen in full from the lower ground. We then moved along by the white-faced bluffs of Drake's Bay to Big Rock Point. The name is most appropriate. There are many rocks scattered or grouped, all the way, but the rocks at Big Rock Point are really big. A good many of them lie out along the shore in disorderly fashion, yet they seem to have an order of their own. They do not confuse their individual characteristics, yet they blend together in harmony. Each stands on its own feet to struggle against any odds that may come to it. My friend always enjoyed herself in her own way; I managed to walk on a few big rocks which I could reach. I looked out over the smooth expanse that stretched before my eyes to the horizon without any obstruction. How could a wide and vast ocean be so calm and gentle and flat? But something was moving slowly from afar. Not only one but a number of them in a row, as if marching in goose-step. They did not seem in a hurry. By and by they crept up to me and spread and stretched wide; then in a moment all disappeared in a whispering musical chorus. The waves receded. I looked down below and saw that the water surrounding the rocks was clear, moving forward and backward, patting gently the feet of the rocks and darting gaily over some brightly colored pebbles; I even saw a few fish swimming to the shallower water in order to show me their dexterity. Many tiny plants with small flowers and some objects that looked like living creatures stuck to the rocks were interesting to inspect. All of a sudden, to my amazement the scene changed to a sublime and chaotic uproar for a moment—masses of big waves rushed towards me in quick movement, rolling and foaming and finally dashing their spray over the rocks and also over my face. I had to run back inland. My friend did the same. The next moment, it was all as calm and gentle as before. On this shore I saw many a beautiful, many a wild and many an animated spectacle as well.

Did Sir Francis Drake witness all this just as I did? Am I, a Chinese, so very different from an Englishman? His object in being here was different from mine anyway. It is said that Drake's company, on June 17, 1579, took refuge here in the *Golden Hind.* It had sailed away from England two years previously and had been troubled by tempest, impenetrable fog and bitter cold before finding shelter in the bay at Estero or Creek which now bear Drake's name. The ship stayed for nearly six weeks and many of his men went ashore to explore the land,

while the Californian Indians living there at the time gathered round
to watch them in awe. It is even somewhere recorded that one of the
Indian chieftains, dressed in coney and other skins, followed by his
retinue of tall and warlike men, begged Drake to take their province
and kingdom into his hand and become their king. Had he been a
Scotsman or an Irishman he might have accepted the offer! The
Golden Hind lay at anchor there for six weeks, during which time
there must have been many fine days like this delicious afternoon of
bright sunshine, light summer air and almost cloudless sky which we
were enjoying. Some of the men must have wandered a little farther
to have a look at the land southward where the San Francisco peninsula
lies. Why didn't they sail farther southward after six weeks of recuper-
ating and reconditioning the ship? I do not understand. Many people
have written that San Francisco was not sighted by Drake's company,
the ship being turned away by the heavy fog which had shrouded the
entrance to the harbor. This statement should be modified to say that
Drake and his men must have seen the peninsula from a distance but
for one reason or another did not approach it, though they stayed
nearly six weeks in its neighbourhood. I chuckle to myself at playing
amateur-historian. Who made me so historically-minded? Olive.

"You cannot go away from San Francisco," said Olive, "without
seeing the Valley of the Moon!" So the fourth trip was arranged. Shih-
hsiang Chen joined us. He took the wheel this time and they both had
a great deal to discuss about the route, while I looked aimlessly through
the car windows. Though speeding along on a well-paved road I
managed to trace quite a number of landmarks on the way to Sonoma,
as I had once gone with Shih-hsiang and the Menchens to Napa Valley.
This time we did not make a right turn, but made straight for Glen
Ellen. On the way the Vallejo home, the Boyes Hot Springs and the
Fetters Hot Springs were pointed out to me from the distance. It is
said that the early Californian Indians knew the health-giving proper-
ties of the Hot sulphur Springs. I was also told that there was a place,
not far from Sonoma, where a large number of gigantic petrified redwoods were to be found. We could not go to see either the springs or
the redwoods, for we had come solely to see the Valley of the Moon;
not the whole valley, nor even all the ranch-houses, but only the one

that Jack London built for himself and from which he made the name of the Valley of the Moon known to the world.

In Sonoma the sunshine seemed much brighter and hotter as it shone on the red roofs of the Spanish-Moorish styled houses with their whitewashed walls, while the tall royal palms stood stiffly upright with their umbrella-like leaves sticking out high at the top of the trunk, motionless in the still air. Many prickly opunita cacti growing by the walls and in the yards suggested a tropical temperature. Now, at Glen Ellen, not at all far from Sonoma, the scene changed into quite soft rolling wooded hills of a dark green summer color, with a hazy blue hue over them all—and a fresh yet delicate verdure in the mossy dells. No wonder the Spanish and Mexicans had long made use of the valley for cattle-farming. And the Russians, too, roamed nearby to hunt and trap sea-otters. Some historians even suggest that Sir Francis Drake, in 1579, led a small group of his men over the mountain ranges from the Valley of the Moon. Actually the name "Valley of the Moon" or "Valley of Many Moons" is the translation of the Indian name "Sono-ma." I do not think the Indians meant the "Valley of Many Moons," for if I understand correctly many Indian expressions are quite similar to the Chinese; if so, "Many moons" means "many months." So Jack London rightly used the title "The Valley of the Moon" for one of his books. He built a ranch in Glen Ellen and eventually caused the separation of the "Valley of the Moon" from the town of Sonoma. It is said that the moon shines over the Valley almost every night.

After entering ranch property we expected to be stopped and told whether we might have a look round, but no one appeared. We strolled under the shade of big trees and along under the eaves of the bungalow peeping through the window and seeing a number of books lying on a desk. Later we came to a quarter where only the lower parts of some white walls remained, with much lush grass growing inside and many tall, wide-spreading trees standing outside. "This must be the remains of 'Wolf House' that Jack London built, but which was burnt down six weeks before it was to be completed," said Olive, "He never lived in it."

Shih-hsiang felt thirsty but could not find a water tap. We followed our friend to another row of bungalows, where someone came out to give us each a glass of water. A conversation immediately started. This man told Olive that Mrs. Jack London was still about for a short while each day, though in failing health at nearly eighty and desiring to see no visitors, which was also the doctor's order. He himself had been working on the ranch for a number of years. He pointed out to us a good few cattle standing under the shade of the trees, for the sun was high up in the middle of the sky and it was very hot. No wind stirred. We ourselves even refrained from moving for the moment. It was peaceful all right, but there was too much warmth in the air and it made us sweat. So our minds were not at peace—at least mine was not.

I had imagined Jack London as a very active person, adventurous and forceful, and the Valley did not seem suited to his character. How did he come to choose it for his home? Curiously enough Jack London's name became known to me when I was a college student in China some forty years ago. I went with two of my classmates to see a silent movie about the Russo-Japanese war and the Yellow Fever. It started with a scene on board ship in which a sailor was fighting back against a group of his fellow-sailors who were bullying him; he was trying to do some writing under difficult conditions in crowded living quarters. This sailor, I was told at the time, was Jack London. I was not studying western literature, so his name meant nothing to me. Indeed I forgot all about him for many years until one day I went with a friend to the little Ina Coolbrith Park and was informed how great a poetess she had been, how many noted literary personalities of the time she had known and how much she had encouraged, guided and inspired Jack London to read and write, when she was librarian of the Oakland Public Library. Now Jack London reappeared in my imagination as a local, born and bred near San Francisco Bay. He was born in 1876 and met Ina Coolbrith for the first time when he was twelve. Encouraged by the poetess, he became a self-made writer; his parents were too poor to be able to give him a good education. I was also told that in Oakland there is a First-and-Last-Chance-Saloon, where an unpainted wooden shack was kindly lent by the barkeeper to Jack London to study and write in when he was a budding author. He was still in his teens when his first works were published. I began to read some of his books, including his short stories. From the little I read, I see him as talented and determined, full of imaginative power and forceful ideas but very self-centered. In his young days San Francisco was at the height of her bonanza period when the contrast between rich and poor was far too great. Gold was thrown about and scattered like dust; yet there was some one with too little to eat, and no place to sit down to read and write. Some of the many unusual, and almost unbelievable events of those days—killing, robbing and dueling—are on record, but there must be many happenings we know nothing about. All these things may have imprinted themselves on the minds of people like Jack London, who had imagination and talent and independence of thought. In Europe and Asia many a great man and writer has had a humble start and some even had nothing to eat at times, but they showed no grudge against the ostentation and squanderings of the nobility. But in San Francisco none had much to start with and were no better by birth than he. This is probably why Jack London was so bitter against life in his writings. His active writing years were about twenty altogether, for he died in 1916. When he made money from his books, he wanted to live like the speculators who made fortunes from the gold and silver mines, spending easily, giving easily, possessing a yacht and building a castle. His deep hatred against life seems to have been already formed in the years when he began to visit Ina Coolbrith for inspiration. If he lived nowadays, I am not sure if he would have become so popular. But at that time he had become a world literary figure by the age of thirty. His advocacy of socialism was a great help in spreading his hatred of current conditions. With such an active mind and positive program in his head, he yet decided to return to San Francisco to build Wolf House in the Valley of the Moon at the age of thirty-three or thereabouts. As he had to force himself to write a thousand words every morning to get money with which to pay his debts, could he really feel settled at that time? I wondered. That was why I felt so little peace in the air of the place, although my friends were conversing happily. They did not realize what had been going on in my head even after we came back. Nevertheless, it was a memorable afternoon for me.

Since that afternoon I have thought often about what it is that will make a book last so that it will be read again and again over many years.

It is not merely the way a story is presented, something more is needed. This "something more" is the wholeness of life reflected as in a mirror; though only one side of life may be described, yet one must feel that the other side exists. Merely attacking the worse side of life falls into the category of propaganda or preaching. It cannot last. Take Goldsmith's *An Eastern Tale,* for instance; if only Asem the Man-hater had kept on brooding till death overtook him without the Genius to show him the consequences of what he had neglected it would not be reprinted now for us to read. In Jack London's story *The Chinago,* Ah Cho, Chung Ga, Ah San, and Ah Chow were merely ignorant gamblers; but in Bret Harte's *Heathen Chinee* Ah Sin had a reason for cheating. Therefore, the latter lives while the former is seldom read nowadays. The prophecy in Jack London's *The Unparalleled Invasion,* about China from 1976 till 1987, seems to have betrayed his own advocacy of socialism. Indeed how difficult it is to create a literary work of art, which must be a mirror of the wholeness of life, when the writer is self-centered! Life has two sides, bitter and sweet. Only through a clear look at the bitter side can we enjoy the sweet side fully. It was a pity that Jack London took to alcohol and obscured for himself the sweeter side of life which he had missed in his younger days. I still cannot understand why he should have come to build a castle in the Valley of the Moon when he was thirty-three—so young?

From these four different trips I learnt more about San Francisco and about life too. Whom should I thank most? Olive!

XXIII

Imitating Uproariously

T HOUGH about two hundred miles away, Yosemite supplies fresh water for the daily needs of San Franciscans. How then can I leave it without mention? It was because I came to see San Francisco that I also came to know Yosemite and love it. .

I have paid three visits so far to this lovely National Park: the second and third were made in June and July in two different years, when I went with friends to watch all the summer activities as well as to see the popular beauty spots. At that season it is a show place, with entertainments including fire-throwing from a high peak, an outdoor campfire festival, tales of the human and natural history of the park, community singing, twilight concerts and so on. Being one of the human species I have a natural inclination to be with my fellow-beings at all times of the year. It is not correct to say that I prefer to keep to myself. Nevertheless, my first visit to Yosemite in early Spring, with one companion, is still the most vivid and memorable one.

I had been in San Francisco for three months already, and having made arrangements to see Boston before I sailed to England in June of 1953, I told Shih-hsiang Chen that I would like to see Yosemite before I went to do some "tracing at leisure the origin of the Yankees." (This is the last line of a poem I wrote about Boston in my book *The Silent Traveller in Boston*. I must admit that I had at that time long been used to the English way of calling every American a "Yankee," until one day I met a Georgian in Market Street in San Francisco who exclaimed angrily, "Don't call me a Yankee, I come from the South and was bred there!")

Shih-hsiang, always very obliging, made special arrangements for his classes at Berkeley so that he could take me to Yosemite for three days. The next morning, Sunday April 26, we left Berkeley quite early and reached the town of Merced for lunch. The sun was shining so brilliantly that I could hardly keep my eyes open. All the way, the scenery on both sides was yellow and brown in color, except for a few green patches here and there. The grass on the hills had turned yellow too; they looked like steaming-hot buns in the sunny haze. We were told that there had been no rain since April Fool's day. Apparently March and April are already summer in California, particularly in the Bay region.

Presently a wooden board caught our attention: it bore the name "Cathay," the old name for China in western languages. At this Cathay the hills were green, with many interesting rocks projecting to give a picturesque setting for the rugged pines; the whole scene might have come out of some Chinese painting by a great Sung master. I begged Shih-hsiang to stop. There must have been a stream running somewhere, though we could not see it, for quite a lot of frogs were croaking in the thick grass and marshy land, undisturbed by the noise of any traffic. We appeared to be the only travellers here, and the croaking frogs seemed to heighten the intense stillness of the air. Suddenly I asked Shih-hsiang: "Do you know why the frogs are croaking?" I got a broad smile but no reply; my friend knew that I was referring to an ancient story about a foolish young emperor, Hui of Han dynasty (he reigned in the first century A.D.) . In ancient China, any member of the imperial family, particularly princes and princesses, were kept within the palace and knew very little about the outside world. However, this young emperor had learnt as a boy that everything which produces a sound, such as a boy or girl crying, must have a reason for doing so. One day he was taken for a walk in the country and heard the frogs croaking; the young emperor enquired of his ministers whether the frog were croaking about some *public* or *private* affair. His ministers were at a loss for an answer.

We passed through Mariposa and Summit, where the Bear River appeared very shrunk, no more than a small mountain stream. Not far from Bear Creek Lodge many purple tamarisks were in full bloom. Presently a number of big rocks forming an arch then came into sight, and we entered Yosemite National Park. On our left the roaring foam of the River Merced rushed by, while on the right a massive cliff, the tip of which I could not see, stood out serenely; we were in the midst of action and non-action. I could not tell whether we were moving or standing still. Unexpectedly a sheet of lush, fresh-green meadow appeared behind the now mirror-like river surface, with a waterfall like a strip of white-satin ribbon hanging from the precipice in the distance. What a store of things for us to see! The air had long become clearer, colder and even chilly since we entered the valley. The road we moved along seemed to have been carved out of huge rocks centuries ago, and many beautifully shaped tall trees stood on guard along it. No wind came to disturb their dark-green uniforms nor wide-stretching arms. Nor did the sun penetrate until we reached Yosemite Lodge, where we learned the location of our tent. There it was, shining brilliantly, in the center of the valley.

On our way to supper, we walked towards the base of Yosemite Fall, guided by its sound, which became louder and louder as we approached. The sun had disappeared from the valley by then. Darkness seemed to have already set in at the narrow entrance to the Fall and gradually to spread outside. The tops of the many tall trees were wrapped in a vast black velvet mist. The upper Fall was shaped like a great Chinese sword, cut out of velvet, and the lower one like a small hole. No other people were about. The longer we listened, the clearer grew the roar of the Fall in the intense stillness of the surroundings. "We have come at just the right time," Shih-hsiang remarked, "the water will not be so full two or three months from now."

Funnily enough, one of the first remarks we overheard in the lodge after we had satisfied our hunger was "Oh, we have come at the wrong time; it's so chilly!" That's how we humans differ.

On returning to our tent for the night, Shih-hsiang found he had forgotten to bring his cigarettes. While he went back for them, I began to arrange our things before lying down. Suddenly I heard a commotion at the entrance. I went to open the flap, only to find I was facing an enormous bear! It stopped there, lifted its snout and turned it this way and that as if to enquire if anybody was at home. But it took no notice of me whatever. Presently it turned its huge body round and moved away. The bright light of the lamp may not have been to its liking. In a little while I heard the dustbin by the side of the door-step being knocked down. We had not deposited anything there yet, so it had another disappointment. When he returned Shih-hsiang said that he had met no one on the way and teased me for being a dreamer and a coward. We had a good laugh over it. I lay down and half dozed off, but my thoughts were still occupied with the beautiful scenery we had that day, and eventually I roused myself fully and composed the following poem:

驅車出橡城 東遊此美地
朝日隱雲中 一路風涼意
滿眼四月花 問我誰最媚
忽睹群山松 崇高遠天際
熊澗水潺潺 默汋流莫忘
峰石抗白波 走水藏妖魅
遠遠來巨聲 飛瀑往空墜
不知幾何長 散放新蟑帔
熊流幾何年 何時見人類
渺小我之生 相識甚易易
眈識萬念消 我生此有寄

Driving our car beyond Oakland
We have come to see Yosemite.
The morning sun is hiding in the clouds—
Such a sense of coolness all the way!
The April flowers are feasting our eyes.
They vie in asking me, "who is the most charming?"
Suddenly I see a large cluster of pines
Whose loftiness and height reach the edge of Heaven.
The water in the Bear Creek flows gently,
While the Merced River rushes down without restraint.
Strange rocks combat the white waves;
The ancient redwoods conceal imps and sprites.
From far, far away comes a booming sound;
The flying Fall has climbed down from the sky!

How long it is, I cannot tell;
It sprays and spreads out like a bridal veil.
When did this hanging forest begin?
And when did it first see man?
How infinitesimal is my life;
It is not easy for us to know one another.
Now I have known you and all my thoughts are stilled,
For my life seems to know where it stands.

"Oh! Hello."

I did not make any noise to disturb my friend's sleep and closed my
eyes now with satisfaction. I slept soundly and deeply until six o'clock
the next morning. My friend broke his silence to complain that he had
not slept at all, and when I asked if he would care to have a morning
stroll with me, the answer was that I had better eat something and go
out strolling by myself, for he wanted to make up his lost sleep.

"To hear is to obey." It took me no time to be out of the tent and to draw a deep breath of the absolutely fresh and clear mountain air. I thought I was back on the top of Mount Lu, my birthplace in China. There was some difference, though. Over three thousand feet up on Ku-ling or "Oxen Peak" of Mount Lu I used to have a small hut. There I would get up very early to watch the morning clouds slowly rising from below and gradually engulfing me and my hut, till I was lost in nothingness. I used to think then that people down below must be regarding me as an immortal. But in the Yosemite Valley I was right down on earth still, and the sun had not yet come out. There was a great commotion over my head, with massive black clouds chasing gray ones across to where some pure white wool-like cloud-balls were hanging. While all this was going on above, nothing moved where I was standing. Not the slightest sound could be heard from the nearby tents. In fact, many tents were not yet occupied. Suddenly a black bear loomed up again and tried to knock down a dustbin near one of the empty tents. I stepped forward as if to apologise for my rudeness the night before and to tell him that the camping season had not yet really begun. The creature did not even turn its head to look at me, but moved away. I followed slowly behind as it moved ponderously on.

Before long it had vanished and my eyes were attracted by a pair of beautiful deer nibbling grass in the open. On my left I saw the vague outline of the Ahwahnee building, softened by the morning mist, rising mysteriously out of the tall sequoia. Far ahead stood the impressive Half Dome peak, clear and distinguishable from the surrounding mountains. There were many wide azure patches in the sky, and though the sun was not yet to be seen, it was very bright above and my gaze could reach quite wide and far. Heavy rain had fallen late the previous evening. The warm heart of the earth had heated the surface, sending much thin vapor into the lower part of the air. Everything in sight was thinly veiled and unreal.

At this moment I felt something wet and cold on my right hand, which I involuntarily drew away. Alas, I had frightened a deer! Unobserved it had come to lick my hand for food, as it must have been accustomed to do. It was tame and friendly then. Now it moved away from me as I tried to approach. It misunderstood me and would not wait for explanation. How touchy this deer was! And how many other misunderstandings like this have arisen among human beings! Though deer, unlike men, only move away, and do not deepen misunderstandings by brooding. I was glad to have a closer observation of the gentle movements of the elegant, long legs of the deer. That was my gain from an unintentional misunderstanding.

Before returning to join my friend, I wanted to have another good look at the Yosemite Fall. All the tree-tops of the redwoods were wrapped in white clouds, and so was the upper part of the Fall, though its roaring sound came very clearly. The clouds were on the move too, in the opposite direction, towards me. They touched my face refreshingly. Before long the tree-tops were left free. Now I realized that not all the clouds were sailing my way but that some were moving upwards to reveal the Fall from below, as if some mysterious hands in Heaven were trying to draw up the thinly-veiling curtain and had rested mid-way for a while. The great line of the Yosemite Fall is folded into three sections; the middle section cuts far back and can be easily overlooked. The upper part is the great show piece, a drop of one thousand four hundred and thirty feet, now in its fullest flow with more water from the night rain. For me it became an immeasurable sheet of pure white satin, shining brilliantly in the sun and flapping occasionally as if someone tugged from above. China's satin and brocade have long been known to the west through the Old Silk Road to Rome and through the Manila Galleons plying to Mexico and Spain since the fifteenth Century. But I have never seen much an enormous strip of white satin. This beautiful sheet of satin flapping on the heights of Yosemite was most probably here before our human history began.

A vast thin layer of cloud still lingered round the upper rocks, the rugged face of which was softened and hardly showed. I watched the whole scene with ever-increasing interest, for it became more and more like a beautiful Chinese vertical scroll painted by one of our great Sung masters who purposely used a plain wash in monochrome or light color for the upper part of the scene. In other words, Yosemite is similar to some parts of China in its rock formations, and in fact, it has some resemblance to one section of my native Mount Lu. The scene made my hand itch and I drew up a careful sketch for a big painting. In the course of my teaching I have found difficulty in making clear to my students how Chinese masters arranged their composition. If they were to see Yosemite Falls on such a morning, they would have a fine object lesson in Chinese painting.

Walking close to the bottom of the Fall, I found the water rushing down with dizzy speed, and the sound quite deafening. The spray sprang out with such a force that it nearly knocked me off the ground. I became moody and expressed my feelings in this quick short verse:

Such angry water carries rain and snow;
It strikes on the rocks with blasting sound,
How like the quarrels of the human world;
Noisily clamouring all the while, when will it stop?

Just then a car passed nearby and I realised it was time for me to go back to my friend. Shih-hsiang was in a happy mood, reading something as he always likes to do.

After breakfasting, we set out on our day's exploration. Shih-hsiang's spirit was as high and venturesome as mine, and despite the warning that the road to Glacial Point was treacherous, he turned the car in that very direction. Not even a bird, much less a bear, was to be seen, and the whole landscape that surrounded us seemed to belong to us alone. When we reached a higher level and made a left turn we found a thin white-velvet carpet of snow. Shih-hsiang slowed up, and moved the car forward inch by inch while I enjoyed the heavily-veiled scenery to the full. Faintly ahead of us, hundreds of thousands of snow-flakes like pieces of white taffeta or silk were fluttering in the air. After another left turn we entered a pass between rocky cliffs. Now our view was limited to trees, shrubs, and interesting rock formations. The taffeta-like snowflakes were growing larger and falling faster than before. Our car made a slight skid, for we had never thought of putting on the snow-chains. Shih-hsiang wanted to drive on still, but I suggested we should get out and walk. So having put the car on safer ground, Shih-hsiang led the way up step by step; I never saw him act so energetically before. A tiny mountain chipmunk emerged from the depth of the grass to stare at me with its bead-like eyes anxiously or angrily—otherwise, all was still and silent. Presently Shih-hsiang began to examine the map, brushing off the heavy snowflakes now and then, and finally remarked: "No use to go on; we wouldn't get to Glacial Point to-night." Indeed, I thought, why should we? We were not mountain climbers or Polar explorers; we were here to enjoy the scenery, so we turned back and made our way downwards. Once inside the car again, Shih-hsiang began to smoke his pipe, but my thoughts were whirling round and going back over my life. There is a well-known Chinese story about people who live in south China and have never seen snow. One day there was actually a snow fall and all their dogs dashed out to bark at it in terror! I had imagined the Californians and their dogs would not be very different from the southern Chinese. But this short walk up to Glacial Point refuted my ideas and showed how little I still knew about the world. Presently we were down again to the point where the snow ceased. Massive white clouds were rolling over the valley on our left. The lower we came the clearer some of the mountain peaks appeared. They gave the illusion of being in constant motion as the clouds and mist revealed and hid them by turns.

It was two o'clock when we reached the valley and Camp Curry. Not a trace of snow there, nor a drop of rain; the air was as fresh and pure as ever, though the sun was still covered in cloud. A visit to Vernal Fall was my next suggestion. So on we drove, taking first a glimpse at the Happy Isles. Afterwards we came to an open space where the paved road ended. There were a few dwellings in sight but no sign of occupants. Not far from the largest house, two elegant, tall dogwood trees were in full bloom. The single petals and evenly arranged four-petal blossoms stood out distinctly. The trees were in a rather shady spot; in sunlight they must have looked more enchanting still. The car was given a rest there and we followed the main trail to look for Vernal Fall.

The pathway was quite wet. I imagined that the rapidly-flowing water of Merced River, combatting the many projecting rocks all the way down, might have soaked the path with its spray. This was not so however—it was simply raining. We did not hurry. I spotted quite a few mountain birds; a bluejay, a yellow warbler and one which may have been a red-cardinal though it flew out of sight too quickly for me to be sure.

Mountain birds flutter ahead of us;
The clear stream sounds all the way.
Wild clouds gather together and then spread;
We check our steps to share our enjoyment.

These four lines formed in my mind after we had stood on the bridge over Merced River. We gazed down and down to our right to a gap where we could see clouds moving in and out. From the other side we could hear the roar of a great volume of water pouring down though it was not yet visible. Up above, many huge boulders stood grotesquely in the way of the rapidly moving water, sending spray far and high over our heads like drizzling rain.

Now the path became a track over the rocks, uneven, twisted and slanting too, with oddly-arranged steps. Much water still ran on some of them. We managed to climb up and up happily. Shih-hsiang was far ahead, for I never could resist gazing around me in all directions. We were now far above the bridge on which we had stood a moment ago. I wondered how we could have stood there, for it looked so narrow and small, and it did not seem to connect with the winding trail covered by the heavy spray of the water. We were in the middle of a vast hollowed gap with rocky cliffs sloping down towards the center, divided by a line of white foam. Myriads of minute water-particles were darting, clashing, and fluttering indistinguishably before my eyes, yet they came to touch my face and pat my hands. The roaring sound was now louder than ever. The noise and activity did not disturb me but rather pleased my eyes and ears; how different from the bustle and din during the rush-hour in Times Square!

I looked up and behold! Shih-hsiang was floating in the air! I could only see a faint image of him and an outline of the prominent rock on which he stood. The dense spray-mist thickly veiled the ground beneath and made him and the rock appear suspended in air. Far behind him part of the huge sheet of Vernal Fall appeared above his right shoulder. He had now become an immortal, or an unapproachable Taoist hermit as they are depicted in many early Chinese masterpieces. A little while later I came up to him and found that he had reached a resting place where an iron-railing circled the edge of the rock and a seat was provided. We smiled at each other without speaking. Then I craned my neck to look farther up and noticed a deer or a stag standing in its pale brown coat near the edge of another jutting rock. The Fall was now in full view and what a Fall! so massive and voluminous, rushing down ceaselessly since before the beginning of the human race. With the aged precipice, lofty sequoia, and the tiny image of the deer against the white Fall, a picture had composed itself beautifully, and I moved nearer to make a sketch. Shih-hsiang soon joined me, remarking with satisfaction, the pipe still in his mouth, "We made it." High

Vernal Fall, Yosemite

above the Vernal stood two shapely mountain peaks. At one time one
of them looked a darker blue than the other and in the next moment
they had exchanged their shades of color. Then one would disappear

from sight altogether; next they had both vanished. The clouds were moving very briskly up there, and the two mountain peaks seemed alive. We both watched them intently.

The two peaks kick the tumbling water
Playing hide-and-seek inside the clouds.
How like us, Shih-hsiang and me
Whistling proudly and enjoying our mad capers.

Again a little verse had blown out of my mouth. Shih-hsiang asked why I had become so dreadfully poetic that day. I liked his comic mood. I tried to induce him to play a poetic game with me but to no avail. The game is called "Lien-chü" (or "Join-a-line"). One of the players composes a line of verse and the other joins the next line to it; they continue in this way until the poem is completed. This game has been played at parties by Chinese men of letters since the sixth century if not before. Shih-hsiang and I had often played it with our friends.

The Chinese ancients said: "To yield is to be preserved whole." We wanted our enjoyment to be preserved whole, so we yielded our place to late-comers and started to walk slowly down. We felt satisfied with our day. The car brought us back to the Valley, where we had some supper in the old village and later had a look at the village church. It was not yet quite dark. A large group of clouds sailed past the main pathway from which we had just come and soon rose up over the Half Dome, gradually spreading to veil the other peaks nearby. Out of my head I chanted the following two lines spontaneously:

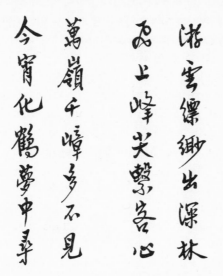

A roaming cloud has just sailed gracefully out of the woods
It rolls up to the top of the mountain, where my heart is bound.

Unexpectedly Shih-hsiang followed with the next two lines:

Thousands of the mountain peaks have almost disappeared;
To-night I will change into a stork and search for them
    in dreams.

There could have been no happier ending to our day. Soon we each
entered our own dream world.

Early the next morning I turned to look out of the window and saw
that my friend was not in his bed. His suitcase and several odd belongings had all vanished with him. Bewildered, I could not believe that
the huge black bear had come to our tent in the night and eaten him
up. I had no Chinese gong on which to beat the call for missing persons,
as the villagers used to do in China's remote countryside. I lay on my
bed thinking of my friend's dream to search for the mountain peaks
and I must have dozed off again. When I next woke up, it was very
bright outside. While washing my face I noticed a slip of paper sticking
out from my pillow, which read "have been *snored* away . . ." Chuckling happily to myself I became enlightened as if I had been punched
by a Ch'an (Zen) master on the head. I must have been imitating the

sound of the waterfalls too uproariously. My imitation of the Yosemite Fall had probably been bad enough to keep my friend awake most of the previous night. But last night, with two falls to imitate, I had driven him right away. It was all my fault for being born with a nose beyond my control. I did not go to look for him immediately but started out on a morning stroll. Suddenly it began to rain and rained heavily. I ran to shelter underneath a huge sequoia but felt instinctively quite unhappy there. In China I had stood under many a rugged pine high up on my native Mount Lu and under the age-old Cypresses of the Confucius Temple in Shangtung Province, without feeling small, but here I simply felt shrunk to nothing. I tried to cast out this despondent thought, but it kept returning to my mind. I had been brought up in an old Chinese Confucian family and taught to aim at being a man, serving my country and mankind. I have never really thought of myself as somebody important, yet I cannot accept the idea of being such a minute creature as I was now, beside the enormous sequoia. Just at that moment a strong gust of wind swirled round and shook all the long branches madly. Big drops of water splashed down all over my face and body as if the tree were exclaiming: "Get out of my shelter! How ungrateful you men are!"

I was out in the open in no time, for the rain had now stopped. And there were a few bright blue patches in the sky. The air was exceedingly fresh. Many loose, thin clouds were being drawn slowly upwards to join the cloud-masses above the mountain peaks. Their playful yet careful motion close to the precipitous cliffs, like rock-climbers groping their way along, was beautiful to watch. Following the faint sound of the Yosemite Fall, I located it far behind thousands of tall trees. From there I tried to pick out the peak of El Capitan, the Bridal Veil Fall, the peak of Three Sisters, the Sentinel Dome, and other landmarks. In a single roving glance over the mountains, the clouds, the trees and the nearby river, I seemed to have surveyed the whole universe. Many birds were active, darting among tree-branches and singing. This was by far the most interesting moment for me in Yosemite. When I quietly opened the door of the Lodge cabin to which my friend had moved, he was still sound asleep. So I sat on the bench outside and amused myself composing the following lines:

天公笑我貪看山
故作靈雨阻我意
詎知山色更濛濛
忽隱忽現逗我戲
怒瀑高與浮雲齊
長松絕頂流青翠
且別飛禽賦歸來
石湘猶自擁衣睡

Heaven laughs at my greediness in enjoying the scenery;
Purposely sends down torrential rain to stop my wandering.
How could I know that the color of the mountains
 would grow more mysterious,
Now visible and now invisible as if luring me
 to play with them?
The uproarious Fall is as high as the floating clouds;
Lofty fir-trees breathe a bluish-green mist over their crests.
I wave my hands to the nearby birds to tell them:
 "I am going back!"

Look! Shih-hsiang is still under the bed-clothes asleep! While we were having breakfast, Shih-hsiang cracked one or two jokes about my ever-lasting mountain peaks, falls, and clouds. He suggested we drive on through the Yosemite Valley and stop wherever we found something of interest. We had a good look at the Cathedral Spires, the Basket Dome, and a very high cliff with pointed top named "Washington Monument!" where Shih-hsiang met a neighbor of Professor Yuan-ren Chao of Cragmont, Berkeley, and engaged in lively talk with him. I amused myself as I always did, sketching roughly this and that. The shapes of the tall redwoods and their intriguing, twisting but powerful branches made my hand scribble all over the little pad I had with me. We then proceeded through dark Wawona Tunnel to face a most unforgettable vista of the towering El Capitan on the left, the shrunken Half Dome in the distant center in the haze, and the slanting bodies of the Three Sisters guarding the Bridal Veil Fall on the right. All down the valley before us and up the hillside beyond grew row upon row of tall, strong pine trees. Their presence enhanced the majestic scenery behind them.

Shih-hsiang insisted on going down to see the Bridal Veil Fall face to face. I agreed, though I felt quite content with what we had already seen. The old Chinese way of visiting beautiful scenery on foot along the mountain paths would never have made Yosemite known to more than a handful of people. Now in a minute Shih-hsiang had parked the car alongside several others on the official parking allotment, and we began to climb up the valley. The way was not so steep as it had been to the Vernal Fall, though we had to walk on huge, irregular boulders. It was interesting to watch the clear mountain water winding its way down between them. To dip our hands in it or even our feet was very tempting. Oh, what a Fall! So high, so unbelievably beautiful, fitly described as the "Bridal Veil." That was just how it looked from a distance. Standing quite near, I had to struggle to keep my foothold. Unlike the gentle bridal veil on a bride's head, the massive spray of the Fall at close quarters was like drenching rain, and very chilly too. It was marvellous to lift our heads and look at that great operation of Nature pouring from the top of the steep, majestic cliff to where we were standing. I got, too, a strange, inexpressible feeling. When one faces Niagara Falls they are grand, immense and unbelievable to the eye but do not give one *a chance* to feel. Close to the foot of the Bridal Veil Fall I did feel and felt wonderfully with an indescribable sense of how my short life was flowing on well.

Shortly we came to the foot of El Capitan. Shih-hsiang and I now found a drier spot to sit down. He smoked his pipe as usual, while I made a rough sketch of the whole scene. I read somewhere that the amount of granite forming El Capitan rock was two or three times as much as the whole Rock of Gibraltar. In order to give life to the picture as well as to indicate the magnitude of El Capitan, I later added a horse drinking water at its foot.

It was still quite early when we returned to the Lodge. My friend

El Capitan

had a drink and I a cup of strong, black coffee, sitting in the lounge to
watch the new arrivals. We discussed what we could do before we returned to Berkeley the next day. Shortly our hunger urged us to have a
meal, and then we strolled back—Shih-hsiang to his Lodge cabin and

I to the tent—for a rest. At a quarter past nine Shih-hsiang came to the tent to chat. When I opened the door and saw the bright dry ground, I took my friend's arm and we went out to stroll under the moon instead. Under the spell of the fresh evening air we did not feel like talking; it was quite easy to find our way under the guidance of the moon. Though the darkness was deep in the distance. Shih-hsiang spied his car and we began to drive slowly. There are a few road-lamps, far apart from one another, near the Lodge and other Camping grounds, but the bright moon dimmed them all. Presently we entered a spot where the moonbeams could not penetrate. The car hit something like a rock and bumped to a stand-still; there we got out. I realized that we had come to Mirror Lake, where we had not lingered very long in the daytime. Moving forward cautiously we approached the edge of the Lake, which was now a deep blue sheet of extremely smooth glass with a moon lying in it. Another Half Dome was in it too, together with its neighboring peaks upside down. There was a wonderful stillness in the air. It was cool, but not chilly, motionless but not inert, breathless but not dead, serene and pleasant indeed. We strolled round the edge of the lake towards the Half Dome, above which the moon was beaming. The footpath was not even, nor quite a semi-circle; sometimes we walked between trees, sometimes behind tall reeds, sometimes the moon led us on, later she was sailing behind us, but all the time the lake surface was an unbroken sheet of intolerable glory in bluish-black jade. I stumbled slightly and immediately a "plop" echoed on the water. I thought I had kicked in a small stone, but Shih-hsiang thought it was a frog that had jumped into the lake. A moment later we heard a chorus of frogs croaking through the tall blades of the reeds, a concert not only pleasing to the ear but intensifying the serenity of the night. At the same time I recalled reading in *Liao-Chai-Chi-Yi*, a seventeenth-century Chinese book of strange stories, about a frog musician. He kept a specially-made music-box, in which there were twelve partitions, each containing a different kind of frog. When he opened the box to play, he took a small stick and tapped on the heads of the frogs in turn in various rhythms and they responded with croaks in different tones.

Presently we followed the same path back to our starting point. Now

One swan chasing another in front of the Palace of Fine Arts.

the moon was directly above the Half Dome and was also directly facing us, keeping a close watch on our steps. We were the only creatures moving and felt very conscious of ourselves, so we moved more and more slowly. Unexpectedly Shih-hsiang seated himself on a large rock. In the darkness, and being so absorbed in the whole scene, I did not notice the flute in his hand. But now, the clear notes of his flute floated out, even clearer in the enchanting purity of the air. I involuntarily began to chant the following verse, written in the third century by some unknown poet:

When the moon moves to the center of the sky,
When the breeze skims over the water surface,
Such a sense of pure joy is there;
Few people can understand this, I fancy.

The wind was in fact flickering the leaves and young branches as if sharing in our ecstasy. Finally Shih-hsiang went off to have his sweet dreams in the cabin and I had the third trial of my uproarious imitation in the tent.

When we came to settle the account at the Lodge the next morning, a young man at the counter smilingly enquired if there was something wrong with the bed as my friend had changed his sleeping quarters. Silence reigned, for delicacy was needed in replying. I eased the situation by saying that I had been trying to imitate the sound of Yosemite Fall too uproariously in the night! So our trip ended with a smile.

California and Yosemite Falls.

XXIV

Twisting Grotesquely

WHEN I LIVED IN Europe, chiefly in the British Isles, I relied solely on my legs for travel, except for very long distances. Unlike American cities, where the traveller stays overnight and moves on again, no European town or city let me pass through easily. The roads there were originally constructed for walking and twist and turn at short intervals so that one just could not dash through in a minute. At each turn neither a supermarket nor a drugstore is to be found but something of life, human life in one of its many aspects, functioning naturally. Man's own identity remains there. Recently I spent two weeks in Venice, and went to a dinner party attended by many different nationalities. One of the guests, the American Consul-general, looked rather tired. He told some of us that during the summer season he was always being bombarded by shouts from the other end of the telephone: most of his fellow countrymen called the Venetians "idiots" and "nuts" for not letting them drive their cars into the city! He related it with such humorous mimicry that we all roared with laughter. Smilingly I remarked that Venice was a place where he could do a service to humanity by compelling men to make full use of their legs, and thus discover their individuality. I told him, half-jokingly, that he should persuade his compatriots to come to Venice, not for its historical background only, but for their own benefit.

However, there is something good to be said for American city plans: they prevent the passerby from casting glances sideways, or deviating from his route. Without these straightest-possible highways I would not have been able to see Monterey and Carmel in a few hours, driving from San Francisco. By the standards of European travel, Monterey and Carmel could not have been included in my impressions of the San Francisco region. But in the sense of travelling in the United

States, most people who come to San Francisco have either been in Monterey and Carmel first or would go there afterwards.

Three sets of friends took me to these places, and each time it was a daytime trip, though the distance each way is more than two hundred miles. On the first and second trip we were unable to see as much as we had hoped. Either the season was wrong or there was an incredibly thick sea-fog covering much of the coast line. However, all deficiencies were made up for by the third trip.

After two hours' straight driving from San Francisco, we reached Pacific Grove. Sunshine lit up everything brilliantly all the way. The City of Pacific Grove does not look like any city I know of in China or Europe. The wide motor road goes straight through with a number of neat-looking houses on both sides, surrounded by lawns, green and fresh, where water sprays were at work. Many tall palm trees stood gazing down at us lazily with waving arms stretched out. There was hardly any breeze to be felt from the ocean. The sunshine must have been very hot, for there was nobody about. We could not find anyone to give us directions for what we wanted to see. Rudolph Schaeffer slowed down his car and at that moment I noticed many golden spots shimmering in the sun by a group of eucalyptus trees. "That's the place!" exclaimed Rudolph and swung over in that direction. On entering a gate, above which a large notice fastened to a redwood announced "Butterfly Trees," we parked and then walked cautiously and slowly towards the myriad golden spots. Each was a Monarch butterfly with its brown-orange wings stretched out, fluttering up and down in the sun. They seemed to be performing an elaborate ballet-dance on a stage in space. We had arrived just after twelve o'clock and many of the butterflies, warmed by the hot sun, were in a frenzy of movement. Many more of them, thousands more, still had their wings folded and clung to the drooping eucalyptus leaves. The inner side of their brown-orange wings is pale yellow with clear, jet-black patterning. Against the bright sunlight they were like the woven design on a Chinese silk-hanging on the green satin base of the eucalyptus leaves, a product of Hanchou in Chekiang Province, famous for its silks. Only they were not immobile like silk-hangings: with the countless fluttering wings like shimmering golden pieces, the whole scene was a lively one, impossible to describe. I have never seen such myriads of butter-flies of one species together before.

This was not our accidental discovery, but the object of our trip. The "butterfly trees" in Pacific Grove along Monterey Peninsula are well-known, and this was just the right time to see them, for the butter-flies usually come to stay for a few months from October till March. These trees were discovered in 1907, I was told, though the butterflies could have been there from time immemorial without having been noticed. The belief persists that these myriad Monarch butterflies return from great distances to the same few trees year after year. Scientists have concluded that they start their annual mass migration from South Alaska, and are joined by many more from British Colum-bia, Washington, Oregon, and North California. Many have observed them taking three days to reach a given point, covering about forty or fifty miles each day, and about two or three months to reach Monterey from South Alaska. They fly fifty or sixty feet from the ground. Unlike bird migrants that travel in flocks, they fly singly. And they are never seen flying at night. They arrive all together like a glint of gold in the afternoon sun about the middle of October. In recent years, these butterfly trees have made Pacific Grove into quite a famous place, and also kept the inhabitants flourishing with gift-shops full of little souvenirs in butterfly designs. The City even stages a parade—"Wel-come the Monarchs back to Pacific Grove"—each fall, with children from elementary schools and kindergartens dressed up with yellow wings.

This delightful visit roused many queries in my mind. Why should the Monarchs specially choose Pacific Grove instead of the many other warmer places, say, South America or Africa, if they can use their fragile wings for such a long distance? Perhaps they cannot cross the ocean. But why should they have to go back several thousand miles to the Canadian rockies and south Alaska in the Spring when the climate of Monterey Peninsula is almost unchangeable the whole year round? If I understand correctly, most butterflies cannot live more than two or three months and some only a few days. The longest life-span for the Monarchs is under nine months. How do they tell their offspring to come back by the same route and to the same trees? I wonder if this

Migration of the Monarchs

bears out the Oriental belief in reincarnation? It is a mystery of nature. The following story from a well-known Chinese book *Liao Chai Chih Yi* or "Unusual Stories recorded in Something-interesting Studio," by Pu Sung-ling, circa A.D. 1710, might be another explanation:

A Mr. Wang of Ch'ung-shan, being a District Magistrate, was habitually commuting the fines and penalties of the Penal Code, inflicted on the various wrongdoers, for a number of butterflies according to the degree of offence. He had a strange passion for butterflies and would let them go all at once in his courtyard, rejoicing to see them fluttering hither and thither as if they were tinsel snippings borne about by a gentle wind. However, a young lady in a brightly colored dress came into his dream one night and rebuked him saying: "Your cruel practice causes many an un-natural death to my sisters; you shall pay for this penalty you extract to satisfy your own passion." Then the young lady changed into a butterfly and flew away. Next morning, as Mr. Wang was enjoying a cup of wine alone in his office, he unexpectedly re-ceived the announcement of a caller, the Imperial Censor was at the door. He hurriedly put on his official cap and dashed out to welcome his Superior. Unfortunately he did not notice a white flower on the cap, which had been stuck in there by a mischievous maid-servant. The Censor, being a great man from the Imperial Palace, was angry at his undignified conduct and censured him severely in his report.

Thereafter, Mr. Wang was no longer allowed to commute penalties for butterflies. What a delicate and delicious revenge! This is only a story, of course, and China has far too many tales like this handed down from the early days. Nevertheless, there is a moral in this little piece, for the Chinese ancient thinkers have always advocated that every creature, not only man, has the right to live in its own way. This story is a warning to children and adults alike not to molest butterflies, instead of putting up a big notice-board. Pacific Grove is far away from China, and centuries beyond Mr. Wang's days. Besides, the Monarchs come to visit the eucalyptus trees of their own accord. The owners of motels nearby need not fear any revenge by the harmless creatures. After all, you would never expect to find the Imperial Censor at your doors; even if he did appear, your cap with a white flower or any other ornament would only tickle his sense of humor!

Butterflies have always a happy association in the Chinese mind; in fact they symbolize happiness. Butterflies often appear as "happy" symbols in almost any form of Chinese art. Our great poets from the fourth century downwards, if not earlier, have sung about them, and many of the stories about them in Chinese literature and art come from a famous passage in the works of the great Chinese Taoist philosopher, Chuang Tzu (died about B.C. 275). He describes how he once dreamed of becoming a butterfly fluttering round happily hither and thither. When he was about to wake up, he did not know whether he was still a butterfly dreaming of becoming a man, or a man who had dreamt of being a butterfly. "Man" is only a name. So is "butterfly." We should not make too much difference between "man" or "butterfly" or anything else. All are illusions. We can only try to enjoy life during our flash of existence.

Presently Rudolph and I started on a very smooth drive for the famous seventeen miles. Rudolph reminded me that this seventeen-mile drive was being kept as a national park, and no building was allowed within its boundaries. I was not very responsive, for I was still happily remembering the Pacific Grove Monarchs. I had given up questioning why the Monarchs had chosen that spot. They appeared at Pacific Grove just as I had done. I began to gaze intently all around from the window, and saw a large stretch of moorland full of luxuriant vegetation on my left, like the most colorful Persian carpet of enormous size. There were masses of Californian succulent grasses of many colors, chiefly pink, red and fresh green. They were woven together with other wild flowers on such a grand scale as could only have been found along the Seventeen-Mile Drive, nowhere in Persia, I believe. Turning to the scenery on my right—the great expanse of the Pacific Ocean—I drew a deep breath and felt almost twice my usual size. The contrast from looking at the minute patterns on the wings of the Monarchs was so great, I could almost hear my eye-balls complaining at the sudden expansion. Suddenly I broke my silence by chanting the following lines by David McCord:

> Now think of words, Take *sky*
> And ask yourself just why—
> Like sun, moon, star, and cloud—
> It sounds so well out loud,
> And pleases so the sight
> When printed black on white.

"Good" remarked Rudolph. "It is good," I replied. David's poem "Take Sky" has become very well-known from his many books of verses for young readers and has also been printed on the front page of The *New York Times Book Review*. I have known David for more than ten years and always like to read his poems aloud. The sound of them appeals to me, and they are easy to remember. This little verse with its catchy rhymes led me on to compose four more lines:

> The sky is so blue,
> The clouds so few,
> The sun so bright,
> Seagulls painted all rocks white.

"That's good, too," laughed Rudolph. I never dare try to write verse in English: this was only a joke. A number of odd-sized rocks stood out a little way off the shore; they were not brown-black like the rest, but white. It is interesting to know that seagulls are also painters, using their own special technique. How long did they take to paint the whole rock white all over, I wonder?

My friend halted his car and suggested we should get out to have a look round and a rest. A huge piece of rocky cliff stretched out into the sea, while the ocean water battled vigorously against the foot of it on both sides without ceasing. Along the cliffs further inshore were many tall trees, including pines, and other abundant vegetation. Only a lonely cypress stood with dignity on the outstretched rocky peninsula. A man-made footpath wound its way to the point. We strolled along leisurely. I thought I was examining a Chinese landscape painting by some Sung master. The scene, so like an old Chinese masterpiece, could prove to the Occidentals that Chinese painters do not create their work entirely out of fantastic images in their own mind as many seem to believe. Actually the Chinese aesthetic theory indicates that the artist can evolve his own compositions, but his creation must not deviate from reality. How glad I was to find this example! The Lonely Cypress

Lonely Pine Rock

is also a favorite subject of the Chinese artist who enjoyes the character of individual trees rather than a luxuriant growth of indiscriminate green foliage. How long has this lonely, old cypress been standing here? Its majestic, undaunted look belittles everything else around it. Even the ocean is only its back-cloth. There must have been wild weather along the Monterey Peninsula at times, yet it shows no sign of withering or weariness. The ancient Chinese have long used the cypress as an emblem of "a strong-willed gentleman"; as such it has figured in Chinese literature and art for hundreds of years. While my friend was enjoying himself examining the landmarks, I composed the following little poem:

孤　四　千　經　下　上　岩　豈
秀　望　載　年　有　與　喬　容
海　芝　自　任　濤　日　當　幽
天　雲　為　抨　聲　月　大　岸
空　霧　雄　擊　洪　友　風　隱

Can it be obscured along these quiet shores?
At the rock's tip it faces mighty winds!
Above it has the sun and moon for companions;
Beneath it has the roaring of great waters.
Year after year it is heedless of battle and assault:
Through the centuries it has stood proudly alone.
There is no cloud or mist to be seen anywhere—
Just a solitary beauty in the expanse of sea and sky!

Just before passing through the gate into the area of Carmel near the end of the Seventeen-mile drive, a number of cypress trees with un-usually twisted shapes by the ocean shore fascinated me. My friend laughed at my impatience to see them, for there would be many more to examine at Carmel's Point Lobos.

Carmel is considered a beautiful all-year-round resort. Many of her inhabitants are in retirement and it is full of "gentlemen of leisure." Perhaps Carmel can be termed a "City of Leisure"; it looked so to me when we arrived. There is quite a British atmosphere in Carmel; the climate is always mild, never too hot, like the warm summer days in the British Isles, only it has none of the dampness of Britain. Many English and Scottish people in retirement have come to live here, I was told.

The sea-fog rolls in from time to time and can be very dense, as I had experienced on my last two trips. Luckily we arrived this time while the sun shone brilliantly in the sky. We paid a visit to Carmel Mission, founded in 1771 by Father Serra who died there after eighteen years. Typically Spanish in appearance, the Mission buildings are orange-brown in color, set at a little distance from the heart of the city. Later we had to find an Inn for lunch. Any food when it is badly needed is always delicious, but we really had a very satisfying meal. This not only renewed our energy, but also refreshed our eyes for sight-seeing. The streets in Carmel are not too straight and many side-roads have curves and turns. The houses and shops on the whole are of only two stories. To my personal interest, I found quite a number of people sitting at tea, and enjoying the British style of tea-drinking with buttered bread or toast, and cakes. Carmel is not representative of modern America in the strict sense.

It was a perfectly soft, warm afternoon. The shore breezes drove away any oppressive heat. The sky was completely free of clouds. We were heading for Carmel's Point Lobos, and it took no time to leave the city behind. The area around Point Lobos is a State Park, and it has been left completely open and natural except for a few well-paved roads for driving. We first came to a rather secluded quarter—I mean "secluded" because the water was still and far away from the open ocean. It looked somewhat like a lagoon, where a few sailing boats were anchored; two were being aired or *careened* on the shore. A family of five was picnicking not far from a big bunch of prickly-pear cacti growing on a rocky slope. At the next turn I was attracted by the name on a signboard—"Little China Cove." My friend suggested that he would lie on a jutting rock and watch the wide expanse of the ocean while I went up to discover the cove's connection with my native land. I climbed up a small mound, and turned on to a wide stretch of land above the water. An elderly gentleman sat on a stone dozing in the warm sun. There was nobody else in sight. The ocean water extending to the infinite horizon looked absolutely calm. Yet my ears were full of sound. Spray showered and splashed upwards against the rocks where the land was split by many cracks. Some gaps were quite big. This must have happened centuries ago. It was a faraway, enchanted scene.

I then traced the trail back and came down a long ladder-like set of steps to a quiet little cove in a horseshoe shape, filled with fine sand. Luxuriant vegetation grew around: shining green of various shades on one side where the sun caught it and darker shades of green on the other. There were many tall, wide-spreading trees on the cliffs, too. It must have been a lovely spot for swimming or bathing. For me it was a perfect place for meditation, and I lingered there a good while. When I stood up again and stretched my arms widely like those of the tall trees, I still had not discovered why this little cove was called "China Cove."

I rejoined Rudolph and we followed the road a good distance past one large group of shrubs after another. Finally Rudolph exclaimed: "There you are!" and pointed at the many cypress trees. Never had I seen so many grotesquely-twisted tree-trunks and branches in such intriguing designs. Each cypress had one or two strong trunks, not straight but curved and twisted at irregular intervals. They looked like groups of virile Greek Apollos exercising each in his own way his robust arms and legs with their bluish embossed veins winding along them. No two were exactly alike. Each trunk had many long-armed branches, full of dark green-blue leaves. Every branch twisted and wound in natural yet fantastic ways, always intertwining with or passing the others as if knowing its exact part in the composition. From any angle and in every aspect all this presented me with new forms, new compositions, new paintings, and new sculptures far more sophisticated than any of the modern works of art I have seen in exhibitions at Rome, Venice, Paris, London, and New York. In the chapter about "Abstract Beauty" in my book *Chinese Calligraphy,* I say:

> There is a beauty which appeals immediately to the heart—in natural scenery, for instance, and in some pictures. There is also a beauty which more than half conceals itself within or behind Form and is revealed only to the "informed" and searching eye. The first we can trace to its origin and analyse. The second is generated neither by powerful thought nor reason, nor has it any particular source: it is the "abstract" beauty of line. . . .
>
> To the Chinese themselves, calligraphy is the most fundamental artistic manifestation of the national mind . . . the enthusiasm of

those Chinese connoisseurs who lost their heads over a single line or groups of lines that have no apparent logical meaning, will seem little short of madness; but such enthusiasm is not misplaced. . . .

The Chinese value calligraphy . . . purely for the sake of the satisfactory nature of its lines and groups of lines; they acknowledge no necessity for the thought expressed to be beautiful. The aesthetic of Chinese calligraphy is simply this: that a beautiful form should be beautifully executed. . . .

The choice and construction require, of course, good taste, and good taste had to be cultivated, and this is done by observing beautiful forms in nature. . . . The fundamental inspiration of calligraphy, as of all the arts in China, is Nature.

Cypresses on Point Lobos

Many Chinese books record how some of the great masters gained inspiration for new calligraphic styles by observing old rugged pines and cypresses, the swaying of the willow branches, the muscles of a tiger's limb, the galloping legs of a horse, etc. They watched them intensely and then tried to achieve the full, masculinely-firm strength in a few rapid strokes of their brush. The spontaneity of the brush-stroke in achieving a natural form without any additional touching up as if it were alive is the aesthetic aim of all Chinese calligraphers as well as painters, and their unspeakable joy, too, if they achieve it. That is the essence of our calligraphy and painting. At Carmel I met my chance as a painter and my challenge too. I lingered, made rough sketches, and then strolled on.

Suddenly most of the thick trunks and branches became red-washed in different gradations. The transformation of their grayish-whiteness into pink, light red, and purple happened in a flash, as if by magic. "Ah, I can use red-ink for them instead of the usual Chinese black ink made of pine-soot," I whispered to myself. The sun had been gradually sinking. My friend and I moved into the cypress grove. Arching overhead, like the roof and columns of a cathedral, or like the vermilion wooden beams and pillars of a Palace in Peking, or rather those of a Chinese thatched house in the countryside, or a hut fit for a hermit to live in, the cypresses had better designs than any architect could have devised. Encrusted with masses of tiny dark-green-blue leaves, some became bright red in the lingering sun and some blacker in the shade. How magical it all was!

On we moved and exchanged no word. After a while we came to a rather shady area and could not even see the ocean water. Again a brilliantly sparkling shaft of light probed in and many cypress trunks revealed interesting shapes in purplish color against a deep-blue background of the sea. Under the rather low canopy of dark-green cypress leaves I could not get a full view of what lay ahead. Then a wonderful pink rock screen appeared. In a minute it turned out to be a large group of white rocks clustered together and stretching out into the ocean between two rocky arms of the land. The soft rays of the setting sun fell on the screen of rocks to make them look like massive corals or pinky quartz of enormous size. The greater part of the rocks was bare, but on the top a number of beautifully-shaped cypresses and pines stood out triumphantly in procession. Yet again the whole scene resembled a Sung landscape painting.

We then walked down a hollow curve along a rocky footpath until we found ourselves on a jutting rock, where I leaned back against a partly-dead cypress trunk. The same coral-like group of rocks stretched out into the ocean but their forms had changed, for I was facing them from a new angle. At each step they presented a new aspect. I soon realised that it is mainly to the labyrinthine intricacy of these high rocky banks that Carmel's Point Lobos owes its singular character of wildness and variety. The cypress here is *The Cupressus Macrocarpa* or Monterey cypress. It is the hardiest of all cypresses and used to be called "rugged veteran." It is confined to two groves near the Pacific, south of Monterey. The larger, Cypress Point Grove, is two miles long and just less than a mile wide; the other, Point Lobos Grove, where we were, is much smaller. My friend caught sight of a local guard and went to talk to him. He said that nobody knew how long the cypresses have been on Point Lobos. "They must have been here thousands and thousands of years," said he. "They have always looked the same to me year in and year out. They stand firm and they never change. One might think some of the branches and trunks are dead. But they are not; they are very much alive. I know that I shall go off this earth eventually," he added with a wink, "but I also know these trees will *never* go from these rocky cliffs."

I remember seeing the famous cypress avenue, specially planted, along the approach to Confucius' grave in Shantung Province. Both sides of the longish path were lined with old and rugged-looking cypress trees, which are known to have been planted as far back as Han dynasty (206 B.C.-A.D. 220) . One of them was pointed out to me as having been planted by Confucius himself (he lived in the sixth century B.C.) . In the Chinese classic *Analects*, Confucius is reported as saying, "When the year becomes cold, we know that the pine and cypress will be the last to change their colors." He seems to indicate the pines and cypresses as having all the characteristics of a superior man, erect, strong, standing firm though twisted and buffeted by tempest and storm. Confucius never did much to spread his ideas for mankind in his lifetime, but his principles prevail till this day.

Again I wrote a little poem to express my feeling for Carmel's cypresses.

俯　日　　　下　四　浩　臨　似　天　造　屈　風　銅　嗟
仰　夜　　　有　週　浩　危　笑　生　出　曲　神　筋　美
萬　跳　群　亂　碎　乎　己　人　傲　異　相　有　鐵　古
古　珠　浴　石　金　斷　忘　間　骨　形　依　時　脈　柏
莫　不　兒　爭　滿　此　斷　織　搖　少　難　肆　竞　樹
窮　知　　　濤　滄　　　此　嫩　青　俗　為　狂　雄　中
期　己　　　　　海　　　遊　質　枝　態　稿　惡　姿　奇

Carmel's ancient cypresses are a wonder among all trees,
Vying with each other in their brass muscles and iron veins!
The God of Wind rages at times in great wrath;
Bending and twisting, they cling together and cannot be shifted.
They create grotesque forms, not a trace of vulgarity:
Their proud bones, Heaven-given, shake their green branches.
They seem to laugh at the human world, at its pettiness and timidity,
Like floating threads that break in an instant at the touch of danger.
Oh grand, grand!
Around them is an oceanful of gold pieces;
Beneath them jumbled rocks struggle against
        waves like a flock of swimmers.
Masses of tumbling pearls know no rest day or night.
Over the centuries they rise and fall without ceasing!

XXV

Concluding Temporarily

W HEN I HAVE COME to know a place for some time, I have usually formed a fixed impression of it, though new details may be added to my picture in later visits. I feel that great, ancient cities like London, Paris and Oxford have a *past* which dominates them. Once I had been impressed by their *past,* what happened in my lifetime and what might develop in the future only tip-toed over my brain, leaving a very slight or even no footprint. The *past* of London, Paris or Oxford is too overwhelming; it obsessed me at times so that I almost lost my own identity as a modern man. But in San Francisco I never dreamed of myself as one of the thousands shipped there to build the Pacific Railroad, nor as a heathen Ah Sin described in Bret Harte's *Heathen Chinee,* nor as an Oriental conjurer. San Francisco has an impressive *past,* but its *present* and *future* count for far more, where I am concerned. In every city unavoidable changes take place from time to time, but few cities can have changed so much within so short a time as San Francisco; it is always marching forward. Therefore I can only conclude writing my impressions of it "temporarily."

I do not care much for the names of San Francisco's hills—the Telegraph, the Russian and the Nob—except that of Twin Peaks. Twin Peaks are drawn like the top part of a Bikini on any map I have seen, but if the Nob means the head, the neck would be too long to meet the breasts, the Twin Peaks.

Seal Rocks sounds good to my ears. I wish Alcatraz could have remained a huge Pelican Rock in the Bay. Though I never have the inclination to be a prophet, I did feel somehow that Alcatraz would be a mere rock again sooner or later, perhaps renamed "Pelican Rock."

Though it was in one way appropriate to borrow from Robert Louis Stevenson the name, Treasure Island, for the ground of the 1939

352

The church on Nob Hill

International Exposition, yet it was misleading, for the exhibition ground was man-made and not really an island unless one thinks of it as joined to Yerba Buena. There are many things there now, unknown to the outside world, but no treasure. Besides, no layman could have any hope of a share, if treasures were there. It became a U.S. Naval Reservation Base during the Second World War. Now that the war has long ended, I suspect some change will take place on Treasure Island in the future. I hope to have a look at it one day.

Angel Island has always been an angel to me. It has always been there for me to see from a distance, sometimes half-hidden in thick fog, and sometimes thinly-veiled by haze or mist, and at times clearly revealed under the bright sun, but I was never on it nor near it. I saw it very close at hand once from Mr. and Mrs. Booth's house at the tip of Belvedere, which is another prominent, huge rock sticking out into the Bay, but a narrow piece of land attaches it to the Tiburon penin-sula. Angel Island stands not far from Belvedere. I was taken to see Belvedere on several occasions. Jimmy and Juanita Lawson wanted me to see the Doll's House there, which was occupied by Mrs. Hewitt at the time. The House was built exactly like a picture from a children's story book. The builder must have had a free hand with his money to build anything he fancied at a time when few people ventured to live far away from the city boundary of San Francisco. On another occasion Mrs. Dekin asked Rudolph Schaeffer to take me to tea with her, so that she might show me her Japanese garden. While taking me down the steps to see the Japanese maple trees and bamboos and other plants beautifully arranged in Japanese style, Mrs. Dekin told me that her forebears had been early pioneers in Pasadena. Her mother used to keep a good many Shetland ponies in her grounds, a picture of which was shown to me afterwards. But Mr. Dekin has business in the Bay area, so they bought a house on Belvedere and designed this garden. Afterwards we were taken over to see Mrs. Booth's place. We walked through a rather narrow road—I mean narrow by comparison with San Francisco streets. On Belvedere the road is just wide enough for a single car, from the bottom up to the top of the rocky hill. In the early days it must have been a simple footpath, like some country lane with high hedges in Devonshire, England. Apart from the road, every bit of the soil seems to belong to private owners. Mrs. Dekin told me more about her interest in design and art until we reached a tall wrought-iron gate. Entering, our eyes were immediately confronted with beauti-fully-arranged flower-beds and well-trimmed shrubs sloping down right to the edge of the Bay water; the reddish image of the Golden Gate Bridge was looking over at us. On the tip of the prominent portion of the hill-rock stood a large whitewashed house with a long balcony commanding a view of the Bay. We did not go up to the house at once, for Mrs. Booth wanted to show us the garden and to let us wander about. There were a number of colored Canton-ware figures and birds dotted about as ornaments in the garden. Many kinds of flowers were in bloom and two big orange trees had countless little gold-balls hanging among their glossy green leaves. Rudolph and I walked on down to a rhododendron grove and enjoyed at the same time listening to the gentle sound of a running stream. Later Rudolph went back to join the ladies and left me by an enormous pine tree on the edge of the hill-slope. Now the reddish image of the Golden Gate Bridge in the distance was in full view. The afternoon sun-haze brightening the re-flection of the water made the bridge seem an unearthly structure. The Bridge can be beguiling from any angle, but it is definitely finer from a good distance. My eyes followed a tiny red dot approaching from far off. Gradually the dot took the shape of a sailing boat with deep red sails, though it still looked as small as a toy from where I stood.

It began moving in between me and the hilly land opposite. This was Angel Island. I could not see its whole extent, for it is the largest island in the Bay. I could pick out a few white houses with red roofs along the far edge of it and that was all I could see of man-made things. Many trees and shrubs, rocks, and other natural things there looked so inviting for a lovely stroll all round. Presently a big shroud of gray clouds moved up the strait of water, as if pushing Angel Island back from me to make way for their passage. Later it resumed its original position, smiling at me under the sun as before. Then another group of clouds came by, doing somersaults as they passed. Mrs. Booth told me that she never tired of watching the movement of the mists over Angel Island. I had thought that San Francisco fog came into the Bay through the Golden Gate, but Mrs. Booth explained that fine clouds gathered from Mount St. Helena down to San Pablo Bay passed over Angel Island too. Mrs. Dekin assured me that an arrangement could be made for me to visit Angel Island one day. "That will be a special day for me," I told them gratefully.

"Angel" was the name given to this large piece of land by Juan Manuel de Ayala when he sailed into the Bay in 1775. He must have had a poetic eye; it was there, yet not there—so he could only describe it as an Angel. I doubt whether Ayala ever managed to set foot on Angel Island. Nothing was known about it until a prison brig was anchored off it, for three years, from 1851 till 1853. By 1854 it had become known as a dueling ground. Those were the days when San Francisco was full of strong men and self-made men, thinking much of their honor and prestige. Had there been more women about then and women of strength and self-made women too, there might not have been so many fatal quarrels. But the men were always quarrelling. Bancroft wrote in his *History of California*:

> During the year 1854 there appeared to be a mania for duels. Editors fought, Lawyers, judges, shoulder-strikers, doctors, loafers fought. . . . If a week or two passed without the notice of a hostile meeting in the public journals, men looked at each other as if something were wrong.

Oak Grove (no longer in existence) near Sacramento, rather than San

Francisco, was the scene of the duel between Editor Edward Gilbert and General James W. Denver. San Francisco's Pioneer race-track witnessed the duel between Lawyer George T. Hunt and his friend, Numa Hubert. Another famous duel took place at a site on the southerly shore of Lake Merced between United States Senator David C. Broderick and David S. Terry, Chief Justice of the State Supreme Court in 1859. But most of the duels were carried out on Angel Island. Each time a duel took place there, hundreds of the inhabitants of San Francisco pushed along on sailing-boats or rowed to the scene. Perhaps the most famous of these encounters on Angel Island was between State Senator William I. Ferguson and George P. Johnston, Clerk of the United States Circuit Court in San Francisco. They had quarrelled over some trifling matter involving the latter's girl-friend one evening in August, 1858. A few days later the duel took place, with pistols as weapons. The State Senator was hit in the right thigh and died a few weeks later, after his leg had been amputated. Why did so many duels take place in the San Francisco area? I found no records of dueling in the annals of Boston, for instance. A good many stories about duels in England and France were known to me. I even heard of dueling taking place on Hampstead Heath two or three years before my arrival in London in 1933. Dueling was a European practice until the beginning of this century, I believe. So apparently just as the early settlers in New England had brought many other things with them from the Old World, "including the fear of witchcraft—a wholesale, body-and-spirit exportation from England or a wholesale importation to America," as I wrote in *The Silent Traveller in Boston,* the early settlers in San Francisco also imported the duel practice to that region.

In those gold-rush days and afterwards, the Island was easily accessible. Mrs. Grayson Kirk, wife of the President of Columbia University, told me that thirty or forty years ago she used to be taken on a ferryboat from San Francisco to Belvedere and Angel Island for picnics. In recent years the San Franciscans seem to have made very little use of it. If the Island belonged to a private owner or a company, it would no doubt have been fully developed and covered with houses like fish-scales long ago. How fortunate that it is not privately owned! The future of the great San Francisco Bay lies in the development of this Island, too. Its present use as the district headquarters and detention barracks of the Immigration and Naturalization Service seems to me a passing phase. I may be a dreamer but so were many of the early pioneers of San Francisco. My particular dream is of seeing Angel Island turned into a great art center as an unforgettable monument to twentieth-century America. There are still thirty-odd years to go before this most interesting and memorable Century of ours comes to an end. Nothing may come of my dream but something new will develop on Angel Island, I am sure. I hope no bridge of any kind nor tunnel will ever be built to join it to the shore, nor any motorcar be allowed on it either!

In recent years I have heard and read controversies about the standard of the performing arts in San Francisco. This is not unnatural as long as these arts are tied up with economic conditions. New York can attract the best artists by its floating dollar-notes. But Lotta Crabtree insisted on coming back to act in San Francisco, and the world-famous Luisa Tetrazzini sang under a San Francisco fountain one Christmas Eve, though she jokingly remarked that she had never expected to be a street-singer. Aren't there actresses and singers of today, who love San Francisco as much as Lotta and Luisa did? In the seventeenth and eighteenth centuries the arts were supported by the noblemen of Europe; in the nineteenth century they came under the patronage of the new-rich; now it is time that they should be well-provided and cared for by the public. Only if all performing arts can rid themselves of their dependence on the purses of the audience will the highest and purest standards of achievement be reached.

During the few visits I have paid to San Francisco I have managed to attend a number of presentations of the performing arts. The performance of Cantonese drama in the Chinese Theatre in Chinatown on Grant Avenue was spectacular enough to attract many Americans' curiosity. But showy costumes alone will not give a true picture of Chinese culture.

The author of *The Flower Drum Song,* C. Y. Lee, used San Francisco's Chinatown for his theme. It was a great success. Hammerstein and Rodgers made a musical out of Lee's story and scored another great success. But the real Chinatown of San Francisco was so near at hand for comparison, that this musical show could not stay long in the city.

I spent an evening in Berkeley to see the performance of Madam Devi Dja and her Bali Java dancers of Indonesia at Wheeler Auditorium. She danced a few short Bali temple dances with great dexterity of hand and body and also performed some versions of other Indonesian dances modified by her western training.

There are many places to hear good music in San Francisco. I must admit that though I have been living away from China for almost thirty years, I still do not enjoy western music as much as other western arts. Nevertheless, I try to learn to appreciate it and my enjoyment is increasing. I have paid a visit to the S.F. Conservatory of Music on Mariposa Street, and also attended a recital in the Stern Grove of beautiful eucalyptuses. The Palace of the Legion of Honor in Lincoln Park is near where I stayed in Lake Street, so Lincoln Park has taken me as a visitor on several occasions. One morning as I strolled there and watched a few people playing golf on the Municipal Golf Links, I suddenly noticed a few tombstones bearing Chinese names and realized that the Links must be on the Old Chinese Cemetery where the early Chinese, brought over to build the railroad and to work in the mines, were buried. No westerner, I am sure, could understand how great a crime it would be in Chinese eyes and Chinese law if an ancestor's tomb was disturbed, for "ancestor worship" has for centuries been the faith of all Chinese. The Chinese on Grant Avenue must have put up a terrific fight for the preservation of this old Chinese Cemetery when Lincoln Park was made. Someone pointed out to me the stone structure which we call "Pailou" or "Paifang," an honorific arch, with two huge Chinese words painted in red on the top of the upper beam and explained that underneath was the sacrificial stone and a stone oven used for roasting pigs to propitiate the gods. I smilingly looked at him and asked: "What gods?" We Chinese have been taught to give our highest respect to our forefathers according to the principles of "Ancestor Worship," and therefore we pay homage to our family tombs annually with food and wine, presenting them ceremonially in front of the deceased as if they were alive to enjoy them. The roast pig is a Cantonese delicacy and so those who were buried in Lincoln Park must have been Cantonese and must have loved roast pig in their lifetime. After the ceremony the descendants could enjoy the roast pig and other food and wine to their hearts' content.

There are always interesting exhibitions in the Palace of the Legion of Honor, but I also greatly enjoyed one of a series of seven concerts presented by the Singers' Guild of San Francisco. The evening began with *Das Marienleben* by Rainer Maria Rilke with music by Paul Hindemith, sung by Soprano Dorothy Renzi; then followed five American poems by Edna St. Vincent Millay with music by Arthur Bliss, sung by Baritone Edgar Jones. After the intermission came three songs by William Blake with music by Leonard Ralston, sung by Contralto Henrietta Harris. The last song was entitled "London," and was sung enchantingly. I did not know Henrietta personally then. A year later I was taken to see her acting in an Opera Bouffe: *The Reformed Drunkard or The Devil's Marriage.* She played Mathurin, the wife. Afterwards we visited her back-stage. After she had changed, five of us went to hunt for beatniks in one café after another. We did not see many unusual characters, but before the night was out, each of us came to look like one ourselves! The following year Henrietta came to Europe and stopped in London first. I gave a dinner party for her at the Hong Kong Restaurant near Piccadilly. My friend the proprietor of the restaurant, Chang Meng Young, provided the most sumptuous dishes he had ever served, so he told me, but all my guests feasted on the Chinese soya-sauce-like skin of Henrietta's face and her eyes, which sparkled at every one. Even after five years or so, those friends of mine will still ask about her when I meet them.

The name of Arthur Bliss had not been known to me before, but the word "Bliss" as a family name interests me. It may have been taken as a good omen name by the first family concerned. I have two friends with that family name, JoAnn and Anthony Bliss. Anthony is the President of the New York Metropolitan Opera Association. Apart from her duties at home and in society, JoAnn is an energetic scholar at Columbia University. Western opera is still rather a mystery to me, but I should like to be able to appreciate it. I was specially intrigued by the idea of seeing *Turandot,* whose story is based on an ancient Chinese legend, but missed it when it came to San Francisco. JoAnn

Bliss's mother, Mrs. Henry Davis, lives in San Francisco and when I met JoAnn, our conversation often touched the Bay area. As I had missed this particular opera there, JoAnn Bliss insisted on taking me to a new presentation of it under a Japanese director at the New York Metropolitan Opera House. It was arranged for me and other guests to meet our host and hostess in the dining hall for dinner. Anthony Bliss anxiously awaited the arrival of the Japanese Ambassador, who was busy at the UN Assembly meetings at the time. From our box we had a full view of the stage. The ladies sat in front with the Ambassador and the two other guests behind. I was fortunate in having not only a view of the stage but also of the audience in our box. Cecil Beaton's new stage designs as well as the exotic costumes fascinated me. I particularly liked the grotesque dresses for Ping, the Grand Chancellor, Pang the General Purveyor, and Pong the Chief Cook, who always appeared together. When there was too much singing which I could not follow very well, I turned my eyes to the members of the audience in front of me and found each wore a tense expression: lips tight, eyes fixed, as if in a state of trance. I think the themes: "Hope for what is born each night and dies each dawn, Blood for what flickers like a flame yet is not fire and *Turandot* for what is like ice but burns" and also Calaf for "the power of love and life" have been known to the human heart since mankind began, but it needed Gozzi to dramatize them and Puccini to write the powerful music. I doubt if acting alone could work so powerfully upon an audience, without music. I was reminded that in Puccini's score there were several Chinese melodies of the *pentatonic,* i.e., five-note scale. It is said that when Puccini was composing the music for this opera, he searched for Chinese music everywhere—old, new, every form. But he died before his *Turandot* had its premiere at La Scala in 1926. Later in the evening, when Emperor Altoum of China appeared on the stage, I scratched my head and went through all the dynasties of China's history but could remember no emperor of such a name. Suddenly one of our party said to me "You could be the emperor over there." "I could, for he doesn't have to sing a word!" was my joking reply.

Many changes have taken place in San Francisco since my first visit in 1953. For instance, there used to be very few houses from Sausalito

The Silent Traveller as Emperor Altoum
(After a Sung Painting of an emperor)

all the way around the Bay to Tiburon, but now there is almost no
space left for another house, and a lagoon has been built behind
Belvedere. I saw the first houses being put up in the new Stonetown
and now it is an old place. In those days I went with Don McPherson
to see his friend practicing rifle-shooting at Sharp Park, and then
walked on to see Pillar Point at Half Moon Bay, which was first sighted
by Francisco de Galli in 1585—it was easy going, but now many new
towns have sprouted up like Chinese bamboo shoots everywhere. One
of my most interesting walks was along the rugged coast from Seacliff
on a sunny day. The morning fog had lifted some time before. I found

a well-paved footpath through a gap in some trees bordering a Golf Links. Apparently no car could come that way. I walked on and kept looking back for a glimpse of the Golden Gate Bridge, and occasionally stopped to make sketches. From time to time I climbed on to some rocks by the shore and got many fine aspects of the Bridge for paintings. Other sightseers found their way along the footpath too, but only to go back to the road and their cars. I stopped to watch hundreds of small water birds, like some kind of plover, dashing along the sand in all directions like people on urgent business in New York's Times Square. The footpath was a little inland from the shore, which was rugged with various rocks and broken branches. The sea breeze, the sea color and the wide expanse of water added to the pleasure of the walk. Then I followed a side footpath to the tip of Land's End where I saw the Golden Gate Bridge in soft haze looking quite mysterious. After turning a corner on the path far down below Lookout Point, I saw a young man lying on a rock reading: this must have been Point Lobos and I stepped past him to have a look at the Searocks. It was a most enjoyable walk and I always wanted to repeat it each time I returned to San Francisco, but for a long time I did not manage to do so, either because of dense fog or because I had too many other engagements. In April 1958 I retraced my steps through the same gap in the golf links, which now looked rather dilapidated with much debris piled up on the edge, and walked along the footpath, which was no longer well-paved. I suspected nothing and met nobody. I lowered my head and scrambled through a thicket with countless trees intertwined in most intricate patterns, of which I made a sketch. Then following the twisting and waterwashed narrow path, I reached the end and stood there for a good look round. On my return as I emerged from the thicket I heard a whistle blowing and a mounted policeman beckoned to me. He asked why I had taken no notice of the sign board at the entrance. I had not seen it. I told him that I had come to enjoy a walk I had taken some years before. He looked rather cross, saying that two people had been washed away from that path in a big storm and that it was dangerous. He implied that I had broken the law. I asked if he wanted to take me to the police station, but he only smiled. Now this little more than a mile of coast line is cut off and a paved road runs round the outside of Lincoln Park while El Camino del Mar goes through the Park. I wonder if Nature will have caused changes on another part of the coast line in a few years' time?

Change means *Chance*. This is how I interpret the *changes* in the *Yi Ching* or *Book of Changes*, a most profound book of Chinese ancient philosophy, now translated into English from Dr. Richard Wilhelm's German translation with a Foreword by Dr. C. G. Jung. Through chance comes Change; without chance, change will not be sought. From the very early days of China's history, as far back as the eleventh century B.C., we learn that the Chinese have used the *Book of Changes* for divination and also for the interpretation of events resulting from chance. Every process in Nature is subject to chance interference either partially or wholly. The *chance* discovery of San Francisco Bay, the *chance* discovery of gold, the *chance* building-up of San Francisco into a big city were all interferences with the original Nature of the land. The *chances* for gold needed the *chance* men, known in American history as *pioneers*. Only pioneers took the *chance* of coming to San Francisco for the *chance* of gold. According to the *Book of Changes, Sheng sheng chih wei yi,* or "Life produces life" and this is called *change*. Wherever the pioneers went, their way of living introduced a new way of living and brought about change. Many pioneers took the chance of leaving New England when the Pilgrims had driven their roots in too deeply and left little chance for the new generations. In the end new life spread everywhere and produced a new nation—the United States of America. Of those early *pioneers* who took the *chance* of coming to San Francisco, many died a natural or unnatural death without having a *chance* to see a single nugget of gold. I have admired those who battled hard against death to get out of Death Valley, where I spent a night at the only ranch, with my friends, Bob and Thelma Morris. I visualized those early days when the pioneers were stranded there and had no idea which way to go in the deadly scorching heat. I have also extended my personal sympathy, no matter how small and useless, to those who met their end at Donner Pass in Mother-Lode Country. They came to die there in seeking a *chance* to live. And what made them do so? They could have managed to live where they were, but they wanted to achieve something better.

Angel Island where my dream lies

This is what I call the "Pioneer Spirit." Not many people possess this pioneering spirit nowadays. But in San Francisco I have felt it filling the Bay air.

In my book *The Silent Traveller in Boston* I related how I found the *Pilgrim's spirit* still lingering round Boston and sufficiently alive there to have survived the uneasy year created by the measures against un-American activities in 1953 and 1954. Now in San Francisco I have found the *Pioneer's spirit* persisting, though on the surface we may be more conscious of an easy-going way of life, night clubs with paintings of nudes on the walls, and bison-like faces. Only recently I heard that some San Franciscans became so scared by the threat of nuclear warfare that they began to build air-raid shelters in a hysterical and childish manner. But the deep-rooted *Pioneer spirit* soon righted them and brought them through their imaginary Death Valley to emerge and enjoy the Bay fog, mist, haze and sunset with as cheerful spirits as before.

How fortunate it is for the United States of America to possess not one but two lasting spirits, the *Pilgrim's* and the *Pioneer's*, each supplementing and complementing the other. I am no historian nor politician, but I think the great potentiality and strength of America lies not in her natural resources, nor her gold, but in the fusion of these two spirits. The *Pilgrim's spirit* has helped her to establish a nation devoted to the principle of universal liberty; none of the other, older nations were built on such a foundation. This Pilgrim's spirit might, however, have led to stagnation and the United States would have fallen into the same pattern as any of these older nations in Europe or Asia; no one could uphold puritanical theories on the Assembly floor of the United Nations nowadays. Fortunately the *Pioneer's spirit* remains alive to spur her into taking *chances*. The *Pioneer's spirit* alone without the *Pilgrim's spirit* to hold it in check might mean chaos. The *Pilgrim's spirit* in the early days of San Francisco's history saw to the setting up of Committee Vigilance, raised the cry against Chinese cheap labor, the not-too-long life of the fabulous Ralston way, and the rebuilding after the great fire and earthquake. The Pioneer's spirit supported and steadied by the *Pilgrim's spirit* eventually created Golden Gate Park over the sand dunes, the Bay Bridge and the Golden Gate Bridge, all of which might have seemed impossible. With the *Pilgrim's spirit* and the *Pioneer's spirit* working side by side, nothing is impossible in America nowadays. That is her strength.

Perhaps I am straying too far into abstract topics, but in a very concrete way I feel that San Francisco is still full of *chances* and the Pioneering spirit is still alive there today. One of the *chances* I foresee is that San Francisco may become a famous national-and-international park within the three big bridges, the Bay, the Golden Gate, and now the San-Rafael-and-Richmond. Geneva with her beautiful lake has had her chance to become a world park. Istanbul could be another with its wonderful bay, but unlike San Francisco it has little chance of such a future. Only the combination of the Pilgrim's and the Pioneer's spirit can make the San Francisco of my dreams. I cannot say how long the Cable cars will stay. But I dream that Angel Island may become a famous Art Center for the Twentieth Century and that the rest of the Bay region—Belvedere, Sausalito, Treasure Island, Alcatraz Rock, etc., each contribute to the formation of a great National-International

Park. I hope to see something like this one day. That is why I say it is the future of San Francisco that counts.

Many people I met in San Francisco exclaimed how wonderful San Francisco was and found my emotionless face too unresponsive. Good friends of mine pressed me to tell them why I kept coming back to San Francisco during the last ten years, but I could not. I never look for perfection. I can only say that San Francisco's progress fascinates me. I know it will progress further and improve still more. Therefore I can only conclude my writing on this City temporarily.

The foundation of the country that Columbus discovered